P · O ·

SPELLING
DICTIONARY

DORLING KINDERSLEY

London • New York • Moscow • Sydney

www.dk.com

A DORLING KINDERSLEY BOOK

Produced for Dorling Kindersley by
PAGE*One*, Cairn House, Elgiva Lane, Chesham,
Buckinghamshire HP5 2JD

PAGE*One* team Chris Clark, Bob Gordon, Thomas
Keenes, Neil Kelly, Helen Parker,
Charlotte Stock, Sarah Watson

DK Managing editor Jane Yorke

Dictionary consultant Sheila Dignen
Dictionary editor David Morrow

Published in Great Britain by
Dorling Kindersley Limited, 80 Strand, London WC2R 0RL

6 8 10 9 7 5
Copyright © 1998 Dorling Kindersley Limited, London
Text copyright © 1976, 1985, 1990, 1993, 1995, 1997 Cassell
Text revision and additions
© 1998 Dorling Kindersley Limited, London

This edition published in 2002

See our complete catalogue at **www.dk.com**

A CIP catalogue record for this book is available from
the British Library.

ISBN 0-7513-5688-3

Printed and bound by LegoPrint, Italy

INTRODUCTION

Using this dictionary

The words featured in this dictionary have been chosen because they can be difficult to spell. Since there is a limit to the total number of words that can be included, only words most likely to be used by the general reader or writer are given. Very few proper nouns appear and foreign terms are included only if they are in common usage. Thus, you will find words such as "chauffeur" and "début", but not "hors combat" or "gîte". A few common slang words have also been given.

Alphabetical order

Headwords in this dictionary are all arranged in alphabetical order. Root words are not automatically followed by their derivatives, which are listed separately.

Abbreviations

In this dictionary, abbreviations have been kept to a minimum. You will, however, find the following:

Am	American English
pl	plural
m	masculine
f	feminine

Alternative spellings

For headwords that have variant spellings, both forms are given, separated by a comma.

e.g. mediaeval, medieval
     medieval, mediaeval

In the above example, the two forms are some distance apart in the text, so an entry is given for each spelling.

When the two variants are next to each other, or fairly close together on the page, only one entry is given at the more common spelling.

e.g. judgement, judgment
     abridgement, abridgment

INFLECTIONS OF VERBS

As verbs are often formed inconsistently in English, verb inflections, such as the –ed, –ing, and –s forms, are given for verbs that could be irregular and, therefore, difficult to spell. Inflections are listed alphabetically under the headword.

- Verbs ending in –e are followed by the past and present participle to show whether or not the –e is dropped in the –ing form.

e.g. debate
      debated
      debating

- Verbs ending in a single consonant such as –t,– n, or –r are followed by –ed, –ing, and –s inflections to make clear whether they take a double or single consonant when inflected.

e.g. ban
      banned
      banning
      bans

budget
budgeted
budgeting
budgets

- Verbs ending in –y are accompanied by inflections to show whether the –y changes to –i–.

e.g. bury
      buried
      buries
      burying

   try
      tried
      tries
      trying

- Inflections of irregular verbs have their own entry with a cross-reference in brackets.

e.g. broke (*from* break)
      flung (*from* fling)

- Inflections are given for verbs that have regular inflections but look as if they might be irregular.

e.g. echo
      echoed
      echoes
      echoing

PLURALS

Plurals are not listed when they are formed regularly by simply adding –s to the root word (see p. 8). However, irregular noun plurals are always listed immediately after the headword and are followed by *pl*. This is true even where verb inflections are also listed under the same headword.

e.g. man
    men *pl*
    manned
    manning
    mans

- Plurals of words ending in –y are always given to distinguish whether or not the –y becomes –ies

e.g. baby
    babies *pl*

    play
    plays *pl*

- Plurals are always given of words that end in –um, –us, or –a because these words often look as if they might have an irregular plural.

e.g. auditorium
    auditoria *pl*

    circus
    circuses *pl*

- Plurals of words ending in –o are always given as there are no strict rules to say whether these take –oes or –os.

e.g. calypso
    calypsos *pl*

    potato
    potatoes *pl*

AMERICAN SPELLINGS

Throughout the dictionary American spellings are listed alphabetically as separate headwords followed by the abbreviation *Am*. The inflections that follow an American spelling are not labelled as American.

e.g. anesthetize *Am*
    anesthetized
    anesthetizing

    labor *Am*
    labored
    laboring

SHARED BRITISH AND AMERICAN SPELLINGS

Sometimes British English and American English share the same headwords but have different inflections. Where this is the case, the British inflections are listed alphabetically first, followed by the American forms, each of which is labelled *Am*.

e.g. bevel
     bevelled
     bevelling
     beveled *Am*
     beveling *Am*

−S OR −Z SPELLINGS

Some verbs have an optional ending of −ise or −ize (see p. 13). American English always uses the −ize ending and today this is becoming increasingly accepted in the rest of the English-speaking world. Both the −ise and −ize versions are listed in the dictionary as separate entries with their own inflections.

e.g. realise
     realised
     realising

     realize
     realized
     realizing

MEANINGS AND DEFINITIONS

This is not a dictionary of definitions, so the meanings of words are given only to avoid confusion in the case of some words that sound the same but have completely different meanings according to the way they are spelled.

e.g. paw (animal's foot)
     poor (lacking wealth)
     pore (of skin)
     pour (liquid)

- For the sake of simplicity, where words with the same spelling can also have different meanings, only one entry is included.

e.g. loaf – which as a noun means bread, and as a verb means to laze around.

COMMON SPELLING RULES

English spelling is notoriously inconsistent, and spellings can often seem illogical. Here are a few basic rules, with examples and exceptions, that will help to make spelling easier.

VERB INFLECTIONS

- To form the past tense of a regular verb add –ed to the root. To form the present continuous, simply add –ing. Many of these inflections are also used as adjectives.

e.g. hunt+ed   hunted
     laugh+ing   laughing

ADVERBS

- Adverbs are formed regularly by adding –ly to the root of the adjective:

e.g. free+ly   freely
     foolish+ly   foolishly

- Adjectives ending in –ic add –ally to form the adverb.

e.g. basic+ally   basically
     historic+ally   historically
     cynic+ally   cynically

Exception: publicly

- When –ly is added to an adjective that ends in a consonant followed by –le, the –le is usually dropped.

e.g. gentle+ly   gently
     subtle+ly   subtly

PLURALS

- Regular plurals are formed by simply adding an s.

e.g. heart   hearts
     book   books

- The plurals of nouns that end in a consonant+y are formed by substituting –ies for –y.

e.g. ambiguity   ambiguities
     category   categories
     penny   pennies

- Nouns ending in a vowel + y form plurals regularly by adding an s.

e.g. array	arrays
key	keys
chimney	chimneys

- If a word ends in –sh, –ch, –s, or –x, the plural is formed by adding –es.

e.g. wish	wishes
finch	finches
boss	bosses
fox	foxes

DOUBLING CONSONANTS IN COMPOUND WORDS

- When an ending that begins with a vowel is added to a word that ends in a single vowel plus a consonant, the consonant is doubled.

e.g. dot+ed	dotted
admit+ance	admittance
excel+ent	excellent

- When an ending that begins with –e, –i, or –y is added to a word that ends in –c, a –k– is inserted between the two to keep the hard sound.

e.g. frolic+ing	frolicking
panic+y	panicky

LOSING A CONSONANT IN COMPOUND WORDS

- Compound words made up of smaller words ending in –ll often drop an –l–.

e.g. all+mighty	almighty
un+till	until
full+fill	fulfil
well+fare	welfare

Exceptions: farewell, fullness, illness, wellbeing

I BEFORE E EXCEPT AFTER C

- The rule –i– before –e– except after –c– can generally be relied upon where the sound is "ee".

e.g. believe, friend, receive

Exceptions: either, weird, seize, caffeine; proper names such as Keith and Sheila

- Where words are not pronounced "ee", –ei– is always correct.

e.g. deign
freight
weight
veil

Y TO I

- When an ending is added
  to a word that ends in a
  consonant+y, the –y changes
  to –i. If the ending begins
  with –i, the –y– is retained.

e.g. pretty+est   prettiest
    pity+ful   pitiful
    pity+ing   pitying

THE SILENT E

- Verbs that end in a silent –e
  generally drop the –e when
  an ending that begins with a
  vowel is added, such as –ed,
  –ing, –er, or –able.

e.g. line+ed   lined
    chase+ing   chasing
    argue+able arguable

- The silent –e is retained
  before a consonant.

e.g. value+less   valueless
    pave+ment pavement

Exception: argument, truly

- In words that end in –ce or
  –ge the silent –e is usually
  retained to keep the soft
  sound of the consonant.

e.g. change+able changeable
    age+ing   ageing
    courage+ous courageous

APOSTROPHES

- The apostrophe is used
  mainly to indicate possession
  or relationship. When
  the noun is singular, an
  apostrophe+s are added
  to the word.

e.g. the boy's school (the
    school of the boy)

    the dog's bone (the
    bone of the dog)

- When the noun is plural
  and already ends in –s, the
  apostrophe follows the whole
  word, after the final –s.

e.g. the boys' school (the
    school of the boys)

    the dogs' bones (the
    bones of the dogs)

- If a noun is already a plural
  without an –s, such as
  "men", "women", "children",
  or "people" an apostrophe+s
  is added.

e.g. the women's office
     the children's books
     the people's flag

- If a singular noun of one syllable ends in –s, it is usual to add another –s after the apostrophe.

e.g. St James's Street
     the Jones's house

- If a singular noun of two syllables ends in –s, it is acceptable to omit the final –s.

e.g. Mr Jenkins' office
     Mrs Peters' house

- Possessive pronouns do not have an apostrophe.

e.g. mine, his, hers, its, ours, yours, theirs, whose

Exception: one's

- An apostrophe is used also to signify that something has been left out of a word.

e.g. don't   do not
     it's   it is, it has
     o'clock   of the clock

NB Don't be tempted to put an apostrophe in the possessive pronoun "its" meaning "of it" – it's wrong!

e.g. even though **it's** raining, the dog eats **its** bone

HYPHENS

Many people are confused when it comes to using hyphens, however, there are one or two simple rules that can make it easier.

- Hyphens are generally used to avoid ambiguity by showing that two or more words are to be treated as a single unit.

e.g. He is my father-in-law.

     She is a good-looking woman.

     There were 20-odd people in the waiting room.

- A compound adjective of which the second ends in –ing or –ed is normally hyphenated.

e.g. a good-natured child
     a hard-working team
     a blue-eyed girl

- When the first word of a compound adjective is well, better, best, ill, worse, or worst, a hyphen is inserted only when the compound adjective precedes a noun. At all other times the hyphen is omitted:

e.g. He is a well-known author

   She is well known for her comedy roles.

   It is clearly an ill-treated animal

   The child was ill mannered and rude.

- Certain phrases, when used as adjectives preceding a noun, require hyphens.

e.g. She said it was a never-to-be-forgotten experience

   He produced a set of up-to-date accounts

- Use hyphens when writing out numbers and fractions from 21 to 99.

e.g. forty-five
   two-thirds
   ninety-eight

ALTERNATIVE SPELLINGS

Some words are accepted with various spellings, both of which are correct. You will often find that one spelling is more common than the other, however, the most important thing when writing is to be consistent. Decide which spelling to use and stick to it.

abridgement	abridgment
briar	brier
disc	disk
dispatch	despatch
encyclopedia	encyclopaedia
extravert	extrovert
gypsy	gipsy
hello	hallo (or hullo)
inquire	enquire
jewellery	jewelry
judgement	judgment
loth	loath
medieval	mediaeval
rateable	ratable
reflection	reflexion
spelled	spelt

WORDS THAT NEVER USE –IZE

The words listed below never use –ize, even in American English. Many of these end in –cise, –mise, –prise, and –vise. As a rule, if the part of the word preceding the ending is not recognizable as an English word, the ending is unlikely to be –ize. For example, there is no such word as ad, appr, surpr or prem.

e.g.
advertise	exercise
advise	expertise
apprise	franchise
arise	guise
braise	improvise
chastise	incise
circumcise	merchandise
comprise	misadvise
compromise	misprise
concise	precise
demise	premise
despise	prise
devise	reprise
disfranchise	revise
disguise	supervise
emprise	surmise
enfranchise	surprise
enterprise	televise
excise	treatise

CHOOSING THE RIGHT WORD

LAY OR LIE?

to lay (laid, laying) – to place, set, or arrange something (this verb always has an object).

e.g. I always lay the table for breakfast.

He laid his cards on the table.

They were still laying the carpet at four o'clock.

She had laid the matter before the committee.

to lie (lay, lying, lain) – to be in a horizontal position (as in bed) or to take that position.

e.g. I lie down on my bed every afternoon.

The apples lay in the long grass.

The book was lying on the table.

The dog had lain in the same position all day.

to lie (lied, lying) – to tell untruths.

e.g. Do not lie to me!

I lied to you about the money.

The accused is lying about his actions.

RAISE OR RISE?

to raise (raised, raising) – to lift (this verb always has an object).

e.g. I raise my hand in a salute.

He is raising all our salaries on Friday.

to rise (rose, rising, risen) – to get up, move higher.

e.g. In winter she rises after the sun has risen.

The star slowly rose above the horizon.

The water level is rising.

WHO, WHOM, OR WHOSE?

• Who is the subject and whom is the object.

e.g. The man who came to dinner is my cousin.

The man whom I invited to dinner was late.

• In questions, whom is rarely used in spoken English, as it tends to sound clumsy. We are much more likely to say "who" even if it is not grammatically correct.

e.g. "Who did you meet?" rather than "Whom did you meet?"

• Unless it is being used to start a question, whom is rarely used without a preceding preposition.

e.g. to whom
by whom
with whom
of whom

• In spoken English, it is usual to omit the word whom altogether.

e.g. "the girl it belongs to" rather than "the girl to whom it belongs".

"the boy I sat with" rather than "the boy with whom I sat".

• In both written and spoken English, whose is often used instead of whom:

e.g. "Whose is this coat?" rather than "Of whom is this coat?"

WHICH OR THAT?

• Which should be used with non-defining clauses, or those that can stand alone without it. That is used with defining clauses, or those where that cannot be removed without altering the meaning of the sentence.

e.g. The film that I saw last night was better than the one on Friday.

The film, which I saw last night, made me feel very sad.

COMMONLY CONFUSED WORDS

In English, there are many words that sound the same, but have completely different spellings and meanings. Here are some of the words that are most commonly confused.

accede (to agree to)
exceed (to go beyond)

accept (to take)
except (to exclude)

access (right of way)
excess (too much)

adapter (someone who adapts)
adaptor (piece of equipment that adapts)

addition (something added)
edition (number of copies of a book, newspaper, etc.)

adverse (unfavourable)
averse (disinclined)

advice (recommendation)
advise (to recommend)

affect (to influence)
effect (to accomplish, result)

aid (help)
aide (assistant)

allay (to make less)
alley (a narrow street)
ally (friendly country or person)

all ready (completely ready)
already (previously, so soon)

allude (to mention in passing)
elude (to escape or avoid)

allusion (a brief mention)
illusion (a false impression)

altar (platform in a church)
alter (to change)

arc (a curved line)
ark (a type of boat)

artist (a person who is skilled in fine arts)
artiste (a theatre performer)

ascent (climb, rise)
assent (agreement, permission)

aural (by ear)
oral (by mouth)

bail (money given to release
a prisoner)
bale out (to remove water
from a boat)

ballet (a form of dancing)
ballot (a method of voting)

base (basis, foundation)
bass (a lower part in music)

bazaar (marketplace, fair)
bizarre (strange)

birth (being born)
berth (a mooring place)

bloc (a group of nations)
block (a solid mass)

born (given birth)
borne (carried, produced)

bough (a tree branch)
bow (form of greeting)

boy (a male child)
buoy (a floating object)

brake (to slow and stop)
break (to fracture, damage)

breach (to break)
breech (rear part of a gun)

bridal (belonging to the bride)
bridle (a horse's harness)

broach (to bring up a subject)
brooch (a piece of jewellery)

cannon (gun)
canon (law)

canvas (cloth)
canvass (to solicit opinions,
votes, etc.)

choose (to select)
chose (past tense of to choose)

chord (musical tones)
cord (thin rope)

cite (to quote)
sight (power of seeing)
site (place)

coarse (rude, rough)
course (series, route)

complement (something that completes or balances)
compliment (praise)

dairy (milk farm)
diary (daily record book)

desert (arid region, to leave or abandon)
dessert (final course of a meal)

dual (of two, double)
duel (fight)

flair (aptitude, style)
flare (to burn, burst out)

foreword (introduction to a written work)
forward (onward, ahead)

idle (inactive)
idol (image of a god)

immigrant (person coming into a country)
emigrant (person leaving a country)

its (belonging to it)
it's (it is)

lead (a metal, to guide)
led (past tense of lead)

lightening (becoming lighter)
lightning (as in thunder)

miner (one who mines)
minor (underage person)

moral (relating to good behaviour)
morale (level of spirits)

naval (of the navy)
navel (umbilicus)

palate (roof of mouth, taste)
palette (artist's paintboard)
pallet (crude bed, platform)

passed (past tense of pass)
past (former time)

pastel (artist's crayons)
pastille (type of sweet)

pedal (foot lever)
peddle (to sell)

personal (belonging to
  someone, intimate)
personnel (staff)

plane (aeroplane, level)
plain (ordinary; open land)

precede (to go before)
proceed (to continue)

prey (animal killed for food)
pray (to say a prayer)

prise (to open with a tool)
prize (award for winner)

principal (chief, head person
principle (rule)

rapped (knocked)
rapt (fascinated)
wrapped (covered)

raze (to destroy totally)
raise (to lift up, increase)

reign (of a monarch)
rein (part of a horse's harness)

review (a report)
revue (amusing theatre show)

rhyme (short poem)
rime (frost)

sceptic (unbeliever)
septic (infected)

stationary (fixed)
stationery (paper supplies)

stile (steps over a wall)
style (manner of doing things)

their (belonging to them)
there (at that place)
they're (they are)

to (toward)
too (also, excessive)
two (number)

waive (to give up)
wave (to salute; on sea)

weather (state of atmosphere)
whether (if)

who's (who is)
whose (of whom)

you're (you are)
your (belonging to you)

DICTIONARY
OF SPELLINGS

aback
abacus
  abacuses *pl*
abandon
  abandoned
  abandoning
  abandons
abandonment
abase
abasement
abash
abate
  abated
  abating
abatement
abattoir
abbess (nun)
abbey (building)
  abbeys *pl*

abbot
abbreviate
  abbreviated
  abbreviating
abbreviation
abdicate
  abdicated
  abdicating
abdication
abdomen
abdominal
abduct
  abducted
  abducting
abduction
abductor
aberrant
aberration
abet

abets
abetted
abetting
abetter, abettor
abeyance
abhor
  abhorred
  abhorring
  abhors
abhorrence
abhorrent
abidance
abide
  abided
  abiding
ability
  abilities *pl*
abject (miserable)
abjection
abjectly
abjure
  abjured
  abjuring
abjuration
ablative
ablaze
able
able-bodied
ablution
ably
abnegate
  abnegated
  abnegating

abnegation
abnormal
abnormality
  abnormalities *pl*
abnormally
abnormity
  abnormities *pl*
aboard
abode
abolish
abolition
abolitionary
abominable
abominably
abominate
  abominated
  abominating
abomination
aboriginal
aborigine
abort
abortion
abortionist
abortive
abound
about
about-face
above
above-board
abracadabra
abrade
  abraded
  abrading

abrasion
abrasive
abreast
abridge
  abridging
  abridged
abridgement,
  abridgment
abroad
abrogate
  abrogated
  abrogating
abrogation
abrupt
abscess
  abscesses *pl*
abscissa
  abscissas,
    abscissae *pl*
abscond
absent
absence
absentee
absenteeism
absently
absent-minded
absinth (plant)
absinthe (drink)
absolute
absolutely
absolve
  absolved
  absolving

absolution
absorb
absorbency
absorbent
absorption
absorptive
abstain
  abstained
  abstaining
abstainer
abstention
abstemious
abstemiously
abstinence
abstinent
abstract
abstraction
abstruse
abstrusely
abstruseness
absurd
absurdity
  absurdities *pl*
absurdly
abundance
abundant
abundantly
abuse
  abused
  abusing
abusive
abusively
abut

abuts
abutted
abutting
abutment
abysmal
abysmally
abyss (deep hole)
  abysses *pl*
acacia
  acacias *pl*
academy
  academies *pl*
academia
academic
academically
academician
accede (to agree)
  acceded
  acceding
accelerate
  accelerated
  accelerating
acceleration
accelerator
accent
accentuate
  accentuated
  accentuating
accentuation
accept
acceptability
acceptable
acceptance

access
accessary (crime)
  accessaries *pl*
accessibility
accessible
accessibly
accession
accessory (extra)
  accessories *pl*
accident
accidental
accidentally
acclaim
acclamation
acclimatisation
acclimatise
  acclimatised
  acclimatising
acclimatize
  acclimatized
  acclimatizing
acclimatization
accolade
accommodate
  accommodated
  accommodating
accommodation
accompany
  accompanied
  accompanies
  accompanying
accompaniment
accompanist

accomplice
accomplish
accomplishment
accord
accordance
accordion
accordionist
accost
account
accountability
accountable
accountancy
accountant
accouterments *Am*
accoutrements
accredit
  accredited
  accrediting
accreditation
accretion
accrual
accrue
  accrued
  accruing
accumulate
  accumulated
  accumulating
accumulation
accumulator
accuracy
accurate
accurately
accursed

accusation
accusative
accusatory
accuse
  accused
  accusing
accuser
accustom
  accustomed
  accustoming
ace
acerbate
  acerbated
  acerbating
acerbic
acerbity
acetate
acetic (acid)
acetylene
ache
  ached
  aching
achievable
achieve
  achieved
  achieving
achievement
achromatic
acid
acidic
acidify
  acidified
  acidifies

  acidifying
acidity
acidosis
acknowledge
  acknowledged
  acknowledging
acknowledgement,
  acknowledgment
acme
acne
acolyte
aconite
acorn
acoustic
acoustical
acoustically
acoustics
acquaint
acquaintance
acquaintanceship
acquiesce
  acquiesced
  acquiescing
acquiescence
acquiescent
acquire
  acquired
  acquiring
acquisition
acquisitive
acquit
  acquits
  acquitted

  acquitting
acquittal
acre
acreage
acrid
acridity
acrimonious
acrimoniously
acrimony
acrobat
acrobatic
acrobatically
acronym
acrophobia
acropolis
across
acrostic
acrylic
act
action
actionable
activate
  activated
  activating
activation
active
actively
activism
activist
activity
  activities *pl*
actor
actress

actual
actuality
  actualities *pl*
actually
actuary
  actuaries *pl*
actuarial
actuate
  actuated
  actuating
actuation
acuity
acumen
acupuncture
acupuncturist
acute
acutely
acuteness
adage
adagio
  adagios *pl*
adamant
adapt
adaptability
adaptable
adaptation
adapter, adaptor
adaption
adaptive
add
addendum
  addenda *pl*
adder

addict
addiction
addictive
addition (sum)
additive
addle
  addled
  addling
address
addressee
adduce
  adduced
  adducing
adenoid
adenoidal
adept
adequate
adequacy
adequately
adhere
  adhered
  adhering
adherence
adherent
adhesion
adhesive
ad hoc
adieu
  adieus, adieux *pl*
ad infinitum
adipose
adiposity
adjacency

adjacent
adjacently
adjectival
adjectivally
adjective
adjoin
adjourn
adjournment
adjudicate
  adjudicated
  adjudicating
adjudication
adjudicator
adjunct
adjust
adjustable
adjuster
adjustment
adjutant
adjuvant
ad-lib
  ad-libbed
  ad-libbing
  ad-libs
adman
  admen *pl*
administer
administrate
  administrated
  administrating
administration
administrative
administrator

admirable
admirably
admiral
admiralty
admiration
admire
admired
admiring
admirer
admissibility
admissible
admissibly
admission
admit
admits
admitted
admitting
admittance
admixture
admonish
admonition
admonitory
ad nauseam
ado
adolescence
adolescent
adopt
adopter
adoption
adoptive
adorable
adorably
adoration

adore
adored
adoring
adorer
adorn
adornment
adrenalin, adrenaline
adrift
adroit
adsorb
adsorbent
adsorption
adulate
adulated
adulating
adulation
adult
adulterant
adulterate
adulterated
adulterating
adulteration
adultery
adulterer
adulteress
adulterous
adulterously
advance
advanced
advancing
advancement
advantage
advantageous

advantageously
advent (arrival)
Advent (time before
Christmas)
adventitious
adventitiously
adventure
adventurer
adventurous
adventurously
adverb
adverbial
adversary
adversaries pl
adverse
adversely
adversity
advert
advertise
advertised
advertising
advertisement
advertiser
advice (suggestion)
advisability
advisable
advise (to give
advice)
advised
advising
advisedly
adviser, advisor
advisory

advocacy
advocate
  advocated
  advocating
advocation
aegis
  aegises *pl*
aeon
aerate
  aerated
  aerating
aeration
aerator
aerial
aerially
aerobatics
aerobic
aerobics
aerodrome
aerodynamics
aerofoil
aeronaut
aeronautical
aeronautics
aeroplane
aerosol
aerospace
aesthete
aesthetic
aesthetically
aestheticism
aetiologist
aetiology

afar
affability
affable
affably
affair
affect (to influence)
affectation
affection
affectionate
affectionately
affidavit
affiliate
  affiliated
  affiliating
affiliation
affinity
  affinities *pl*
affirm
affirmation
affirmative
affirmatively
affix
afflict
affliction
affluence
affluent
afford
afforest
  afforested
  afforesting
afforestation
affray
  affrays *pl*

affront
aficionado
afield
afloat
aforesaid
afraid
afresh
Afrikaans
after
aftermath
afternoon
afterthought
afterwards
again
against
agape
agate
age
  aged
  ageing, aging
ageless
agelessness
agency
  agencies *pl*
agenda
agent
agglomerate
agglomeration
aggrandise
  aggrandised
  aggrandising
aggrandisement
aggrandize

aggrandized
aggrandizing
aggrandizement
aggravate
  aggravated
  aggravating
aggravation
aggregate
  aggregated
  aggregating
aggregation
aggression
aggressive
aggressively
aggressiveness
aggressor
aggrieve
  aggrieved
  aggrieving
aghast
agile
agilely
agility
aging (*from* age)
agitate
  agitated
  agitating
agitation
agitator
aglow
agnostic
agnosticism
ago

agog
agony
  agonies *pl*
agonise
  agonised
  agonising
agonize
  agonized
  agonizing
agoraphobia
agrarian
agree
agreeable
agreeably
agreement
agriculture
agricultural
agriculturist,
  agriculturalist
aground
ague
ahead
ahoy
aid
aide (helper)
aide-de-camp
  aides-de-camp *pl*
AIDS
ail (to be ill)
ailing
aileron
ailment
aim

aimless
aimlessly
aimlessness
air
airborne
air-conditioned
aircraft
airdrome *Am*
airfield
air force
air hostess
airily
airiness
airing
airless
airlessness
airlift
airline
airliner
airlock
airmail
airman
  airmen *pl*
airplane *Am*
airport
air raid
airspace
air steward
air stewardess
airtight
airworthiness
airworthy
airy

airy-fairy
aisle
ajar
akimbo
akin
alabaster
à la carte
alacrity
à la mode
alarm
alarmist
alas
albatross
albeit
albino
  albinos *pl*
albinism
album
albumen (white of
  egg)
albumin (protein)
alchemy
alchemist
alcohol
alcoholic
alcoholism
alcove
alderman
  aldermen *pl*
ale (beer)
alert
alertly
alertness

alfresco
alga
  algae *pl*
algebra
algebraic
algebraical
algebraically
alias
  aliases *pl*
alibi
  alibis *pl*
alien
alienable
alienate
  alienated
  alienating
alienation
alienator
alight
align
alignment
alike
aliment (food)
alimentary (food)
alimony
alive
alkali
  alkalis, alkalies *pl*
alkaline
alkalinity
all (every)
allay (to reduce,
  lessen)

allegation
allege
  alleged
  alleging
allegedly
allegiance
allegory (story)
  allegories *pl*
allegorical
allegorically
allegretto
  allegrettos *pl*
allegro
  allegros *pl*
alleluia, halleluiah,
  hallelujah
allergic
allergy
  allergies *pl*
alleviate
  alleviated
  alleviating
alleviation
alley
  alleys *pl*
alliance
alligator
alliteration
allocate
  allocated
  allocating
allocation
allocution (a speech)

allot
  allots
  allotted
  allotting
allotment
allow
allowable
allowance
alloy
  alloys *pl*
all right
allude (to mention)
  alluded
  alluding
allure
allurement
alluring
allusion (mention)
allusive (mentioning)
alluvial
ally
  allies *pl*
  allied
  allying
alliance
alma mater
almanac
almighty
almond
almoner
almost
alms (charity)
aloe

aloft
alone
along
aloof
aloofly
aloofness
aloud (speak)
alp
alpine
alpaca
alphabet
alphabetical
alphabetically
already
also
also-ran
altar (in church)
alter (to change)
alterable
alteration
altercate
  altercated
  altercating
altercation
alternate
  alternated
  alternating
alternation
alternative
alternatively
alternator
although
altimeter

altitude
alto
  altos *pl*
altogether
altruism
altruist
altruistic
altruistically
alum
aluminium
aluminum *Am*
always
Alzheimer's
am (*from* be)
amalgam
amalgamate
  amalgamated
  amalgamating
amalgamation
amanuensis
  amanuenses *pl*
amass
amateur
amateurish
amateurishly
amateurishness
amateurism
amaze
  amazed
  amazing
amazement
ambassador
ambassadorial

amber
ambidextrous
ambience
ambient
ambiguity
  ambiguities *pl*
ambiguous
ambiguously
ambit
ambition
ambitiously
ambivalence
ambivalent
amble
  ambled
  ambling
ambulance
ambulant
ambush
ameliorate
  ameliorated
  ameliorating
amelioration
amen
amenable
amenably
amend
amendment
amenity
  amenities *pl*
American
Americana
Americanisation

Americanise
  Americanised
  Americanising
Americanism
Americanization
Americanize
  Americanized
  Americanizing
amethyst
amiable
amiability
amiably
amicable
amicability
amicably
amid
amidships
amidst
amiss
amity
ammeter
ammonia
ammunition
amnesia
amnesty
  amnesties *pl*
amniocentesis
  amniocenteses *pl*
amniotic
amoeba
  amoebas,
    amoebae *pl*
amoebic

amok, amuck
among
  amongst
amoral
amorally
amorous
amorously
amorousness
amorphous
amortisation
amortise
  amortised
  amortising
amortization
amortize
  amortized
  amortizing
amount
amour
amp
amperage
ampere
ampersand
amphetamine
amphibian
amphibious
amphitheater *Am*
amphitheatre
ample (enough)
amplitude
amplifier
amplify
  amplified

amplifies
amplifying
amplification
amplifier
amply
ampoule (bottle)
amputate
  amputated
  amputating
amputation
amputee
amuck, amok
amulet
amuse
  amused
  amusing
amusement
anachronism
anachronistic
anaemia
anaemic
anaerobic
anaesthetic
anaesthesia
anaesthetisation
anaesthetise
  anaesthetised
  anaesthetising
anaesthetist
anaesthetization
anaesthetize
  anaesthetized
  anaesthetizing

anagram
anal
analgesia
analgesic
analogous
analog (computer)
analogical
analogue (similar)
analogy
  analogies pl
analyse
  analysed
  analysing
analyze
  analyzed
  analyzing
analysis
  analyses pl
analyst
analytic
analytical
analytically
anarchic
anarchical
anarchism
anarchist
anarchy
anathema
  anathemas pl
anatomic
anatomical
anatomically
anatomise

anatomised
anatomising
anatomist
anatomize
  anatomized
  anatomizing
anatomy
  anatomies pl
ancestor
ancestral
ancestry
  ancestries pl
anchor
  anchored
  anchoring
anchorage
anchovy
  anchovies pl
ancient
ancillary
  ancillaries pl
anecdotal
anecdote
anemometer
anemone
aneroid
anesthesia Am
anesthetic Am
anesthetist Am
anesthetization Am
anesthetize Am
  anesthetized
  anesthetizing

aneurysm
anew
angel (spiritual)
angelic
angelical
angelically
anger
angina
angle (fishing; maths)
angler
Anglican
Anglicanism
anglicisation
anglicise
  anglicised
  anglicising
anglicization
anglicize
  anglicized
  anglicizing
Anglomania
Anglophile
Anglophobe
Anglophobia
angostura
angry
  angrier
  angriest
anguish
angular
angularity
anhydrous
aniline

animal
animalcule
animate
  animated
  animating
animatedly
animation
animosity
  animosities pl
animus
aniseed
ankle
anklet
annal (story of one
  year)
annalist
anneal (to toughen, eg
  metal)
annex (join)
  annexed
  annexes
  annexing
annexation
annexe (building)
annihilate
  annihilated
  annihilating
annihilation
anniversary
  anniversaries pl
annotate
  annotated
  annotating

annotation
annotator
announce
  announced
  announcing
announcement
announcer
annoy
  annoyed
  annoying
annoyance
annual (yearly)
annually
annuity
  annuities pl
annuitant
annul (cancel)
  annulled
  annulling
  annuls
annular (ring-like)
annularity
annulment
annunciate
  annunciated
  annunciating
annunciation
anode
anodyne
anoint
anomalous
anomalously
anomaly

anomalies *pl*
anon. (anonymous)
anon (soon)
anonymity
anonymous
anonymously
anorak
another
answer
  answered
  answering
answerable
answerphone
antacid
antagonise
  antagonised
  antagonising
antagonize
  antagonized
  antagonizing
antagonism
antagonist
Antarctic
antecedence
antecedent
antechamber
antedate
  antedated
  antedating
antediluvian
antelope
antenatal
antenna (of insect)

antennae *pl*
antenna (radio)
  antennas *pl*
anterior
anteriority
ante-room
anthem
anther
anthology
  anthologies *pl*
anthologist
anthracite
anthrax
anthropoid
anthropology
anthropological
anthropologist
anthropomorphic
anthropomorphism
anti-aircraft
antibiotic
antibody
  antibodies *pl*
antic
antichrist
anticipate
  anticipating
  anticipated
anticipation
anticipative
anticipatory
anticlimactic
anticlimax

anticlockwise
anticyclone
anticyclonic
antidepressant
antidote
antifreeze
antigen
antihistamine
antilogarithm
antimacassar
antimony
antipathy
  antipathies *pl*
antipathetic
antipodean
antipodes
antiquarian
antiquary
  antiquaries *pl*
antiquated
antique
antiquity
  antiquities *pl*
antirrhinum
  antirrhinums *pl*
anti-Semite
anti-Semitic
anti-Semitism
antiseptic
antiseptically
antisepsis
antisocial
antisocially

antithesis
  antitheses *pl*
antitoxic
antitoxin
antler
antonym
anus
anvil
anxiety
  anxieties *pl*
anxious
anxiously
any
anybody
anyhow
anyone
anything
anyway
anywhere
aorta
  aortas *pl*
apace
apart
apartheid
apartment
apathetic
apathetically
apathy
ape
aperient
aperitif
aperture
apex

apexes, apices *pl*
aphasia
aphid
aphorism
aphoristic
aphrodisiac
apiary
  apiaries *pl*
apiarist
apiculture
apiece
aplomb
apocalypse
apocalyptic
apocrypha
apocryphal
apogee
apologia
  apologias *pl*
apologetic
apologetically
apologise
  apologised
  apologising
apologize
  apologized
  apologizing
apology
  apologies *pl*
apophthegm
apoplectic
apoplectically
apoplexy

apostasy
  apostasies *pl*
apostate
apostatise
  apostatised
  apostatising
apostatize
  apostatized
  apostatizing
a posteriori
apostle
apostolate
apostolic
apostrophe
apostrophise
  apostrophised
  apostrophised
apostrophize
  apostrophized
  apostrophizing
apothecary
  apothecaries *pl*
apotheosis
  apotheoses *pl*
appal
  appalled
  appalling
  appals
appall *Am*
  appalled
  appalling
  appalls
apparatus

apparatuses *pl*
apparel
apparent
apparently
apparition
appeal
  appealed
  appealing
appear
  appeared
  appearing
appearance
appease
  appeased
  appeasing
appeasement
appeaser
appellant
appellation
append
appendage
appendicitis
appendix (addition to
  a book)
  appendices *pl*
appendix (in
  anatomy)
  appendixes *pl*
appertain
appetite
appetiser, appetizer
appetising, appetizing
applaud

applause
apple
apple-cart
appliqué
apply
  applied
  applies
  applying
appliance
applicable
applicant
application
appoint
appointment
apportion
apposite (apt)
appraisal
appraise
  appraised
  appraising
appraisement
appreciable
appreciably
appreciate
  appreciated
  appreciating
appreciation
appreciative
apprehend
apprehension
apprehensive
apprentice
apprenticeship

apprise
  apprised
  apprising
apprize
  apprized
  apprizing
approach
approachable
approbation
appropriate
  appropriated
  appropriating
appropriately
appropriateness
appropriation
appropriator
approve
  approved
  approving
approval
approximate
  approximated
  approximating
approximately
approximation
appurtenance
apricot
a priori
apron
apropos
apt
aptitude
aptly

aptness
aqualung
aquarium
  aquaria, aquariums *pl*
aquatic
aquatint
aqueduct
aqueous
aquiline
arabesque
Arabian
Arabic
arable
arbiter
arbitrage
arbitrarily
arbitrariness
arbitrary
arbitrate
  arbitrated
  arbitrating
arbitration
arbitrator
arbour (garden bower)
arbor (axis; garden
  bower *Am* only)
arc (curve)
arcade
arch
archaeological
archaeologically
archaeologist
archaeology

archaic
archaism
archaistic
archangel
archbishop
archbishopric
archdeacon
archdeaconry
archdiocese
archduke
archducal
archduchess
archduchy
  archduchies *pl*
arch-enemy
  arch-enemies *pl*
archer
archery
archetypal
archetype
archiepiscopal
archiepiscopate
archipelago
  archipelagos,
    archipelagoes *pl*
architect
architectural
architecturally
architecture
architrave
archive
archivist
archly

archness
arctic
ardent
ardently
ardour
ardor *Am*
arduous
arduously
are (*from* be)
aren't
area (space)
arena
  arenas *pl*
argosy
argot
arguable
arguably
argue
  argued
  arguing
argument
argumentative
aria (song)
  arias *pl*
arid
aridity
aright
arise
  arisen
  arises
  arising
  arose
aristocracy

aristocracies
aristocrat
aristocratically
arithmetic
arithmetical
arithmetically
arithmetician
ark
arm
arms (weapons)
armada
  armadas *pl*
Armageddon
armament
armature
armchair
armful
armistice
armlet
armor *Am*
armorer *Am*
armory *Am*
  armories *pl*
armour
armourer
armoury
  armouries *pl*
armorial
arms
army
  armies *pl*
aroma
  aromas *pl*

aromatherapy
aromatic
arose (*from* arise)
around
arousal
arouse
  aroused
  arousing
arpeggio
  arpeggios *pl*
arraign
arraignment
arrange
arrangement
arrant (utter,
  thorough)
array
arrears
arrest
arrive
  arrived
  arriving
arrival
arrogance
arrogant
arrogantly
arrogate
  arrogated
  arrogating
arrogation
arrow
arrowroot
arsenal

arsenic
arsenical
arsenious
arson
arsonist
art
artefact
arterial
artery
  arteries *pl*
artesian
artful
artfully
artfulness
arthritic
arthritis
artichoke
article
articulate
  articulated
  articulating
articulately
articulation
artifact *Am*
artifice
artificer
artificial
artificiality
artificially
artillery
artilleryman
  artillerymen *pl*
artisan

artist (*eg* painter)
artiste (performer)
artistic
artistically
artistry
artless
artlessly
artlessness
arty
Aryan
asbestos
asbestosis
ascend (to go up)
ascendancy,
  ascendency
ascendant
ascension
ascent (going up)
ascertain
ascertainable
ascertainment
ascetic (hermit)
ascetically
asceticism
ascribable
ascribe
  ascribed
  ascribing
ascription
asepsis
aseptic
asexual
asexuality

asexually
ash
ashamed
ashen
ashore (on the beach)
ashtray
ashy
Asia
Asiatic
aside
asinine
asininity
ask
askance
askew
asleep
asp
asparagus
aspect
aspen
asperity
  asperities *pl*
aspersion
asphalt
asphyxia
asphyxiant
asphyxiate
  asphyxiated
  asphyxiating
asphyxiation
aspic
aspidistra
  aspidistras *pl*

aspirant
aspirate
  aspirated
  aspirating
aspiration
aspire
  aspired
  aspiring
aspirin
ass
assail
assailant
assassin
assassinate
  assassinated
  assassinating
assassination
assault
assaulter
assay (to test)
  assays *pl*
assayer
assemblage
assemble
  assembled
  assembling
assembly
  assemblies *pl*
assent (agreement)
assert
assertion
assertive
assess (measure)

assessable
assessment
assessor
asset
assiduity
assiduous
assiduously
assign
assignable
assignation
assignee
assignment
assimilate
  assimilated
  assimilating
assimilation
assist
assistance
assistant
assizes
associate
  associated
  associating
association
assonance
assonant
assort
assorted
assortment
assuage
  assuaged
  assuaging
assuagement

assume
  assumed
  assuming
assumption
assurance
assure (to guarantee)
  assured
  assuring
assuredly
assurer
aster (plant)
asterisk
asteroid
astern
asthma
asthmatic
astir (moving about)
astigmatism
astigmatic
astonish
astonishment
astound
astral
astrakhan
astray
astride
astringency
astringent
astrologer
astrology
astronaut
astronautics
astronomy

astronomer
astronomic
astronomical
astronomically
astroturf
astute
astutely
astuteness
asunder
asylum
  asylums *pl*
asymmetric
asymmetrical
asymmetrically
asymmetry
ate (*from* eat)
atheism
atheist
athlete
athletic
athletics
atlas
atmosphere
atmospheric
atoll
atom
atomic
atomically
atomisation
atomise
  atomised
  atomising
atomiser

atomization
atomize
  atomized
  atomizing
atomizer
atone
  atoned
  atoning
atonement
atrocious
atrociously
atrocity
  atrocities *pl*
atrophy
  atrophied
  atrophies
  atrophying
attach
attachable
attaché
attaché case
attachment
attack
attacker
attain
attainable
attainment
attempt
attend
attendance
attendant
attention
attentive

attentively
attenuate
  attenuated
  attenuating
attenuation
attenuator
attest
attestation
attestor, attestator
attic
attire
  attired
  attiring
attitude
attorney
  attorneys *pl*
attract
attraction
attractive
attractiveness
attributable
attribute
  attributed
  attributing
attribution
attributive
attributively
attrition
attune
  attuned
  attuning
atypical
atypically

aubergine
auburn
auction
auctioneer
audacious
audaciously
audacity
audibility
audible
audibly
audience
audiometer
audiometric
audiometry
audio-typist
audio-visual
audit
  audited
  auditing
auditor
audition
auditorium
  auditoriums,
  auditoria *pl*
au fond
auger (tool)
augment
augmentation
au gratin
augur (to predict)
augury
  auguries *pl*
August (month)

august (noble)
auk
aunt (relation)
auntie, aunty
au pair
aura
  auras *pl*
aural (by ear)
aurally
auspices
auspicious
auspiciously
austere
austerely
austerity
  austerities *pl*
autarchy (absolute
  power)
  autarchies *pl*
autarky (self-
  sufficiency)
authentic
authentically
authenticate
  authenticated
  authenticating
authentication
authenticity
author
authorship
authorisation
authorise
  authorised

authorising
authority
  authorities *pl*
authoritarian
authoritative
authoritatively
authorization
authorize
  authorized
  authorizing
autism
autistic
autobiographic
autobiographical
autobiographically
autobiography
  autobiographies *pl*
autocracy
  autocracies *pl*
autocrat
autocratic
autocratically
autogenous
autogiro, autogyro
  autogiros,
    autogyros *pl*
autograph
automatic
automatically
automation
automatism
automaton
  automatons,

automata *pl*
automobile
automotive
autonomous
autonomy
autopilot
autopsy
  autopsies *pl*
autostrada
  autostrade *pl*
auto-suggestion
autumn
autumnal
auxiliary
  auxiliaries *pl*
avail
availability
available
avalanche
avant-garde
avarice
avaricious
avenge
  avenged
  avenging
avenger
avenue
aver
  averred
  averring
  avers
average
averse

aversion
avert
avertable, avertible
aviary
  aviaries *pl*
aviation
aviator
avid
avidity
avidly
avocado
  avocados *pl*
avocation
avoid (evade)
avoidable
avoidably
avoidance
avuncular
await
awake
  awakes
  awaking
  awoke
  awoken
award
aware
awareness
away
awe (fear)
awesome
awful
awfully
awfulness

awhile
awkward
awkwardly
awkwardness
awl
awning
awry
ax *Am*
axe
  axed
  axing
axial
axially
axiom
axiomatic
axiomatically
axis
  axes *pl*
axle
ay, aye
ayah
ayatollah
azalea
  azaleas *pl*
azimuth
azimuthal
azure

B

babble (to chatter)
  babbled
  babbling
babbler
babe
Babel (tower of)
baboon
baby
  babies *pl*
babyish
babysit
  babysat
  babysits
  babysitting
babysitter
baccarat
bacchanalia
bachelor
bachelorhood

bacillary
bacillus
  bacilli *pl*
back
backache
backbench
backbencher
backbenches
backbite
backbiter
backbiting
backbone
back-breaking
backdate
  backdated
  backdating
backer
backfire
  backfired

  backfiring
backgammon
background
backpack
backstairs
backup
backward
backwardness
backwater
bacon
bacterial
bacteriological
bacteriologist
bacteriology
bacterium
  bacteria *pl*
bad (not good)
bade (*from* bid)
badge
badger
badly
badminton
bad-tempered
baffle
  baffled
  baffling
bag
  bagged
  bagging
  bags
bagatelle
baggage
baggy

baggier
baggiest
bagpipe
baguette
bail (to scoop water)
  bailed
  bailing
bailiff
  bailiffs *pl*
bairn
bait (fishing)
  baited
  baiting
baize
bake
  baked
  baking
baker
bakery
  bakeries *pl*
baksheesh,
  backsheesh
balaclava
  balaclavas *pl*
balalaika
  balalaikas *pl*
balance
  balanced
  balancing
balcony
  balconies *pl*
bald (hairless)
balderdash

bald-headed
baldness
bale (to bundle)
  baled
  baling
baleful
balefully
ball (round shape)
ballad
ballast
ball-bearing
ballerina
  ballerinas *pl*
ballet
ballistic
balloon
  ballooned
  ballooning
ballot
  balloted
  balloting
ball-point
ballyhoo
balm
balmy (weather)
  balmier
  balmiest
baloney, boloney
balsam
baluster
balustrade
bamboo
bamboozle

bamboozled
bamboozling
ban (to prohibit)
  banned
  banning
  bans
banal
banality
  banalities *pl*
banally
banana
  bananas *pl*
band (strip; group)
bandage
  bandaged
  bandaging
bandit
banditry
bandoleer, bandolier
bandsman
  bandsmen *pl*
bandy
  bandied
  bandies
  bandying
bandy-legged
bane
baneful
banefully
bang
  banged
  banging
bangle

banish
banishment
banister, bannister
banjo
  banjos *pl*
bank
banker
banknote
bankrupt
bankruptcy
  bankruptcies *pl*
banner
banns (for marriage)
banquet
  banqueted
  banqueting
banshee
bantam
banter
  bantered
  bantering
baptise
  baptised
  baptising
baptism
baptize
  baptized
  baptizing
bar
  barred
  barring
  bars
barb

barbarian
barbaric
barbarism
barbarous
barbarously
barbecue
  barbecued
  barbecuing
barbed wire
barber
barbitone
barbiturate
barbituric
bard (poet)
bare (uncovered)
  bared
  baring
bareback
barefaced
barefoot
bareheaded
barelegged
barely
bareness
bargain
barge
  barged
  barging
bargee
barge-pole
baritone
barium
bark

bark, barque (ship)
barley
barmaid
barman
  barmen *pl*
barmily
barmy (silly)
  barmier
  barmiest
barn
barnacle
barnyard
barometer
barometric
baron (nobleman)
baroness
baronet
baronial
barony
  baronies *pl*
baroque
barque, bark (ship)
barrack
barrage
barrel
  barrelled
  barrelling
  barrels
  barreled *Am*
  barreling *Am*
barren (sterile)
barrenness
barricade

barricaded
barricading
barrier
barrister
barrow
bartender
barter
　bartered
　bartering
barterer
basalt
base (to found)
　based
　basing
baseball
baseless
basely
basement
baseness
bashful
bashfully
bashfulness
basic
basically
basil
basin
basis
　bases *pl*
bask
basket
basketball
bas-relief
　bas-reliefs *pl*

bass (fish; music)
bass, bast (fibre)
basset
bassoon
bastard
bastardy
baste
　basted
　basting
bastion
bat
　bats
　batted
　batting
batch
bate (to hold)
　bated
　bating
bated breath
bath
bathe (to go
　swimming)
　bathed
　bathing
bather
bathos
batik
baton (conductor's)
batsman
　batsmen *pl*
battalion
batten (to close)
batter

battery
　batteries *pl*
battle
　battled
　battling
battleax *Am*
battleaxe
battledress
battlement
battleship
batty
　battier
　battiest
bauble
baulk, balk
bauxite
bawdy
　bawdier
　bawdiest
bawl (to shout)
　bawled
　bawling
bay
　bayed
　baying
　bays
bay leaf
bayonet
bazaar (market)
bazooka
　bazookas *pl*
be (to exist)
　am

are
been
being
is
was
beach (shore)
  beaches *pl*
beachcomber
beachhead
beacon
bead
  beaded
  beading
beadle
beady
beagle
beak
beaker
beam
  beamed
  beaming
bean (vegetable)
beanfeast
beansprout
beanstalk
bear (animal; to carry)
  bearing
  bears
  bore
  borne
bearable
beard
bearer

bearing (of a
  machine)
beast
beastliness
beastly
  beastlier
  beastliest
beat (to hit)
  beaten
  beating
  beats
beater
beatific
beatnik
beau (suitor)
  beaux *pl*
beauty
  beauties *pl*
beauteous
beautician
beautiful
beautifully
beautify
  beautified
  beautifies
  beautifying
beaver
becalm
because
beckon (to signal)
  beckoned
  beckoning
become

became
becomes
becoming
bed
  bedded
  bedding
  beds
bedaub
bedclothes
bedevil
  bedevilled
  bedevilling
  bedevils
  bedeviled *Am*
  bedeviling *Am*
bedlam
Bedouin
bedraggle
  bedraggled
  bedraggling
bedridden
bedrock
bedsit
bee (insect)
beech (tree)
  beeches *pl*
beef
  beefed
  beefing
beefeater
beefsteak
beefy
  beefier

49

beefiest
beehive
beeline
been (*from* be)
beer (ale)
beeriness
beery
beeswax
beet (vegetable)
beetle (insect)
beetroot
befall
  befallen
  befalling
  befalls
  befell
befit
  befits
  befitted
  befitting
before
beforehand
befoul
befriend
beg
  begged
  begging
  begs
beget
  begets
  begetting
  begot
  begotten

begetter
beggar
beggarliness
beggarly
beggary
begin
  began
  beginning
  begins
  begun
beginner
begone
begonia
  begonias *pl*
begrudge
  begrudged
  begrudging
beguile
  beguiled
  beguiling
beguilement
beguiler
behalf
behave
  behaved
  behaving
  behavior *Am*
  behaviour
behead
  beheaded
  beheading
behind
behindhand

behold
  beheld
  beholding
  beholds
beholden
beholder
behoove *Am*
  behooved
  behooving
behove
beige
being (*from* be)
belabor *Am*
  belabored
  belaboring
belabour
  belaboured
  belabouring
belated
belay
  belayed
  belaying
  belays
belch
beleaguer
belfry
  belfries *pl*
belie
  belied
  belies
  belying
belief
believable

believe
  believed
  believing
believer
belittle
  belittled
  belittling
belittler
bell (for ringing)
belladonna
  belladonnas *pl*
belle (pretty girl)
belles lettres
bellicose
bellicosity
belligerence
belligerent
bellow
bellows
belly
  bellies *pl*
bellyful
belong
beloved
below (under)
belt
bemoan
  bemoaned
  bemoaning
bemuse
  bemused
  bemusing
bench

bencher
bend
  bending
  bends
  bent
beneath
benediction
benefaction
benefactor
benefactress
benefice
beneficence
beneficent
beneficial
beneficially
beneficiary
  beneficiaries *pl*
benefit
  benefited
  benefiting
benefiter
benevolence
benevolent
benevolently
benighted
benign
benignancy
benignant
benison
bent
benumb
benzene (coal tar)
benzine (petrol)

bequeath
bequest
berate
  berated
  berating
bereaved
bereavement
bereft
beret (cap)
berry (fruit)
  berries *pl*
berserk
berserker
berth (nautical)
beryl
beseech
beset
  besets
  besetting
beside
besides
besiege
  besieged
  besieging
besom
besotted
besought (*from*
  beseech)
bespeak
  bespeaking
  bespeaks
  bespoke
  bespoken

best
bestial
bestialism
bestiality
  bestialities pl
bestially
bestir
  bestirred
  bestirring
  bestirs
bestow
bestowal
bestride
  bestrides
  bestriding
  bestrode
bet
  bets
  betted
  betting
better
bête noire
  bêtes noires pl
betel nut
betide
betoken
betray
  betrayed
  betraying
betrayal
betroth
betrothal
betrothed

better
  bettered
  bettering
betterment
between
betwixt
bevel
  bevelled
  bevelling
  bevels
  beveled Am
  beveling Am
beverage
bevy
  bevies pl
bewail
beware
bewilder
bewilderment
bewitch
beyond
bhaji, bhajee
biannual (twice a
  year)
biannually
bias
  biased, biassed
  biases
  biasing, biassing
bible (general)
Bible (Christian or
  Jewish scriptures)
biblical

bibliography
  bibliographies pl
bibliographer
bibliographic
bibliographical
bibliographically
bibliophile, bibliophil
bibulous
bicarbonate
bicentenary
  bicentenaries pl
bicentennial
biceps
bicker
bicycle
bicyclist
bid
  bade
  bidden
  bidding
  bids
bide
  bided
  biding
bidet
biennial (every two
  years)
biennially
bier (coffin stand)
bifocal
bifurcate
  bifurcated
  bifurcating

bifurcation
big
  bigger
  biggest
bigamist
bigamous
bigamously
bigamy
bight (bay)bigot
bigoted
bigotry
bigwig
bijou
  bijoux *pl*
bike
bikini
bilateral
bilaterally
bilberry
  bilberries *pl*
bile
bilge
biliary
bilingual
bilingualism
bilinguist
bilious
biliousness
bilk
bill
billet
billet doux
  billets doux *pl*

billetee
billeter
billiards
billion
billionaire
billow (of a wave)
billowy
bimonthly
bin
  binned
  binning
  bins
binary
binaural
bind
  binding
  binds
  bound
binder
bindery
  binderies *pl*
binge
  binged
  binging
bingo
binnacle
binocular
binomial
biochemical
biochemist
biochemistry
biodegradable
biodegrade

biodegraded
  biodegrading
biodiversity
biography
  biographies *pl*
biographer
biographical
biographically
biological
biologically
biologist
biology
bionics
biopsy
  biopsies *pl*
biorhythms
bipartisan
bipartite
biped
biplane
bipolar
birch
bird
birdie
bird's-eye
biriani, biryani
birth (born)
birthday
birthplace
birthrate
birthright
biscuit
bisect

bisection
bisector
bisexual
bisexually
bishop
bishopric
bismuth
bison
bistro
bit
bitch
  bitches *pl*
bite (with teeth)
  bit
  biter
  bites
  biting
  bitten
bitter
bitterly
bittern (bird)
bitterness
bitumen
bituminous
bivalve
bivouac
  bivouacs
  bivouacked
  bivouacking
bizarre (unusual)
bizarrely
bizarreness
blab

blabbed
blabbing
blabs
black
blackberry
  blackberries *pl*
blackbird
blackboard
blacken
blackguard
blackguardly
blackmail
blackmailer
black market
black marketeer
blackness
blackout (loss of
  consciousness)
black out (to lose
  consciousness)
blacksmith
bladder
blade
blame
  blamed
  blaming
blameless
blamelessly
blanch
blancmange
bland
blandish
blandishment

blandly
blank
blanket
blare
  blared
  blaring
blarney
blasé
blaspheme
blasphemer
blasphemous
blasphemy
  blasphemies *pl*
blast
blast-off
blatancy
blatant
blatantly
blaze
  blazed
  blazing
blazer
blazon
bleach
bleak
bleakly
bleakness
blear
blearily
bleariness
bleary
bleary-eyed
bleat

bleated
bleating
bleed
  bled
  bleeding
  bleeds
blemish
  blemishes *pl*
blench
blend
blender
bless
  blessed (sacred)
  blesses
  blessing
  blest
blew (*from* blow)
blight
blighter
blind
blind alley
  blind alleys *pl*
blindfold
blindly
blink
blinkered
bliss
blissful
blissfully
blissfulness
blister
  blistered
  blistering

blithe
blithely
blitheness
blithering
blizzard
bloat
  bloated
  bloating
bloater
blob
  blobbed
  blobbing
  blobs
bloc (group)
block (to stop; solid
  piece)
blockade
blockage
blockbuster
blockhead
bloke
blond (male)
blonde (female)
blood
bloodcurdling
bloodhound
blood pressure
bloodshed
bloodshot
bloodthirsty
blood vessel
bloody
  bloodied

bloodies
bloodying
bloodier
bloodiest
bloom
  bloomed
  blooming
bloomer
blossom
  blossomed
  blossoming
blot
  blots
  blotted
  blotting
blotch
  blotches *pl*
blotchy
  blotchier
  blotchiest
blotter
blouse
blow
  blew
  blown
  blows
blower
blowzy (red-faced)
blub
  blubbed
  blubbing
  blubs
blubber (of whale)

blubbery
bludgeon
blue (colour)
bluebell
blueberry
  blueberries *pl*
blue-chip
blue-collar
blue-eyed
blueness
blue-pencil
  blue-pencilled
  blue-pencilling
  blue-pencils
  blue-penciled *Am*
  blue-penciling *Am*
bluff
bluffness
blunder
blunderbuss
blunderer
blunt
bluntly
bluntness
blur
  blurred
  blurring
  blurs
blurb
blurriness
blurry
blurt
blush

bluster
blustery
boa
  boas *pl*
boa constrictor
boar (male pig)
board (wooden plank)
boarder (lodger)
boast
boaster
boastful
boastfully
boastfulness
boat
boatswain, bosun
bob
  bobbed
  bobbing
  bobs
bobbin
bobby
  bobbies *pl*
bobsled, bobsleigh
bode
  boded
  boding
bodice
bodied
bodiless
bodily
bodkin
body
  bodies *pl*

bodyguard
bogey (golf; goblin;
    nasal mucus)
  bogeys *pl*
boggle
  boggled
  boggling
bogie (wheeled
    undercarriage)
  bogies *pl*
bogus
boil
  boiled
  boiling
boiler
boisterous
boisterously
bold (brave)
bolder
boldly
bole (tree trunk)
bollard
boloney, baloney
Bolshevik
Bolshevism
Bolshevist
bolster
  bolstered
  bolstering
bolt
bomb
bombard
bombardier

bombardment
bombast
bombastic
bombastically
bomber
bombshell
bona fide (in good
  faith)
bona fides (good
  faith)
bonanza
  bonanzas *pl*
bond
bondage
bone
  boned
  boning
boneless
bonfire
bonhomie
bonnet
bonny
  bonnier
  bonniest
bony
  bonier
  boniest
bonsai
bonus
  bonuses *pl*
bon voyage
boo
  boos *pl*

booed
booing
boos
booby
  boobies *pl*
book
  booked
  booking
bookable
bookie
bookkeeper
bookkeeping
booklet
boom
  boomed
  booming
boomerang
boor (lout)
boorish
boost
booster
boot
  booted
  booting
bootee (baby's shoe)
booth
bootlace
bootleg
  bootlegs
  bootlegged
  bootlegging
bootlegger
bootless

booty (plunder)
booze
  boozed
  boozing
boozer
boozy
boracic
borax
border (edge)
bore
  bored
  boring
boredom
born (of a baby)
borne (*from* bear)
borough (town)
borrow (*eg* money)
borrower
bosh
bosom
boss
bossily
bossiness
bossy
  bossier
  bossiest
bosun, boatswain
botanical
botanist
botany
botch
both
bother

botheration
bothersome
bottle
  bottled
  bottling
bottleneck
bottom
  bottomed
  bottoming
bottomless
bottommost
botulism
boudoir
bough (branch)
bought (*from* buy)
boulder
boulevard
bounce
  bounced
  bouncing
bound
boundary
  boundaries pl
bounder
boundless
bounteous
bountiful
bounty
  bounties pl
bouquet
bourbon
bourgeois
bourgeoisie

bout
boutique
bovine
bow (to bend)
bowdlerise
  bowdlerised
  bowdlerising
bowdlerize
  bowdlerized
  bowdlerizing
bowel (intestine)
bower
bow-legged
bow-legs
bowl (dish)
bowler
bowling
bow-tie
box
boxer
Boxing Day
boy (male child)
  boys pl
boycott
boyfriend
boyhood
boyish
boyishly
boyishness
bra (brassiere)
  bras pl
brace
  braced

bracing
bracelet
bracken
bracket
brackish
brad
bradawl
brag
  bragged
  bragging
  brags
braggart
braid
  braided
  braiding
Braille
brain
brainless
brainwashed
brainwashing
brainwave
brainy
  brainier
  brainiest
braise (to cook)
  braised
  braising
brake (to slow down)
  braked
  braking
bramble
bran
branch

brand
brand-new
brandy
  brandies *pl*
brash
brass
brassard
brasserie (restaurant)
brassiere (bra)
brat
bravado
brave
  braved
  braving
bravely
bravery
bravo (cry of
  approval)
  bravos *pl*
bravo (ruffian)
  bravoes *pl*
bravura
brawl
brawn
brawny
bray
  brayed
  braying
  brays
braze (to solder)
  brazed
  brazing
brazen

brazenness
brazier (burner)
breach (break)
  breached
  breaches
  breaching
bread (food)
breadth (width)
break (to split)
  breaking
  breaks
  broke
  broken
breakable
breakage
breakfast
breakthrough
bream (fish)
breast
breastfeed
  breastfed
  breastfeeding
  breastfeeds
breath (air)
breathalyse
  breathalysed
  breathalysing
breathalyser
breathalyze
  breathalyzed
  breathalyzing
breathalyzer
breathe (to take

  breaths)
  breathed
  breathing
breather
breathless
breathtaking
breech (of gun)
breeches (trousers)
breech-loader
breech-loading
breed
  bred
  breeding
  breeds
breeze
  breezed
  breezing
breezily
breezy
  breezier
  breeziest
brethren
brevity
brew (to make beer)
brewer
brewery
  breweries *pl*
briar, brier
bribe
  bribed
  bribing
bribeable, bribable
bribery

bric-a-brac
brick
brickbat
bricklayer
bricklaying
bridal (of bride)
bride
bridegroom
bridesmaid
bridge
  bridged
  bridging
bridgehead
bridle (of horse)
  bridled
  bridling
bridle-path
Brie
brief
  briefed
  briefing
  briefs
briefcase
briefly
brier, briar
brigade
brigadier
brigand
bright
brighten
  brightened
  brightening
brightly

Brighton
brilliance
brilliant
brilliantly
brim (to fill)
  brimmed
  brimming
  brims
brimful, brimfull
brimstone
brine
bring
  bringing
  brings
  brought
brink
briny
briquette
brisk
brisket
briskly
bristle
  bristled
  bristling
bristly
Britain (country)
Britannia
Britannic
British
Briton (British
  subject)
Brittany
brittle

brittleness
broach (to open)
broad
broadcast
broadcaster
broaden
broadly
broadminded
broadside
brocade
broccoli
brochure
brogue
broil
  broiled
  broiling
broiler
broke (*from* break)
broken (*from* break)
broken-hearted
broker
brokerage
bromide
bronchial
bronchitic
bronchitis
bronco
  broncos *pl*
bronze
bronzed
brooch (jewellery)
  brooches *pl*
brood (to worry)

brooded
brooding
broody
brook
brooklet
broom
broth
brothel
brother
brotherhood
brother-in-law
  brothers-in-law *pl*
brotherliness
brotherly
brougham (carriage)
brought (*from* bring)
brow (eyebrow; edge)
browbeat
  browbeaten
  browbeating
brown
Brownie
browse
  browsed
  browsing
  bruise
  bruised
  bruising
bruiser
bruising
brunette
brunt
brush

brusque
brusquely
brusqueness
Brussels (city)
Brussels sprouts
brutal
brutalisation
brutalise
  brutalised
  brutalising
brutality
  brutalities *pl*
brutalization
brutalize
  brutalized
  brutalizing
brutally
brute
bubble
  bubbled
  bubbling
bubbly
buccaneer
buck
bucket
bucketful
  bucketfuls *pl*
buckle
  buckled
  buckling
buck rarebit (food)
buck-passer
buckpassing

buckram
buck-toothed
bucolic
bud
  budded
  budding
  buds
Buddha
Buddhism
Buddhist
buddleia
  buddleias *pl*
budge
  budged
  budging
budgerigar
budget
  budgeted
  budgeting
budgetary
buff
buffalo
  buffaloes *pl*
buffer
buffet
  buffeted
  buffeting
buffoon
buffoonery
  buffooneries *pl*
bug
  bugged
  bugging

bugs
bugbear
buggy
  buggies *pl*
bugle
bugler
build
  building
  builds
  built
builder
building
bulb
bulbous
bulge
  bulged
  bulging
bulimia
bulk
bulkhead
bulky
  bulkier
  bulkiest
bull
bulldoze
  bulldozed
  bulldozing
bulldozer
bullet
bullet-proof
bulletin
bullfighter
bullfinch

bullfinches *pl*
bullion
bullish
bullock
bull's-eye
bully
  bullies *pl*
  bullied
  bullies
  bullying
bullyrag
bulrush
bulwark
bum
  bummed
  bumming
  bums
bumble-bee
bump
bumper
bumpily
bumpiness
bumpy
  bumpier
  bumpiest
bumpkin
bumptious
bumptiously
bumptiousness
bun
bunch
  bunches *pl*
bundle

bundled
bundling
bung
bungalow
bunged up
bungle
  bungled
  bungling
bungler
bunion
bunk
bunker (in golf)
bunkum
bunny
  bunnies *pl*
Bunsen burner
bunting
buoy (float)
  buoys *pl*
buoyancy
buoyant
buoyantly
bur, burr (of a plant)
burble
  burbled
  burbling
burden
  burdened
  burdening
burdensome
bureau
  bureaux, bureaus *pl*
bureaucracy

bureaucracies *pl*

ureaucrat

ureaucratic

ureaucratically

ourgeon

urgeoning

burglar

burglary

  burglaries *pl*

burgle

  burgled

  burgling

burgomaster

burgundy

  burgundies *pl*

burial

burlesque

burliness

burly

  burlier

  burliest

burn

  burned

  burning

  burns

  burnt

burner

burnish

burnished

burnisher

burr (sound)

burrow

bursar

bursary

  bursaries *pl*

burial

burst

bury

  buried

  buries

  burying

bus

  buses *pl*

busby

  busbies *pl*

bush

  bushes *pl*

bushel

bushy

  bushier

  bushiest

business

  businesses *pl*

business-like

businessman

  businessmen *pl*

businesswoman

  businesswomen *pl*

bus-stop

busk

busker

bust

bustle

  bustled

  bustling

busy

busied

busies

busying

busier

busiest

busybody

  busybodies *pl*

busyness (being busy)

but (contrary)

butcher

butcherer

butchery

  butcheries *pl*

butler

butt (to adjoin;

    container)

  butted

  butting

  butts

butter

  buttered

  buttering

buttercup

butter-fingered

butter fingers

butterfly

  butterflies *pl*

buttery

  butteries *pl*

buttock

button

  buttoned

  buttoning

buttress
buxom
buxomness
buy (to purchase)
  bought
  buying
  buys
buyer
buzz
buzzard
buzzer
by (close to)
by and by
bye (in cricket)
by-election
bygone
by-law
by-line, byline
bypass
bypath
by-play
by-product
byre (cow-house)
byroad
bystander
byte (computer)
byword

cab
cabaret
cabbage
cabby
  cabbies *pl*
cabin
cabinet
cable
  cabled
  cabling
cablegram
cache (hide)
cackle
  cackled
  cackling
cacophonous
cacophony
  cacophonies *pl*
cactus

cacti, cactuses *pl*
cad
cadaver
cadaverous
caddie, caddy (golf)
  caddied
  caddies
  caddying
caddis
caddish
caddishly
caddis-worm
caddy (tea)
  caddies *pl*
cadence
cadenza
  cadenzas *pl*
cadet
cadet corps

cadge
  cadged
  cadging
cadmium
Caesar
caesarean
café
  cafés *pl*
cafeteria
  cafeterias *pl*
caffeine
cage
caged
cagey
  cagier
  cagiest
  cagily
  caginess
cagoule
cairn
caisson
cajole
  cajoled
  cajoling
cajolery
cake
  caked
  caking
calabash
calamine
calamity
  calamities *pl*
calamitous

calcification
calcify
  calcified
  calcifies
  calcifying
calcium
calculable
calculate
  calculated
  calculating
calculation
calculator
calculus
calendar (table
  of dates)
calender (machine)
calends, kalends
calf
  calves pl
caliber Am
calibrate
  calibrated
  calibrating
calibration
calibre
calico
  calicoes, calicos pl
caliper Am
caliph
caliphate
call (to shout out)
caller
calligrapher

calligraphic
calligraphist
calligraphy
calliper
callisthenic,
  calisthenic
callisthenics,
  calisthenics
callosity
callous (unfeeling)
callously
callousness
callow
callus (hard skin)
  calluses pl
calm
calmly
calmness
calomel
calorie
  calories pl
calorific
calorimeter
calorimetric
calorimetry
calumniate
  calumniated
  calumniating
calumniator
calumnious
calumny
  calumnies pl
calve (give birth

to a calf)
  calved
  calving
calypso
calyx
  calyxes, calyces pl
cam
camaraderie
camber
cambered
cambric
camcorder
came (from come)
camel
camel-hair
Camembert
cameo
  cameos pl
camera
  cameras pl
camisole
camomile
camouflage
  camouflaged
  camouflaging
camp
campaign
camphor
camphorated
campsite
campus
  campuses pl
can (to put in tins)

canned
canning
cans
can (to be able to)
could
anal
analisation
analise
canalised
canalising
analization
analize
canalized
canalizing
canary (bird)
canaries *pl*
can-can
cancel
cancelled
cancelling
cancels
canceled *Am*
canceling *Am*
cancellation
cancer
cancerous
candelabra,
candelabrum
candelabra,
candelabras,
candelabrums *pl*
candid (open)
candidacy

candidacies *pl*
candidate
candidature
candidly
candle
candlelight
candlestick
candor *Am*
candour
candy
candies *pl*
candied
candies
candying
cane
caned
caning
canine
canister
canker
cannabis
cannery
canneries *pl*
cannibal
cannibalisation
cannibalise
cannibalised
cannibalising
cannibalism
cannibalization
cannibalize
cannibalized
cannibalizing

cannily
canniness
cannon (gun)
cannonade
cannot
canny
cannier
canniest
canoe
canoes *pl*
canoeing
canoeist
canon (law)
canonical
canonisation
canonise
canonised
canonising
canonization
canonize
canonized
canonizing
canonry
canopied
canopy
canopies *pl*
can't (cannot)
cant (hypocrisy)
cantabile
cantaloup, cantaloupe
cantankerous
cantankerously
cantata

cantatas *pl*
canteen
canter
  cantered
  cantering
cantilever
canto
  cantos *pl*
canton
cantonal
cantonment
cantor
canvas (cloth)
  canvases *pl*
canvass (for votes)
  canvassed
  canvasses
  canvassing
canvasser
canyon
caoutchouc
cap
  capped
  capping
  caps
capability
  capabilities *pl*
capable
capably
capacious
capacitance
capacitive
capacitor

capacity
  capacities *pl*
cape
caper (to jump)
caper-sauce
capillary
  capillaries *pl*
capital (city, letter)
capitalisation
capitalise
  capitalised
  capitalising
capitalism
capitalist
capitalistic
capitalization
capitalize
  capitalized
  capitalizing
capitally
capitation
Capitol (building)
capitulate
  capitulated
  capitulating
capitulation
capon
cappuccino
caprice
capricious
capriciously
capsizable
capsize

capsized
capsizing
capstan
capsular
capsule
captain
captaincy
  captaincies *pl*
caption
  captioned
  captioning
captious
captiously
captiousness
captivate (to delight)
  captivated
  captivating
captivation
captive
captivity
capture
  captured
  capturing
captor
car
carabiniere
  carabinieri *pl*
carafe
caramel
carat (weight)
caravan
caravanning
caraway

caraways *pl*
arbide
arbine
arbohydrate
arbolic
arbon
arbon dioxide
arbonaceous
arbonate
arbonic
arbonisation
arbonise
  carbonised
  carbonising
carbonization
carbonize
  carbonized
  carbonizing
carborundum
carboy
  carboys *pl*
carbuncle
carburetor *Am*
carburettor
carcass, carcase
  carcasses, carcases *pl*
carcinogenic
carcinoma
  carcinomas *pl*
card
cardboard
card-carrying
cardiac

cardigan
cardinal (of Church)
cardiogram
cardiograph
cardiographer
cardiographic
cardiography
care
  cared
  caring
careen
  careened
  careening
career
  careered
  careering
careerist
carefree
careful
carefully
careless
carelessly
carelessness
caress
caretaker
careworn
cargo
  cargoes *pl*
caricature
  caricatured
  caricaturing
caricaturist
caries (decay)

carillon
carjack
carjacking
carminative
carmine
carnage
carnal
carnally
carnation
carnival
carnivorous
carol
  carolled
  carolling
  carols
  caroled *Am*
  caroling *Am*
  caroler *Am*
  caroller
carotid
carousal (drinking
  bout)
carouse
  caroused
  carousing
carousel (roundabout)
  carousing
carp
carpenter
carpentry
carpet
  carpeted
  carpeting

carriage
carrion
carrot (vegetable)
carrier
carry (to bear)
  carried
  carries
  carrying
cart
cartage
carte blanche
cartel
carter
cartilage
cartilaginous
cartographer
cartographic
cartography
carton (cardboard)
cartoon (drawing)
cartoonist
cartridge
carve (to cut up)
  carved
  carving
caryatid
cascade
  cascaded
  cascading
cascara
case
  cased
  casing

casein
casement
cash (money)
cashew
cashier
cashmere
casino
  casinos pl
cask
casket
casserole
cassette
cassock
cast (throw)
castanets
castaway
  castaways pl
caste (social class)
casteless
castellated
cast-off
castigate
  castigated
  castigating
castigation
castle
castor, caster
castor oil
castrate
  castrated
  castrating
castration
castrato (singer)

castrati pl
casual
casually
casualness
casualty
  casualties pl
casuist
casuistry
cat
catabolism
cataclysm (upheaval)
cataclysmal
cataclysmic
cataclysmically
catacomb
catalepsy
cataleptic
catalog Am
  cataloged
  cataloging
cataloger Am
catalogue
  catalogued
  cataloguing
cataloguer
catalysation
catalyse
  catalysed
  catalysing
catalyser
catalysis
  catalyses pl
catalyst

catalytic
catalyzation
catalyze
  catalyzed
  catalyzing
catalyzer
catamaran
catapult
cataract
catarrh
catarrhal
catastrophe
catastrophic
catastrophically
catcall
catch
  catches
  catching
  caught
catchment
catechise
  catechised
  catechising
catechism
catechize
  catechized
  catechizing
categoric
categorical
categorically
categorise
  categorised
  categorising

categorize
  categorized
  categorizing
category
  categories *pl*
cat's eye
cater
caterer
caterpillar
caterwaul
catgut
catharsis
cathartic
cathedral
catheter
cathode
cathodic
catholic
catholicism
catholicity
catkin
catnap
cattily
cattish
catty
  cattier
  cattiest
catsup *Am*
cattle
caucus
  caucuses *pl*
caught (*from* catch)
caul (of a baby)

cauldron
cauliflower
caulk (to make
  watertight)
causal
causation
causative
cause
  caused
  causing
causeway
  causeways *pl*
caustic
caustically
cauterisation
cauterise
  cauterised
  cauterising
cauterization
cauterize
  cauterized
  cauterizing
cautery
  cauteries *pl*
caution
cautionary
cautious
cautiously
cavalcade
cavalier
cavalry
  cavalries *pl*
cave

caved
caving
caveat
cavern
cavernous
caviare, caviar
cavil
  cavilled
  cavilling
  cavils
  caviled Am
  caviling Am
cavity
  cavities pl
cavort
caw (bird sound)
cayenne
CD
CD ROM
cease
ceasefire
ceaseless
ceaselessly
cedar
cede (yield)
  ceded
  ceding
cedilla
  cedillas pl
ceiling (of a room)
celandine
celebrant
celebrate

celebrated
celebrating
celebration
celebrator
celebrity
  celebrities pl
celeriac
celerity
celery (vegetable)
celestial
celestially
celibacy
celibate
cell (eg prison)
cellar (basement)
cellarage
cellist
cello
  cellos pl
cellophane
cellular
cellulite
celluloid
cellulose
Celsius
Celt
Celtic
cement
cemetery
  cemeteries pl
cenotaph
censer (for incense)
censor (official)

censorious
censorship
censure (blame)
  censured
  censuring
census
  censuses pl
cent (money)
centaur
centenary
  centenaries pl
centenarian
centennial
centigrade
centigram
centiliter Am
centilitre
centime
centimeter Am
centimetre
centipede
central
centralisation
centralise
  centralised
  centralising
centralization
centralize
  centralized
  centralizing
centrally
center Am
  centered

centering
centerpiece *Am*
centre
  centred
  centring
centre-forward
centrepiece
centrifugal
centrifugally
centrifuge
centripetal
centrist
centuple
centurion
century
  centuries *pl*
cephalic
cephalitis
ceramic
cereal (grain)
cerebellum
  cerebellums,
  cerebella *pl*
cerebral
cerebral palsy
cerebration
cerebro-spinal
cerebrum
  cerebra *pl*
ceremonial
ceremonially
ceremonious
ceremoniously

ceremony
  ceremonies *pl*
cerise
certain
certainly
certainty
  certainties *pl*
certifiable
certificate
  certificated
  certificating
certification
certify
  certified
  certifies
  certifying
certitude
cervical
cervix
cessation
cession (yielding)
cesspit
cesspool
chafe (rub)
  chafed
  chafing
chaff (straw)
chaffinch
  chaffinches *pl*
chagrin
chain
chair
  chaired

chairing
chairman
  chairmen *pl*
chairwoman
  chairwomen *pl*
chaise longue
  chaises longues *pl*
chalcedony
  chalcedonies *pl*
chalet
chalice
chalk
chalky
challenge
  challenged
  challenging
challenger
chamber
chamberlain
chambermaid
chameleon
chamfer (groove)
chamois
champ, chomp (chew
  noisily)
champagne
champion
championships
chance
  chanced
  chancing
chancel
chancellery

chancelleries *pl*
chancellor
chancery
 chanceries *pl*
chancy
 chancier
 chanciest
chandelier
chandler
change
 changed
 changing
changeable
changeling
channel
 channelled
 channelling
 channels
 channeled *Am*
 channeling *Am*
chant
chantry
 chantries *pl*
chaos
chaotic
chaotically
chap
 chapped
 chapping
 chaps
chapel
chaperon
 chaperoned

chaperoning
chaperonage
chaplain
chaplaincy
chaplet
chapter
char
charred
 charring
 chars
charlady
 charladies *pl*
charwoman
 charwomen *pl*
charabanc
character
characterisation
characterise
 characterised
 characterising
characteristic
characteristically
characterization
characterize
 characterized
 characterizing
charade
charcoal
charge
 charged
 charging
chargeable
chargé d'affaires

chargés d'affaires *pl*
chariot
charioteer
charisma
charismatic
charity
 charities *pl*
charitable
charitably
charlatan
charlotte
charlotte russe
charm
charmer
chart
charter
charterer
charwoman
 charwomen *pl*
charily
chariness
chary
chase (to pursue)
 chased
 chasing
chaser
chasm
chassis
 chassis *pl*
chaste (pure)
chastely
chasten
chastise

chastised
chastising
chastisement
chastity
chat
  chats
  chatted
  chatting
château
  châteaus,
    châteaux *pl*
chatelaine
chatter
chatterbox
chatty
  chattier
  chattiest
chattel
chauffeur
  chauffeurs *pl*
chauffeuse
chauvinism
chauvinist
chauvinistic
cheap (low priced)
cheaper
cheaply
cheapness
cheat
  cheated
  cheating
check (control; stop)
checkered *Am*

checkmate
cheek
cheekily
cheekiness
cheeky
  cheekier
  cheekiest
cheep (chick's chirp)
cheer
cheerily
cheerless
cheery
  cheerier
  cheeriest
cheerful
cheerfully
cheerfulness
cheese
cheese-paring
cheetah (animal)
chef
chef-d'oeuvre
  chefs-d'oeuvre *pl*
chemical
chemically
chemise
chemist
chemistry
cheque (order on
  bank)
chequered
cherish
cheroot

cherry
  cherries *pl*
cherub
cherubic
cherubically
chess
chessboard
chest
chestnut
chevalier
chevron
chevroned
chevy, chivvy, chivy
  chevied, chivvied,
  chivied
  chevying,
  chivvying, chivying
chew (to eat)
  chewed
  chewing
  chews
chewy
  chewier
  chewiest
Chianti
chic (elegant)
chicanery
chichi
chick (young bird)
chicken
chickenpox
chickweed
chicory

chide
  chid
  chidden
  chided
  chiding
chief
  chiefs *pl*
chieftain
chiffon
chilblain
child
  children *pl*
childbirth
childhood
childish
chill
chilled
chilli, chili (spice)
  chillies, chilies *pl*
chilly
  chillier
  chilliest
chime
  chimed
  chiming
chimney
  chimneys *pl*
chimpanzee
chin
China
china (porcelain)
Chinese
chink

chinos
chintz
  chintzes *pl*
chip
  chipped
  chipping
  chips
chipmunk
chiropodist
chiropody
chiropractic
chiropractor
chiropraxy
chirp
chirrup
  chirruped
  chirruping
chisel (tool)
chisel (to cheat)
  chiselled
  chiselling
  chisels
  chiseled *Am*
  chiseling *Am*
chiseler *Am*
chiseller
chit
chit-chat
chivalrous
chivalrously
chivalry
chive
chivvy, chivy, chevy

  chivvied, chivied,
    chevied
  chivvying, chivying,
    chevying
chlorate
chloride
chlorinate
  chlorinated
  chlorinating
chlorination
chlorine
chlorodyne
chlorofluorocarbon
chloroform
chlorophyll
chock
chock-a-block
chocoholic
chocolate
choice
choicely
choiceness
choicest
choir
choke
  choked
  choking
choker
choler (anger)
cholera
choleric
cholesterol
chomp, champ (chew

noisily)
choose (select)
  chooses
  choosing
  chose
  chosen
choosy
chop
  chopped
  chopping
  chops
chopper
choppy
  choppier
  choppiest
chopstick
chop-suey
choral (of a choir)
choral (hymn) *Am*
chorale (hymn)
chorally
chord (music)
chore
choreographer
choreographic
choreography
chorister
chortle
  chortled
  chortling
chorus
  choruses *pl*
chose (*from* choose)

chosen (*from* choose)
chow (dog)
chow mein
Christ
christen
Christendom
christening
Christian
Christianity
Christmas
Christmassy
chromate
chromatic
chromatin
chrome
chromic
chromium
chromosome
chromosphere
chronic
chronically
chronicle
  chronicled
  chronicling
chronological
chronologically
chronology
  chronologies *pl*
chronometer
chrysalis
  chrysalises *pl*
chrysanthemum
  chrysanthemums *pl*

chub
chubby
  chubbier
  chubbiest
chuck
chucker-out
chuckle
chuckling
chuffed
chug
  chugged
  chugging
  chugs
chukker, chukka,
  chukkar
chum
chummy
chump
chunk
chunky
  chunkier
  chunkiest
church (general)
  churches *pl*
Church (Christian)
church-goer
churchwarden
churlish
churn
chute (sloping
  passage)
chutney
  chutneys *pl*

cicada
  cicadas, cicadae *pl*
cicatrice (scar)
cicatrise (to heal)
  cicatrised
  cicatrising
cicatrize
  cicatrized
  cicatrizing
cider
cigar
cigarette
cinder
Cinderella
cinema
  cinemas *pl*
cinematic
cinematograph
cinematography
cineraria
  cinerarias *pl*
cinerarium
  cinerariums *pl*
cinerary
cinerary urn
cinnamon
cipher, cypher
circa
circle
  circled
  circling
circuit
circuitous

circuitry
  circuitries *pl*
circular
circularise
  circularised
  circularising
circularize
  circularized
  circularizing
circulate
  circulated
  circulating
circulation
circumcise
  circumcised
  circumcising
circumcision
circumference
circumflex
circumlocution
circumnavigate
  circumnavigated
  circumnavigating
circumnavigation
circumscribe
  circumscribed
  circumscribing
circumscription
circumspect
circumspection
circumstance
circumstantial
circumstantially

circumvent
  circumvented
  circumventing
circumvention
circus
  circuses *pl*
cirrhosis
cirrus
  cirri *pl*
cist
cistern
citadel
citation
cite (quote)
  cited
  citing
citizen
citizenship
citrate
citric
citron
citrus
city
  cities *pl*
civet
civic
civic center *Am*
civic centre
civil
civilian
civilisation
civilise
  civilised

civilising

civility

civilities *pl*

civilization

civilize

civilized

civilizing

civilly

civvies

clad

cladding

claim

claimable

claimant

clairvoyance

clairvoyant

clam (shellfish)

clamant

clamber

clamminess

clammy

clamor *Am*

clamorous

clamour

clamp

clan

clandestine

clandestinely

clang

clanger (bad mistake)

clangor (noise) *Am*

clangour (noise)

clannish

clap

clapped

clapping

claps

claptrap

claret

clarification

clarify

clarified

clarifies

clarifying

clarinet

clarinettist, clarinetist

clarion

clarity

clash

clasp

class

classic

classical

classically

classicism

classicist

classics

classifiable

classification

classify

classified

classifies

classifying

classless

classroom

classy

classier

classiest

clatter

clattered

clattering

clause

claustral

claustrophobia

claustrophobic

clavichord

clavicle

clavicular

claw

clay

clean

cleaned

cleaning

cleanable

cleaner

cleanliness

cleanly

cleanse

cleansed

cleansing

clear

clearance

clear-cut

clearly

cleave

cleaved

cleaving

cleft

clove

cloven
clef
  clefs *pl*
clematis
clemency
clement
clench
clergy
clergyman
  clergymen *pl*
cleric
clerical
clerk
clever
cleverly
clew, clue (thread)
cliché
click
client
clientele
cliff
climactic
  (culminating)
climate
climatic (of climate)
climatically
climatology
climax
  climaxes *pl*
climb (to ascend)
climbable
climber
clime (region)

clinch
cling
  clinging
  clings
  clung
clinic
clinical
clinically
clink
clinker
clip
  clipped
  clipping
  clips
clipboard
clipper
clique
cliquey
cliquish
clitoris
  clitorises *pl*
cloak
cloakroom
clobber
cloche
clock
clockwise
clockwork
clod
clodhopper
clog
  clogged
  clogging

clogs
cloister
cloistered
cloistral
clone
  cloned
  cloning
close
  closed
  closing
closet
  closeted
  closeting
closure
clot
  clots
  clotted
  clotting
cloth (material)
clothe (to dress)
  clothed
  clothing
clothes (garments)
clothier
cloud
  clouded
  clouding
cloudy
  cloudier
  cloudiest
clout
clove (spice)
cloven

clover
clover-leaf
clown
cloy
club
  clubbed
  clubbing
  clubs
cluck
clue
clue, clew (thread)
clueless
clump
clumsily
clumsiness
clumsy
  clumsier
  clumsiest
clung (*from* cling)
cluster
  clustered
  clustering
clutch
clutter
  cluttered
  cluttering
coach
  coaches *pl*
coachman
coagulate
  coagulated
  coagulating
coagulation

coal
coalesce
  coalesced
  coalescing
coalescence
coalescent
coalition
coarse (rough)
coarsely
coarsen
  coarsened
  coarsening
coarseness
coast
coastal
coaster
coastguard
coat (garment;
  to cover)
  coated
  coating
coax
coaxial
cob
cobalt
cobble
  cobbled
  cobbling
cobbler
cobra
  cobras *pl*
cobweb
cocaine

coccygeal
coccyx
cochineal
cochlea
  cochleae *pl*
cock
cockade
cockatoo
  cockatoos *pl*
cockchafer
cockcrow
cockerel
cock-eyed
cockily
cockle
cockney
  cockneys *pl*
cockpit
cockroach
  cockroaches *pl*
cocksure
cocktail
cocky
  cockier
  cockiest
coco (tree)
cocoa (drink)
coconut
cocoon
cocotte
cod
coda
  codas *pl*

coddle
  coddled
  coddling
code
  coded
  coding
codeine
codger
codicil
codification
codify
  codified
  codifies
  codifying
cod's roe
codling
coeducation
coeducational
coefficient
coerce
  coerced
  coercing
coercion
coexist
coexistence
coffee
coffer
coffin
cog
cogency
cogent
cogently
cogitate

cogitated
cogitating
cogitation
cognac
cognate
cognisance,
  cognizance
cognisant, cognizant
cognition
cognitive
cognomen
cog-wheel
cohabit
  cohabited
  cohabiting
cohabitation
cohere
  cohered
  cohering
coherence
coherent
coherently
coherer
cohesion
cohesive
cohort
coiffeur (hairdresser)
  coiffeurs pl
coiffeuse
  coiffeuses pl
coiffure (hair style)
coil
  coiled

coiling
coin
coinage
coincide
  coincided
  coinciding
coincidence
coincident
coincidental
coincidentally
coiner
coir (fibre)
coition
coitus
coke
col (mountain pass)
colander
cold
cold-blooded
coldly
cold-shoulder
cole (cabbage)
coleslaw
colic
colicky
Coliseum (in
  London)
colitis
collaborate
  collaborated
  collaborating
collaboration
collaborator

collage (patchwork
  picture)
collapse
  collapsed
  collapsing
collapsible
collar (around neck)
  collared
  collaring
collaret
collarette
collate
  collated
  collating
collateral
collation
collator
colleague
collect
collectible,
  collectable
collection
collective
collectively
collectivism
collectivist
collector
colleen
college
collegial
collegian
collegiate
collide

collided
colliding
collie
collier
colliery
  collieries pl
collision
collocate
  collocated
  collocating
collocation
colloid
colloidal
colloquial
colloquialism
colloquially
colloquy
  colloquies pl
collude
  colluded
  colluding
colitis
collusion
collusive
cologne
colon (bowel,
  punctuation)
colonel (military)
colonial
colonialism
colonisation
colonise
  colonised

colonising
coloniser, colonizer
colonist
colonization
colonize
  colonized
  colonizing
colonnade
colony
  colonies pl
color Am
  colored
  coloring
coloration Am
colorful Am
colorfully Am
colorless Am
colossal
colossally
colosseum (in Rome)
colour
  coloured
  colouring
colourful
colourfully
colourless
colt
coltish
columbine
column
columnar
columnist
coma

(unconsciousness)
comas *pl*
comatose
comb
combat
  combated
  combating
combatant
combative
combe, coomb
  (valley)
combinable
combination
combine
  combined
  combining
combustible
combustion
come
  came
  comes
  coming
comedian *m*
comedienne *f*
comedy
  comedies *pl*
comeliness
comely (pretty)
  comelier
  comeliest
comestible
comet
comeuppance

comfit (sweetmeat)
comfort
comfortable
comfortably
comforter
comic
comical
comicality
  comicalities *pl*
comically
comity (friendship)
  comities *pl*
comma (punctuation
  mark)
  commas *pl*
command
commandant
commandeer
  commandeered
  commandeering
commander
commandment
commando
  commandos *pl*
commemorate
  commemorated
  commemorating
commemoration
commemorative
commence
  commenced
  commencing
commencement

commend
commendable
commendably
commendation
commensurable
commensurate
commensurately
comment
commentary
  commentaries *pl*
commentator
commerce
commercial
commercialisation
commercialise
  commercialised
  commercialising
commercialism
commercialization
commercialize
  commercialized
  commercializing
commercially
commiserate
  commiserated
  commiserating
commiseration
commissar
commissariat
commission
commissionaire
commissioner
commit

commits
committed
committing
commitment
committal
committee (group)
commode
commodious
commodity
  commodities *pl*
commodore
common
commoner
commonplace
commonwealth
commotion
communal
communally
commune
  communed
  communing
communicable
communicant
communicate
  communicated
  communicating
communication
communicative
communion
communiqué
communism
communist
community

communities *pl*
commutable
commutation
commutator
commute
  commuted
  commuting
commuter
compact
companion
companionable
company
  companies *pl*
comparable
comparably
comparative
comparatively
compare (to liken)
  compared
  comparing
comparison
compartment
compartmentalisation
compartmentalise
  compartmentalised
  compartmentalising
compartmentalization
compartmentalize
  compartmentalized
  compartmentalizing
compass
  compasses *pl*
compassion

compassionate
compassionately
compatibility
compatible
compatibly
compatriot
compel
  compelled
  compelling
  compels
compendious
compendium
  compendiums,
  compendia *pl*
compensate
  compensated
  compensating
compensation
compensator
compensatory
compère (on stage)
  compèred
  compères
  compèring
compete
  competed
  competing
competence
competent
competently
competition
competitive
competitively

competitor
compilation
compile
  compiled
  compiling
compiler
complacency
complacent (smug)
complacently
complain
  complained
  complaining
complainant
complainer
complaint
complaisance
complaisant (willing)
complement
    (to add to)
  complemented
  complementing
complementary
complete
  completed
  completing
completely
completion
complex
complexion
complexity
  complexities *pl*
compliance
compliant

complicacy
complicate
  complicated
  complicating
complication
complicity
compliment (praise)
complimentary
compline (church
  service)
comply
  complied
  complies
  complying
component
comport
comportment
compose
  composed
  composing
compos mentis
composer (of music)
composition
compositor (in
  printing)
compost (garden
  refuse)
composure (calmness)
compote (of fruit)
compound
comprehend
comprehensibility
comprehensible

comprehensibly
comprehension
comprehensive
comprehensively
compress
compressibility
compressible
compression
compressor
comprise
  comprised
  comprising
compromise
  compromised
  compromising
comptometer
compulsion
compulsive
compulsively
compulsorily
compulsory
compunction
computable
computation
compute
  computed
  computing
computer
computerisation
computerise
  computerised
  computerising
computerization

computerize
  computerized
  computerizing
computing
comrade
comradely
comradeship
con
  conned
  conning
  cons
concave
concavity
  concavities *pl*
conceal
  concealed
  concealing
concealment
concede
  conceded
  conceding
conceit
conceited
conceivable
conceivably
conceive
  conceived
  conceiving
concentrate
  concentrated
  concentrating
concentration
concentrator

concentric
concentrically
concentricity
concept
conception
conceptual
conceptualise
  conceptualised
  conceptualising
conceptualize
  conceptualized
  conceptualizing
concern
concert
concertina
  concertinas *pl*
concerto
  concertos *pl*
concession
concessionaire
concessionary
conch
concierge
conciliate
  conciliated
  conciliating
conciliation
conciliator
conciliatory
concise
concisely
conciseness
conclave

conclude
  concluded
  concluding
conclusion
conclusive
conclusively
concoct
concoction
concomitance
concomitant
concord
concordance
concordant
concourse
concrete
concretely
concreteness
concubinage
concubine
concur
  concurred
  concurring
  concurs
concurrence
concurrent
concuss
  concussed
concussion
condemn
  condemned
  condemning
condemnation
condemnatory

condensation
condense
  condensed
  condensing
condenser
condescend
condescension
condign
condignly
condiment
condition
conditional
conditionally
condolatory
condole
  condoled
  condoling
condolence
condoler
condom
condone (to forgive)
  condoned
  condoning
conduce
  conduced
  conducing
conducive
conduct
conductance
conductivity
conductor
conduit
cone

coney, cony (rabbit)
  coneys, conies *pl*
confabulate
  confabulated
  confabulating
confabulation
confection
confectioner
confectionery
confederacy
  confederacies *pl*
confederate
  confederated
  confederating
confederation
confer
  conferred
  conferring
  confers
conference
conferment
confess
confessional
confessor
confetti
confidant (person)
confidante *f*
confide
  confided
  confiding
confidence
confident (self-
  assured)

confidential
confidentiality
confidentially
confidently
configuration
confine
  confined
  confining
confinement
confirm
confirmable
confirmation
confirmative
confirmatory
confiscate
  confiscated
  confiscating
confiscation
confiscator
confiscatory
conflagration
conflict
conform
conformable
conformance
conformation
conformity
confound
confrère, confrere
confront
confrontation
confuse
  confused

confusing
confusion
confutation
confute
  confuted
  confuting
conga (dance)
  congas *pl*
  congaed
  congaing
congeal
  congealed
  congealing
congelation
congenial
congeniality
congenially
congenital
congenitally
conger
conger-eel
congest
congestion
congestive
conglomerate
  conglomerated
  conglomerating
conglomeration
congratulate
  congratulated
  congratulating
congratulation
congratulatory

congregate
  congregated
  congregating
congregation
congregational
congress
  congresses *pl*
congressional
congruence
congruent
congruity
congruous
conic
conical
conically
conifer
coniferous
conjecturable
conjecturably
conjectural
conjecture
conjoin
  conjoined
  conjoining
conjoint
conjointly
conjugal
conjugate
  conjugated
  conjugating
conjugation
conjunction
conjunctival

conjunctive
conjunctivitis
conjure
  conjured
  conjuring
conjuror
conker (chestnut)
connect
connection,
  connexion
connective
connector, connecter
conning-tower
connivance
connive
  connived
  conniving
connoisseur
connotation
connote
  connoted
  connoting
connubial
connubially
conquer (to win)
  conquered
  conquering
conquerable
conqueror
conquest
consanguineous
consanguinity
conscience

conscientious
conscientiously
conscientiousness
conscious
consciously
consciousness
conscript
conscription
consecrate
  consecrated
  consecrating
consecration
consecutive
consecutively
consensus
consent
consequence
consequential
consequently
conservancy
conservation
conservatism
conservative
conservatoire
conservatory
  conservatories *pl*
conserve
  conserved
  conserving
consider
  considered
  considering
considerable

considerably
considerate
considerately
considerateness
consideration
consign
  consigned
  consigning
consignee
consignment
consignor, consigner
consist
consistence
consistency
  consistencies *pl*
consistent
consolable
consolation
consolatory
console (comfort,
  control panel)
  consoled
  consoling
consoler
consolidate
  consolidated
  consolidating
consolidation
consols (Govt
  securities)
consommé
consonant
consort

consortium
  consortia *pl*
conspicuous
conspicuously
conspicuousness
conspiracy
  conspiracies *pl*
conspirator
conspiratorial
conspire
  conspired
  conspiring
constable
constabulary
  constabularies *pl*
constancy
constant
constantly
constellation
consternation
constipate
  constipated
  constipating
constipation
constituency
  constituencies *pl*
constituent
constitute
  constituted
  constituting
constitution
constitutional
constitutionally

constrain
  constrained
  constraining
constraint
constrict
constriction
constrictive
constrictor
construct
construction
constructional
constructive
constructively
constructor
construe
  construed
  construing
consul (official)
consular
consulate
consult
consultant
consultation
consultative
consumable
consume
  consumed
  consuming
consumer
consummate
  consummated
  consummating
consummately

consummation
consumption
consumptive
contact
contactor
contagion
contagious
contain
  contained
  containing
container
containerisation
containerise
  containerised
  containerising
containerization
containerize
  containerized
  containerizing
containment
contaminant
contaminate
  contaminated
  contaminating
contamination
contemplate
  contemplated
  contemplating
contemplation
contemplative
contemplatively
contemporaneous
contemporary

  contemporaries pl
contempt
contemptible
contemptibly
contemptuous
contemptuously
contend
content
contention
contentious
contentment
contest
contestable
contestant
context
contiguity
contiguous
contiguously
continence
continent
continental
contingency
  contingencies pl
contingent
continual
continually
continuance
continuation
continue
  continued
  continuing
continuity
continuous

continuously
contort
contortion
contortionist
contour
contraband
contraception
contraceptive
contract
contraction
contractor
contractual
contractually
contradict
contradiction
contradictory
contralto
  contraltos *pl*
contraption
contrarily
contrariness
contrary
contrast
contravene
  contravened
  contravening
contravention
contretemps
contribute
  contributed
  contributing
contribution
contributor

contributory
contrite
contritely
contrition
contrivance
contrive
  contrived
  contriving
control
  controlled
  controlling
  controls
controllable
controller
controversial
controversially
controversy
  controversies *pl*
controvert
controvertible
contumacious
contumacy
contumely
contuse
contusion
conundrum
  conundrums *pl*
conurbation
convalesce
  convalesced
  convalescing
convalescence
convalescent

convection
convector
convene
  convened
  convening
convener
convenience
convenient
conveniently
convent
convention
conventional
conventionality
conventionally
converge
  converged
  converging
convergence
convergent
conversant
conversation
conversational
conversationalist
conversationally
converse
  conversed
  conversing
conversely
conversion
convert
converter, convertor
convertibility
convertible

convex
convexity
convey
  conveyed
  conveying
  conveys
conveyance
conveyancer
conveyancing
conveyor belt
conveyor, conveyer
convict
conviction
convince
  convinced
  convincing
convincingly
convivial
conviviality
convivially
convocation
convoke
  convoked
  convoking
convoluted
convolution
convolvulus
  convolvuluses *pl*
convoy
  convoys *pl*
convulse
  convulsed
  convulsing

convulsion
convulsive
convulsively
cony, coney (rabbit)
  conies, coneys *pl*
coo (bird sound)
  cooed
  cooing
  coos
cook
  cooked
  cooking
cooker
cookery
cool
  cooled
  cooling
coolant
cooler
cool-headed
coolie (labourer)
coolly
coolness
coomb, combe
  (valley)
coop (to enclose)
co-op
cooperate
  cooperated
  cooperating
cooperation
cooperative
cooperator

co-opt
co-option
coordinate
  coordinated
  coordinating
coordination
cop (policeman)
cope (to manage)
  coped
  coping
copeck, kopek,
  kopeck
copier
co-pilot, copilot
copious
copiously
copper
copperplate
coppice, copse
copra
copulate
  copulated
  copulating
copulation
copy
  copies *pl*
  copied
  copies
  copying
copyright
copyrighted
coquetry
coquette

coquettish
coral (in sea)
cord (thin rope)
cordage
cordial
cordiality
cordially
cordite
cordon
cordon bleu
cords (trousers)
corduroy
core (centre)
  cored
  coring
co-respondent,
  corespondent (in
    divorce case)
coriander
cork
corkage
corkscrew
corm
cormorant
corn
cornea
  corneas pl
corneal
cornelian
corner
  cornered
  cornering
cornet

cornflour (in cooking)
cornflower (blue
  flower)
cornice
cornstarch
cornucopia
corny
  cornier
  corniest
corollary
  corollaries pl
corona
  coronae, coronas pl
coronary
  coronaries pl
coronation
coroner
coronet
coroneted
corporal
corporal punishment
corporate
corporation
corporeal (not
  spiritual)
corps (group of
  people)
corps de ballet
corpse (dead body)
corpulence
corpulent
corpuscle
corpuscular

corral (to enclose
  cattle)
  corralled
  corralling
  corrals
correct
correction
corrective
correctly
correctness
corrector
correlate
  correlated
  correlating
correlation
correlative
correlativity
correspond
correspondence
correspondent
  (writer)
corridor
corrigendum
  corrigenda pl
corroborate
  corroborated
  corroborating
corroboration
corroborative
corrode
  corroded
  corroding
corrodible

corrosion
corrosive
corrugate
  corrugated
  corrugating
corrugation
corrupt
corrupter
corruptibility
corruptible
corruption
corruptive
corruptly
corruptness
corsage
corset
  corseted
  corseting
cortège, cortege
cortex
  cortices *pl*
cortical
cortisone
corundum
corvée
corvette
cosecant, cosec
cosh
co-signatory,
  cosignatory
co-signatories,
  cosignatories *pl*
cosily

cosine, cos (maths.)
cosiness
cosmetic
cosmetician
cosmic
cosmically
cosmonaut
cosmopolitan
cosmos
cossack
cosset
  cosseted
  cosseting
co-star, costar
cost
costard (apple)
coster
costermonger
costive (constipated)
costlier
costly
costume
costumier
cosy
  cosies *pl*
  cosier
  cosiest
cot
cotangent, cot
  (maths)
coterie
cottage
cottager

cottaging
cotton
cotton wool
cotyledon (botany)
couch
couch-grass
cough
could (*from* can)
couldn't
council (County, etc.)
councillor
counsel (lawyer or
  advice)
  counselled
  counselling
  counsels
  counseled *Am*
  counseling *Am*
counsellor
counselor *Am*
count
countdown
countenance
counter
counteract
counteraction
counter-attraction,
  counterattraction
counterbalance
counterbalancing
counter-clockwise
counterfeit
counterfoil

counter-irritant,
  counterirritant
countermand
countermine
counterpane
counterpart
counterpoint
counterpoise
countersign
  countersigned
  countersigning
countersink
  countersinking
  countersinks
  countersunk
counterweight
countess
countless
countrify
  countrified
  countrifies
  countrifying
country
  countries pl
countryman
  countrymen pl
county
  counties pl
county council
county councillor
coup
coup d'état
coup de grace

couple
  coupled
  coupling
couplet
coupon
courage
courageous
courageously
courgette
courier
course
  coursed
  coursing
court (law; to woo)
  courted
  courting
courtesan
courtesy
  courtesies pl
courteous
courteously
courtier
courtly (polite)
court-martial
  courts-martial pl
  court-martialled
  court-martialling
  court-martials
  court-martialed Am
  court-martialing Am
courtship
courtyard
cousin

cousinly
couture
couturier
couturière
cove
coven
covenant
cover
  covered
  covering
coverage
coverlet
covert
covertly
cover-up
covet
  coveted
  coveting
covetous
covey
  coveys pl
cow
cowboy
  cowboys pl
cowherd
cowhide
cowman
  cowmen pl
coward (scared
cowardice
cowardliness
cowardly
cower (to cringe)

cowered
cowering
cowers
cowl
cowrie, cowry
cowries *pl*
cowslip
cox
coxcomb
coxswain
coy
coyly
coyness
cozen (to cheat)
cozened
cozening
cozenage
cozily *Am*
coziness *Am*
cozy *Am*
cozies *pl*
cozier
coziest
crab
crabbed
crabby
crack
cracker
crackle
crackled
crackling
cradle
cradled

cradling
craft
craftsman
craftsmen *pl*
craftsmanship
crafty
craftier
craftiest
crag
craggy
crake
cram
crammed
cramming
crams
crammer
cramp
cranage
cranberry
cranberries *pl*
crane
craned
craning
cranial
cranium
craniums *pl*
crank
crankcase
crankiness
crankshaft
cranky
crankier
crankiest

cranny
crannies *pl*
crape (black crêpe)
crapulence
crapulent
crapulous
crash
crash-land
crass
crate
crater
cravat
crave
craved
craving
craven
crawfish, crayfish
crawl
crawler
crayon
craze
crazed
crazily
craziness
crazy
crazier
craziest
creak (to squeak)
creaked
creaking
creaky
cream
creamery

creameries *pl*

creaminess

creamy

  creamier

  creamiest

crease

  creased

  creasing

create

  created

  creating

creation

creative

creatively

creativity

creator

creature

crèche

credence

credential

credibility

credible

credibly

credit

  credited

  crediting

creditable

creditably

creditor

credo

  credos *pl*

credulity

credulous

creed

creek (*small stream*)

creep

  creeping

  creeps

  crept

creeper

creepily

creepiness

creepy

  creepier

  creepiest

cremate

  cremated

  cremating

cremation

crematorium

  crematoria,

  crematoriums *pl*

crematory

  crematories

Creole

creosote

crêpe

crepitate

  crepitated

  crepitating

crepitation

crept (*from* creep)

crepuscular

crescendo

  crescendos *pl*

crescent

cress

crest

crestfallen

cretin

cretinism

cretinous

crevasse (*in glacier*)

crevice (*crack*)

crew

crib

  cribbed

  cribbing

  cribs

cribbage

cribber

crick

cricket

cricketer

cried (*from* cry)

crier

cries (*from* cry)

crime

criminal

criminally

criminologist

criminology

crimson

cringe

  cringed

  cringing

crinkle

  crinkled

  crinkling

crinkly
crinoline
cripple
  crippled
  crippling
crisis
  crises *pl*
crisp
crispness
criss-cross
  criss-crossed
  criss-crossing
criterion
  criteria *pl*
critic
critical
critically
criticise
  criticised
  criticising
criticism
criticize
  criticized
  criticizing
critique (critical
  essay)
croak
crochet (knitting)
  crocheted
  crocheting
crock
crockery
crocodile

crocus
  crocuses *pl*
croft
crofter
croissant
crony
  cronies *pl*
crook
crooked
crookedly
croon
crooner
crop
  cropped
  cropping
  crops
cropper
croquet (game)
croquette (rissole)
crosier
cross
cross-breed
  cross-bred
  cross-breeding
  cross-breeds
cross-examination
cross-examine
  cross-examined
  cross-examining
cross-examiner
cross-eyed
cross-legged
crossly

crossness
cross-purpose
cross-question
  cross-questioned
  cross-questioning
cross-questioner
cross-reference
  cross-referenced
  cross-referencing
crossroad
cross-section
crossword
crotch (of body
  or trousers)
crotchet (music)
crouch
croup
croupier
croûton, crouton
crow
crowbar
crowd
  crowded
  crowding
crown
  crowned
  crowning
crucial
crucially
crucible
crucifix
  crucifixes *pl*
crucifixion

crucify
  crucified
  crucifies
  crucifying
crude
crudely
crudity
  crudities *pl*
cruel
  crueller
  cruellest
cruelly
cruelty
  cruelties *pl*
cruet
cruise (on a ship)
  cruised
  cruising
cruiser
crumb
crumble
  crumbled
  crumbling
crumbling
crumbly
crumby
crumpet
crumple
  crumpled
  crumpling
crunch
crunchy
  crunchier

  crunchiest
crupper
crusade
crusader
crush
crushed
crust
crustacean
crustaceous
crustily
crusty
crutch
  crutches *pl*
crux
  cruxes, cruces *pl*
cry
  cries *pl*
  cried
  cries
  crying
cryogenics
crypt
cryptic (obscure)
cryptically
cryptogam (plant)
cryptogram (code)
cryptograph
cryptographic
cryptography
crystal
crystalline
crystallisation
crystallise

crystallised
crystallising
crystallization
crystallize
  crystallized
  crystallizing
crystallographer
crystallography
cut
  cuts
  cutting
cubby-hole
cube
cubed
cubic
cubicle
cuckold
cuckoo
cucumber
cuddle
  cuddled
  cuddling
cuddly
cudgel
  cudgelled
  cudgelling
  cudgels
  cudgeled *Am*
  cudgeling *Am*
cue (signal; hint;
  billiards)
cuff
cuisine

cul-de-sac
  cul-de-sacs *pl*
culinary
cull
culminate
  culminated
  culminating
culmination
culottes
culpability
culpable
culpably
culprit
cult
cultivate
  cultivated
  cultivating
cultivatable
cultivation
cultivator
cultural
culturally
culture
  cultured
  culturing
culver
cumbersome
cummerbund
cumulative
cumulatively
cumulus
  cumuli *pl* .
cunning

cunningly
cup
  cupped
  cupping
  cups
cupboard
cupful
  cupfuls *pl*
cupidity
cupola
  cupolas *pl*
cur
curaçao
curacy
  curacies *pl*
curate
curator
curb (to restrain; road
  edge *Am*)
curbstone *Am*
curd
curdle
  curdled
  curdling
curability
curable
curative
cure
  cured
  curing
curé (priest)
curette (knife)
curfew

curio
  curios *pl*
curiosity
  curiosities *pl*
curious
curiously
curl
curler
curly
  curlier
  curliest
curlew
curmudgeon
currant (fruit)
currency
  currencies *pl*
current (flow)
currently
curriculum
  curricula,
    curriculums *pl*
curriculum vitae
  curricula vitae *pl*
currish
curry
  curried
  curries
  currying
curry-comb
curse
  cursed
  cursing
cursive

cursor
cursorily
cursory
curt
curtail
  curtailed
  curtailing
curtailment
curtain
  curtained
  curtaining
curtly
curtness
curtsey
  curtseyed
  curtseying
  curtseys
curtsy
  curtsied
  curtsies
  curtsying
curvature
curve
  curved
  curving
cushion
cuss
cussedness
custard
custodial
custodian
custody
custom

customarily
customary
custom-built
customisation
customise
  customised
  customising
customization
customize
  customized
  customizing
customer
custom-made
customs
cut
  cutter
  cutting
  cuts
cutaneous
cutback
cute
  cuter
  cutest
cutely
cuteness
cuticle
cutlass
  cutlasses *pl*
cutler
cutlery
cutlet
cuttlefish
cyanide

cyanosis
cybernetics
cyberpunk
cyberspace
cyclamen
cycle
  cycled
  cycling
cyclic
cyclical
cyclically
cyclists
cyclometer
cyclone
cyclonic
cygnet
cylinder
cylindrical
cylindrically
cymbal (gong)
cymbalist
cynic
cynical
cynically
cynicism
cynosure
cypher, cipher
cypress (tree)
  cypresses *pl*
cyst
cystitis
cytology
Czech

dab
 dabbed
 dabbing
 dabs
dabble
 dabbled
 dabbling
dabbler
da capo
dace
dachshund
dad
daddy
 daddies *pl*
dado
 dadoes *pl*
daffodil
daft
dagger

daftly
daftness
dahlia
 dahlias *pl*
daily
 dailies *pl*
daintily
daintiness
dainty
 daintier
 daintiest
dairy (milk)
 dairies *pl*
dairymaid
dais (platform)
 daises *pl*
daisy
 daisies *pl*
dale (valley)

dalliance
dally (to dawdle)
 dallied
 dallies
 dallying
Dalmatian
dam (barrier)
 dammed
 damming
 dams
damage
 damaged
 damaging
damageable
damask
dame
damn (to condemn,
 curse)
 damned
 damning
damnable
damnably
damnation
damp
dampen
 dampened
 dampening
damper
dampness
damsel
damson
dance
 danced

dancing
dancer
dandelion
dandified
dandle
  dandled
  dandling
dandruff
dandy *pl*
  dandies
danger
dangerous
dangerously
dangle
  dangled
  dangling
dank
dankness
daphne (shrub)
dapper
dapple
  dappled
  dappling
dare
  dared
  daring
daredevil
dark
darken
darker
darkly
darkness
darling

darn
dart
dash
dashboard
dastardly
data
date
  dated
  dating
dateless
dative
daub
  daubed
  daubing
dauber
daughter
daughter-in-law
  daughters-in-law *pl*
daunt
dauntless
dauntlessly
Dauphin
davit
dawdle
  dawdled
  dawdling
dawdler
dawn
day
  days *pl*
daybreak
daylight
day to day

daze (to stun)
  dazed
  dazing
dazzle
  dazzled
  dazzling
deacon
deaconess
dead
deaden
  deadened
  deadening
deadline
deadliness
deadlock
deadlocked
deadly
  deadlier
  deadliest
deaf
deafen
  deafened
  deafening
deafeningly
deafer
deafness
deal
  dealing
  dealt
dealer
dean
deanery
  deaneries *pl*

dear (loved)
  dearer
  dearest
dearly
dearness
dearth
death
deathless
deathlike
deathly
death-rate
débâcle
debar
  debarred
  debarring
debark
debarkation
debase
  debased
  debasing
debasement
debatable
debatably
debate
  debated
  debating
debauch
debauchee
debaucher
debauchery
  debaucheries *pl*
debenture
debilitate

debilitated
debilitating
debilitation
debility
  debilities *pl*
debit
  debited
  debiting
debitable
debonair
debouch (to emerge)
debouchment
debrief
  debriefed
  debriefing
  debrief
debris
debt
debtor
debunk
debus
  debussed
  debussing
  debuses
début
débutant *m*
débutante *f*
decade
decadence
decadent
decaffeinated
decamp
decant

decanter
decapitate
  decapitated
  decapitating
decapitation
decarbonisation
decarbonise
  decarbonised
  decarbonising
decarbonization
decarbonize
  decarbonized
  decarbonizing
decathlon
decay
  decayed
  decaying
  decays
decease
  deceased
deceit
deceitful
deceitfully
deceive
  deceived
  deceiving
deceiver
decelerate
  decelerated
  decelerating
deceleration
decency
  decencies *pl*

decent (respectable)
decently
decentralisation
decentralise
  decentralised
  decentralising
decentralization
decentralize
  decentralized
  decentralizing
deception
deceptive
deceptively
decibel
decide
  decided
  deciding
decidedly
deciduous
decimal
decimalisation
decimalise
  decimalised
  decimalising
decimalization
decimalize
  decimalized
  decimalizing
decimate
  decimated
  decimating
decimation
decipher

deciphered
  deciphering
decipherment
decision
decisive
decisively
deck
declaim
  declaimed
  declaiming
declamation
declamatory
declaration
declare
  declared
  declaring
declassification
declassify
  declassified
  declassifies
  declassifying
declension
declinable
declination
decline
  declined
  declining
declivity
  declivities pl
decoction
decode
  decoded
  decoding

decoder
décolletage
décolleté
decomposable
decompose
  decomposed
  decomposing
decomposition
decompress
decompression
decompressor
decongestant
decontaminate
  decontaminated
  decontaminating
decontamination
decontrol
  decontrolled
  decontrolling
decorate
  decorated
  decorating
decoration
decorative
decorator
decorous
decorously
decorum
décor
decoy
  decoys pl
decrease
  decreased

decreasing
decree
  decreed
  decreeing
decrement
decrepit
decrepitude
decry
  decried
  decries
  decrying
dedicate
  dedicated
  dedicating
dedication
dedicatory
deduce (to infer)
  deduced
  deducing
deducible
deduct (to subtract)
deductible
deduction
deed
deem
  deemed
  deeming
deep
deepen
  deepened
  deepening
deeper
deep-freeze

deep-freezing
deep-frozen
deep-freezer
deep-fry
  deep-fried
  deep-fries
  deep-frying
deep-laid
deeply
deep-seated
deer (animal)
de-escalate
  de-escalated
  de-escalating
de-escalation
deface
  defaced
  defacing
de facto
defamation
defamatory
defame
  defamed
  defaming
default
defaulter
defeat
  defeated
  defeating
defeatism
defeatist
defecate
  defecated

defecating
defecation
defect
defection
defective
defector
defence
defenceless
defend
defendant
defender
defense Am
defenseless
defensibility
defensible
defensibly
defensive
defer
  deferred
  deferring
  defers
deference
deferential
deferentially
deferment
defiance
defiant
defiantly
deficiency
  deficiencies pl
deficient
deficit
defied

defier
defies (*from* defy)
defile
  defiled
  defiling
defilement
definable
define
  defined
  defining
definite
definitely
definition
definitive
definitively
deflate
  deflated
  deflating
deflation
deflationary
deflect
deflection
deflector
deflower
  deflowered
  deflowering
defoliant
defoliate
  defoliated
  defoliating
defoliation
defoliator
deform

deformation
deformity
  deformities *pl*
defraud
defray
  defrayed
  defraying
  defrays
defrayable
defrayal
defreeze
  defreezing
  defrozen
defrost
deft
deftly
deftness
defunct
defuse
  defused
  defusing
defy
  defied
  defies
  defying
dégagé
degeneracy
degenerate
  degenerated
  degenerating
degeneration
degenerative
degradation

degrade
  degraded
  degrading
degree
dehydrate
  dehydrated
  dehydrating
dehydration
de-ice
  de-iced
  de-icing
de-icer
deification
deify
  deified
  deifies
  deifying
deign
  deigned
  deigning
deism
deity
  deities *pl*
dejected
dejection
de jure
delay
  delayed
  delaying
  delays
delectable
delegacy
  delegacies *pl*

delegate
  delegated
  delegating
delegation
delete
  deleted
  deleting
deleterious
deletion
deliberate
  deliberated
  deliberating
deliberately
deliberation
delicacy
  delicacies *pl*
delicate
delicately
delicatessen
delicious
deliciously
delight
  delighted
  delighting
delightful
delightfully
delimit
  delimited
  delimiting
delimitation
delineate
  delineated
  delineating

delineation
delineator
delinquency
  delinquencies *pl*
delinquent
deliquesce
deliquescence
deliquescent
delirious
delirium
deliver
  delivered
  delivering
deliverance
deliverer
delivery
  deliveries *pl*
delouse
  deloused
  delousing
delta
  deltas *pl*
delude
  deluded
  deluding
deluge
  deluged
  deluging
delusion
delusive
deluxe
delve
  delved

delving
demagnetisation
demagnetise
  demagnetised
  demagnetising
demagnetization
demagnetize
  demagnetized
  demagnetizing
demagogic
demagogue
demagoguery
demagogy
demand
demarcate
  demarcated
  demarcating
demarcation
démarche
demean
  demeaned
  demeaned
demeanor *Am*
demeanour
demented
dementia
demesne
demilitarise
  demilitarised
  demilitarising
demilitarize
  demilitarized
  demilitarizing

demise
  demised
  demising
demist
demister
demitasse
demobilisation
demobilise
  demobilised
  demobilising
demobilization
demobilize
  demobilised
  demobilizing
democracy
  democracies *pl*
democratic
democratically
democratisation
democratise
  democratised
  democratising
democratization
democratize
  democratized
  democratizing
demolish
demolition
demon
demonic
demonstrable
demonstrate
  demonstrated

demonstrating
demonstration
demonstrative
demonstrator
demoralisation
demoralise
  demoralised
  demoralising
demoralization
demoralize
  demoralized
  demoralizing
demote
  demoted
  demoting
demotion
demount
demur (to object)
  demurred
  demurring
  demurs
demure (modest)
  demurely
demurrage
demurred
den
denationalisation
denationalise
  denationalised
  denationalising
denationalization
denationalize
  denationalized

denationalizing
denaturalise
  denaturalised
  denaturalising
denaturalize
  denaturalized
  denaturalizing
dengue (fever)
denial
denied (*from* deny)
denier (thread
  thickness)
denigrate
  denigrated
  denigrating
denigration
denigrator
denim
denizen
denominate
  denominated
  denominating
denomination
denominational
denominator
denote
  denoted
  denoting
dénouement
denounce
  denounced
  denouncing
denouncement

denouncer
de nouveau
de novo
dense
densely
denseness
denser
density
  densities *pl*
dent
dental
dentifrice
dentine
dentist
dentistry
dentition
denture
denudation
denude
  denuded
  denuding
denunciate
  denunciated
  denunciating
denunciator
denunciatory
deny
  denied
  denies
  denying
deodorant
deodorisation
deodorise

deodorised
  deodorising
deodorization
deodorize
  deodorized
  deodorizing
Deo volente
depart
department
departmental
departmentalise
  departmentalised
  departmentalising
departmentalize
  departmentalized
  departmentalizing
departmentally
departure
depend
dependable
dependant (person)
dependence
  dependencies *pl*
dependent (rely on)
depersonalise
  depersonalised
  depersonalising
depersonalize
  depersonalized
  depersonalizing
depict
depiction
depilatory

depilatories *pl*
deplete
  depleted
  depleting
depletion
deplorable
deplorably
deplore
  deplored
  deploring
deploy
  deployed
  deploying
  deploys
deployment
depopulate
  depopulated
  depopulating
depopulation
deport
deportation
deportee
deportment
  (behaviour)
depose
  deposed
  deposing
deposit
  deposited
  depositing
deposition
depositor
depository

depositories *pl*
depot
  depots *pl*
deprave (to corrupt)
  depraved
  depraving
depravity
deprecate
  deprecated
  deprecating
deprecation
deprecator
deprecatory
depreciate
  depreciated
  depreciating
depreciation
depredation
  (plundering)
depredator
depress
depressant
depressed
depression
depressive
depressurisation
depressurise
  depressurised
  depressurising
depressurization
depressurize
  depressurized
  depressurizing

deprival
deprivation
deprive
  deprived
  depriving
depth
deputation
depute
  deputed
  deputing
deputise
  deputised
  deputising
deputize
  deputized
  deputizing
deputy
  deputies *pl*
derail
  derailed
  derailing
derailment
derange
  deranged
  deranging
derangement
derelict
dereliction
deride
  derided
  deriding
de rigueur
derision

derisive
derisory
derivation
derivative
derive
  derived
  deriving
dermatitis
dermatologist
dermatology
derogate
  derogated
  derogating
derogation
derogatorily
derogatory
derrick
dervish
descant
descendant
descent (going down)
descend
describable
describe
  described
  describing
description
descriptive
desecrate
  desecrated
  desecrating
desecrater
desecration

desecrator
desegregate
  desegregated
  desegregating
desegregation
desensitise
  desensitised
  desensitising
desensitize
  desensitized
  desensitizing
desert (barren region)
deserts (rewards)
deserve
  deserved
  deserving
deservedly
déshabillé, dishabille
desiccate
  desiccated
  desiccating
desiccation
desiccator
desideratum
  desiderata pl
design
designate
  designated
  designating
designation
designer
desirability
desirable

desirably
desire
  desired
  desiring
desirous
desist
desk
desolate
  desolated
desolation
despair
  despaired
  despairing
despatch, dispatch
desperado
  desperadoes pl
desperate
desperately
desperation
despicable
despicably
despise
  despised
  despising
despite
despoil
despoiler
despoliation
despond
despondency
despondent
despondently
despot

despotic
despotically
despotism
dessert (fruit or sweet)
dessertspoon
destination
destine
destiny
  destinies pl
destitute
destitution
destroy
  destroyed
  destroying
  destroys
destroyer
destruction
destructive
destructiveness
destructor
desultorily
desultoriness
desultory
detach
detachable
detachment
detail
  detailed
  detailing
detain
  detained
  detaining
detect

detectable
detection
detective
detector
détente
detention
deter
  deterred
  deterring
  deters
detergent
deteriorate
  deteriorated
  deteriorating
deterioration
determinable
determinant
determination
determine
  determined
  determining
determinism
deterrent
detest
detestable
detestation
dethrone
  dethroned
  dethroning
dethronement
detonate
  detonated
  detonating

detonation
detonator
detour
detract
detraction
detractor
detriment
detrimental
detrimentally
deuce
devaluation
devalue
  devalued
  devaluing
devastate
  devastated
  devastating
devastator
develop
  developed
  developing
developer
development
developmental
deviant
deviate
  deviated
  deviating
deviation
device (thing)
devil
  devilled
  devilling

deviled *Am*
deviling *Am*
devils
devilish
devilishly
devilment
devilry
devious
deviously
deviousness
devise (plan)
  devised
  devising
devoid
devolution
devolve
  devolved
  devolving
devote
  devoted
  devoting
devotee
devotion
devour
  devoured
  devouring
devoutly
devoutness
dew (water)
dewy
dexterity
dexterous, dextrous
dexterously,

dextrously
dextrose (kind of
   glucose)
diabetes
diabetic
diabolic
diabolical
diabolically
diadem
diaeresis
diagnose
   diagnosed
   diagnosing
diagnosis
   diagnoses *pl*
diagnostic
diagnostician
diagonal
diagonally
diagram
diagrammatic
diagrammatically
dial
   dialled
   dialling
   dialed *Am*
   dialing *Am*
   dials
dialect
dialectic
dialer *Am*
dialler
dialogue

diameter
diametric
diametrical
diametrically
diamond
diapason
diaper
diaphanous
diaphragm
diarchy
   diarchies *pl*
diarist
diarrhea *Am*
diarrhoea
diary (daily notes)
   diaries *pl*
diastolic
diastone (heart
   function)
diathermy
diatom
diatomic
diatribe
dibber
dibble
dice
   dice *pl*
   diced
   dicing
dicey
dichotomy
dicker
   dickered

dickering
dicky
   dickier
   dickiest
dicotyledon
dictaphone
dictate
   dictated
   dictating
dictation
dictator
dictatorial
dictatorially
diction
dictionary
   dictionaries *pl*
didactic
didactically
didacticism
diddle
   diddled
   diddling
didn't (did not)
die (tool)
   dies *pl*
die (to cease living)
   died
   dies
   dying
die-hard
dielectric
diesel
diet

dieted
dieting
dietary
dietician, dietitian
differ
  differed
  differing
difference
different
differential
differentially
differentiate
  differentiated
  differentiating
differentiation
difficult
difficulty
  difficulties *pl*
diffidence
diffident
diffidently
diffract
diffraction
diffuse
  diffused
  diffusing
diffuser
diffusion
diffusive
dig
  digging
  digs
  dug

digest
digestibility
digestible
digestion
digestive
digger
digit
digital
digitalin
digitalis
dignify
  dignified
  dignifying
  dignifies
dignitary
  dignitaries *pl*
dignity
digress
digression
digressive
dike, dyke
dilapidate
  dilapidated
  dilapidating
dilapidation
dilatability
dilatable
dilatation
dilate
  dilated
  dilating
dilation
dilator

dilatorily
dilatoriness
dilatory (delaying)
dilemma
  dilemmas *pl*
dilettante
  dilettanti,
    dilettantes *pl*
diligence
diligent
diligently
dill
dilly-dally
  dilly-dallied
  dilly-dallies
  dilly-dallying
diluent
dilute
  diluted
  diluting
dilution
diluvial
dim
  dimmed
  dimming
  dims
dime (coin)
dimension
dimensional
diminish
diminuendo
  diminuendos *pl*
diminution

diminutive
dimity
  dimities pl
dimly
dimple
  dimpled
  dimpling
din
dinar (currency)
dine (to eat)
  dined
  dining
diner (person; café)
dinghy (boat)
  dinghies pl
dingily
dinginess
dingy (dark)
  dingier
  dingiest
dinner (meal)
dinosaur
dint
diocesan
diocese
  dioceses pl
diode
diorama
  dioramas pl
dioxide
dip
  dipped
  dipping

dips
diphtheria
diphthong
diploma
  diplomas pl
diplomacy
  diplomacies pl
diplomat
diplomatic
diplomatically
diplomatist
dipper
dipsomania
dipsomaniac
dire
  direr
  direst
direct
  directed
  directing
direction
directional
directive
director
directorate
directory
  directories pl
direful
dirge
dirigible
dirndl
dirt
dirtily

dirtiness
dirty
  dirtied
  dirties
  dirtying
disability
  disabilities pl
disable
  disabled
  disabling
disablement
disabuse
  disabused
  disabusing
disadvantage
  disadvantaged
  disadvantaging
disadvantageous
disaffected
disaffection
disagree
  disagreed
  disagreeing
disagreeable
disagreeably
disagreement
disallow
disappear
  disappeared
  disappearing
disappearance
disappoint
  disappointed

disappointing
disappointment
disapproval
disapprove
  disapproved
  disapproving
disarm
disarmament
disarrange
  disarranged
  disarranging
disarrangement
disarray
disassociate
  disassociated
  disassociating
disassociation
disaster
disastrous
disastrously
disband
disbandment
disbar
  disbarred
  disbarring
  disbars
disbelief
disbelieve
  disbelieved
  disbelieving
disbeliever
disburden
  disburdened

disburdening
disburse
  disbursed
  disbursing
disbursement
disc
discard
disc-brake
discern
discernible
discernment
discharge
  discharged
  discharging
disciple
disciplinarian
disciplinary
discipline
  disciplined
  disciplining
disc-jockey
  disc-jockeys *pl*
disclaim
  disclaimed
  disclaiming
disclaimer
disclose
  disclosed
  disclosing
disclosure
disco
  discos *pl*
discolor

discolored
discoloring
discoloration
discolour
discoloured
discolouring
discomfit (to thwart)
  discomfitted
  discomfitting
  discomfits
  discomfited *Am*
  discomfiting *Am*
discomfiture
discomfort (pain)
discompose
  discomposed
  discomposing
discomposure
disconcert
disconnect
disconnection
disconsolate
disconsolately
discontent
discontinuance
discontinue
  discontinued
  discontinuing
discontinuing
discontinuity
  discontinuities *pl*
discontinuous
discord

discordance

discordant

discothèque,
  discotheque

discount

discourage
  discouraged
  discouraging

discouragement

discourse
  discoursed
  discoursing

discourteous

discourteously

discourtesy
  discourtesies *pl*

discover
  discovered
  discovering

discoverer

discovery
  discoveries *pl*

discredit
  discredited
  discrediting

discreet (prudent)

discreetly

discrepancy
  discrepancies *pl*

discrepant

discrete (separate)

discretely

discretion

discriminate
  discriminated
  discriminating

discriminatory

discursive

discus (heavy disc)
  discuses, disci *pl*

discuss (to talk over)

discussion

disdain

disdainful

disdainfully

disease

diseased

disembark

disembarkation

disembodied

disembodiment

disembody
  disembodied
  disembodies
  disembodying

disembowel
  disembowelled
  disembowelling
  disembowels

disenchant

disenchantment

disengage
  disengaged
  disengaging

disengagement

disentangle

disentangled

disentangling

disentanglement

disestablish

disestablishment

disfavor *Am*

disfavored *Am*

disfavour

disfavoured

disfigure
  disfigured
  disfiguring

disfigurement

disgorge
  disgorged
  disgorging

disgrace
  disgraced
  disgracing

disgraceful

disgracefully

disgruntled

disguise
  disguised
  disguising

disgust

dish
  dishes *pl*

dishabille, déshabillé

dishearten
  disheartened
  disheartening

disheveled *Am*

dishevelled
dishonest
dishonestly
dishonesty
dishonor Am
　dishonored
　dishonoring
dishonorable Am
dishonorably Am
dishonored Am
dishonour
　dishonoured
　dishonouring
dishonourable
dishonourably
dishwasher
disillusion
disincentive
disinclination
disinclined
disinfect
disinfectant
disinfection
disinherit
　disinherited
　disinheriting
disinheritance
disintegrate
　disintegrated
　disintegrating
disintegration
disintegrator
disinter

disinterred
disinterring
disinters
disinterested
disinterment
disjointed
disk (computer; disc
　Am)
dislikable
dislike
　disliked
　disliking
dislocate
　dislocated
　dislocating
dislocation
dislodge
　dislodged
　dislodging
dislodgement,
　dislodgment
disloyal
disloyally
disloyalty
dismal
dismally
dismantle
　dismantled
　dismantling
dismay
dismayed
dismember
　dismembered

dismembering
dismemberment
dismiss
dismissal
dismount
disobedience
disobedient
disobediently
disobey
　disobeyed
　disobeying
disoblige
disobliging
disorder
disordered
disorderliness
disorderly
disorganisation
disorganise
　disorganised
　disorganizing
disorganization
disorganize
　disorganized
　disorganizing
disorientate
　disorientated
　disorientating
disorientation
disown
disparage
　disparaged
　disparaging

isparagement
isparate (different)
isparity
  disparities *pl*
ispassionate
ispassionately
ispatch
ispatch, despatch
ispatcher
ispel
  dispelled
  dispelling
  dispels
ispensary
  dispensaries *pl*
ispensation
ispense
  dispensed
  dispensing
ispenser
ispersal
isperse
  dispersed
  dispersing
ispersion
ispirit
  dispirited
  dispiriting
isplace
  displaced
  displacing
isplacement
isplay

displayed
displaying
displays
displease
  displeased
  displeasing
displeasure
disport
disposable
disposal
dispose
  disposed
  disposing
disposition
dispossess
dispossession (taking
  away)
disproportion
disproportionate
disproportionately
disprove
  disproved
  disproving
disputable
disputably
disputant
dispute
  disputed
  disputing
disqualification
disqualify
  disqualified
  disqualifies

disqualifying
disquiet
  disquieted
  disquieting
disquieten
  disquietened
  disquietening
disquietitude
disquisition
disregard
disrepair
disreputable
disreputably
disrepute
disrespect
disrespectful
disrespectfully
disrobe
  disrobed
  disrobing
disrupt
disruption
disruptive
dissatisfaction
dissatisfy
  dissatisfied
  dissatisfies
  dissatisfying
dissect
dissection
dissector
dissemble
  dissembled

dissembling
dissembler
disseminate
  disseminated
  disseminating
dissemination
disseminator
dissension
dissent (difference)
dissenter
dissertation
disservice
dissidence
  (disagreement)
dissident
dissimilar
dissimilarity
  dissimilarities *pl*
dissimulate
  dissimulated
  dissimulating
dissimulation
dissimulator
dissipate
  dissipated
  dissipating
dissipation
dissociate
  dissociated
  dissociating
dissociation
dissoluble
dissolute

dissolutely
dissoluteness
dissolution
dissolve
  dissolved
  dissolving
dissolvent
dissonance
dissonant
dissuade
  dissuaded
  dissuading
dissuasion
dissuasive
distaff
  distaffs *pl*
distance
  distanced
  distancing
distant
distantly
distaste
distasteful
distastefully
distemper
  distempered
  distempering
distend
distensible
distension
distil
  distilled
  distilling

distils
distillation
distiller
distillery
  distilleries *pl*
distinct
distinction
distinctive
distinctly
distingué
distinguish
distinguishable
distort
distortion
distortionless
distract
distraction
distrain
distraint
distrait
distraught
distress
distribute
  distributed
  distributing
distribution
distributive
distributor
district
district nurse
distrust
distrustful
disturb

disturbance
disturber
disunion
disunite
disunited
disuniting
disunity
disuse
disused
itch
ditches *pl*
itcher
ither
dithered
dithering
dithery
ditto
ditty
ditties *pl*
diureses
diuretic
diurnal (in a day)
diurnally
diva (prima donna)
divas *pl*
divagate
divagated
divagating
divagation
divan
dive
dived
diving

dove *Am*
diver
diverge
diverged
diverging
divergence
divergent
divers (various)
diverse (different)
diversely
diversification
diversify
diversified
diversifies
diversifying
diversion
diversity
diversities *pl*
divert
divertissement
divest
divide
divided
dividing
dividend
divider
divination
divine
divined
divining
divinely
diviner
diving (*from* dive)

divinities *pl*
divinity
divisible
division
divisional
divisive
divisor
divorce
divorced
divorcing
divorcee
divot
divulge
divulged
divulging
Diwali
DIY, do-it-yourself
dizzily
dizziness
dizzy
dizzier
dizziest
do
did
does
doing
done
docile
docilely
docility
dock
docker
docket

docketed
docketing
dockyard
doctor
  doctored
  doctoring
doctorate
doctrinaire
doctrinal
doctrine
document
documentary
  documentaries *pl*
documentation
dodder
dodderer
doddery
dodge
  dodged
  dodging
dodgy
  dodgier
  dodgiest
dodo
  dodos *pl*
doe (deer)
  does *pl*
doer
does (*from* do)
doesn't
doff
dog
  dogged

dogging
dogs
dog-ear
dog-eared
dogged (stubborn)
doggedly
doggerel
doggy, doggie
dogma
  dogmas *pl*
dogmatic
dogmatically
dogmatise
  dogmatised
  dogmatising
dogmatism
dogmatize
  dogmatized
  dogmatizing
do-gooder
doily
  doilies *pl*
doing (*from* do)
do-it-yourself, DIY
dolce far niente
doldrums
dole (pay)
  doled
  doling
doleful
dolefully
doll (toy)
dollar (money)

dolled
dollop
dolly
  dollies *pl*
dolor *Am*
dolorous
dolour (sorrow)
dolphin
dolt
domain
dome (round roof)
domed
domelike
Domesday-Book
domestic
domestically
domesticate
  domesticated
  domesticating
domesticity
domicile
domiciliary
dominance
dominant
dominantly
dominate
  dominated
  dominating
domination
domineer
  domineered
  domineering
dominical

ominion
omino
dominoes *pl*
on
donned
donning
dons
on't
onate
donated
donating
onation
one (*from* do)
onkey
donkeys *pl*
onnish
onor (giver)
oodle
doodled
doodling
oodler
oom
doomed
dooming
oor
ope
doped
doping
dopey
dormancy
dormant
dormer
dormitory

dormitories *pl*
dormouse
dormice *pl*
dorsal
dorsally
dory
dories *pl*
dosage
dose
dosed
dosing
dosimeter
doss
doss-house
dossier
dot
dots
dotted
dotting
dotage
dotard
dote
doted
doting
dottily
dotty
dottier
dottiest
double
doubled
doubling
double entendre
double-barrelled

double-breasted
doubly
doubt
doubter
doubtful
doubtfully
doubtfulness
doubtless
douche
douched
douching
dough (bread)
doughnut
doughtily
doughtiness
doughty
doughtier
doughtiest
doughy
doughier
doughiest
dour
dourly
dourness
douse (drench)
doused
dousing
dove
dovecot
dovecote
dovetail
dovetailed
dovetailing

dowager

dowdily

dowdiness

dowdy
  dowdier
  dowdiest

dowel

dower

dower-house

down

downcast

downfall

downfallen

downhearted

downpour

downright

Downs

downstairs

downtrodden

downward

dowry
  dowries pl

dowse (search
  for water)
  dowsed
  dowsing

dowser

doyen

doze
  dozed
  dozing

dozen

drab

drachma (Greek
  money)
  drachmas pl

Draconian

draft (preliminary
  writing)

draftsman
  draftsmen pl

drafty Am
  draftier
  draftiest

drag
  dragged
  dragging
  drags

dragoman
  dragomans,
  dragomen pl

dragon

dragonfly
  dragonflies pl

dragoon
  dragooned
  dragooning

drain
  drained
  draining

drainage

drama
  dramas pl

dramatic

dramatically

dramatis personae

dramatisation

dramatise
  dramatised
  dramatising

dramatist

dramatization

dramatize
  dramatized
  dramatizing

drank (from drink)

drape
  draped
  draping

draper

drapery
  draperies pl

drastic

drastically

draught (of air)

draughts (game)

draughtsman
  draughtsmen pl

draughty
  draughtier
  draughtiest

draw
  drawing
  drawn
  drew

drawback

drawer

drawing-room

drawl

read
  dreaded
  dreading
dreadful
dreadfully
dreadness
dreadnought
dream
  dreamed, dreamt
  dreaming
dreamer
dreamily
dreamless
dreamy
  dreamier
  dreamiest
drearily
dreariness
dreary
dredge
  dredged
  dredging
dredger
dregs
drench
drenched
dress
  dresses pl
dressage
dressed
dresser
dressmaker
dressy

drew
dribble
  dribbled
  dribbling
dribbler
driblet
dried (from dry)
drier, dryer (drying
  machine)
dries (from dry)
drift
drill
drily (from dry)
drink
  drank
  drinking
  drunk
drinker
drip
  dripped
  dripping
  drips
drip-dry
  drip-dried
  drip-dries
  drip-drying
drive
  driven
  driving
  drove
drivel
  drivelled
  drivelling

drivels
  driveled Am
  driveling Am
driveler Am
driveller
driven (from drive)
driver
driving
drizzle
  drizzled
  drizzling
drizzly
drogue
droll
drollery
  drolleries pl
drolly
drollness
dromedary
  dromedaries pl
drone
  droned
  droning
droop
  drooped
  drooping
drop
  dropped
  dropping
  drops
droplet
drop-out
  drop-outs pl

dropper

dropsical

dropsy

dross

drought

drove (*from* drive)

drover

droves

drown

drowse
  drowsed
  drowsing

drowsier

drowsily

drowsiness

drowsy
  drowsier
  drowsiest

drudge

drudgery

drug
  drugged
  drugging
  drugs

drugget (fabric)

druggist

drugstore

druid

drum
  drummed
  drumming
  drums

drum-major

drummer

drunk

drunkard

drunken

drunkenly

drunkenness

dry
  dried
  dries
  drying
  drier
  driest

dry-clean
  dry-cleaned
  dry-cleaning

dryer, drier (drying
  machine)

dryly

dryness

dual (double)

dualism

dual-purpose

dub
  dubbed
  dubbing
  dubs

dubbin, dubbing
  (grease)

dubious

dubiously

ducal

ducat

duchess

duchesses *pl*

duchy
  duchies *pl*

duck

duckling

duct

ductile

ductility

ductless

dud

dudgeon

due (payable)

duel (fight)
  duelled
  duelling
  duels
  dueled *Am*
  dueling *Am*

duellist

duenna
  duennas *pl*

duet
  dueted
  dueting

duffel, duffle
  (cloth, coat)

duffer

dug (*from* dig)

dug-out
  dug-outs *pl*

duke

dukery
  dukeries *pl*

dulcet
dull
dullard
dullness
dully
duly (*from* due)
dumb
dumb-bell
dumbfound, dumfound
  dumbfounded,
    dumfounded
  dumbfounding,
    dumfounding
dumbly
dumbness
dumfound
  dumfounded
  dumfounding
dummy
  dummies *pl*
dump
dumpiness
dumpling
dumpy
  dumpier
  dumpiest
dun (demand)
  dunned
  dunning
  duns
dunce
dune
dung

dungarees
dungeon
dunghill
duodecimal
duodecimo
duodenal
duodenum
  duodenums *pl*
duologue
dupe
  duped
  duping
dupery
duplex
  duplexes *pl*
duplicate
  duplicated
  duplicating
duplication
duplicator
duplicity
durability
durable
durably
durance
duration
duress
during
dusk
dust
duster
dustiness
dusty

dustier
dustiest
dutiable
dutiful
dutifully
duty
  duties *pl*
duty-free
duvet
dwarf
  dwarfs, dwarves *pl*
  dwarfed
  dwarfing
  dwarfs
dwell
  dwelled, dwelt
  dwelling
dweller
dwelling
dwindle
  dwindled
  dwindling
dye (to colour)
  dyed
  dyeing
  dyes
dyer
dying (*from* die)
dyke, dike
dynamic
dynamically
dynamite
  dynamited

dynamiting
dynamo
  dynamos *pl*
dynamometer
dynasty
  dynasties *pl*
dyne (unit)
dysentery
dyslexia
dyslexic
dyspepsia
dyspeptic

E

each
eager
eagerly
eagerness
eagle
eagle-eyed
eaglet
ear
earache
earful
earl
earldom
earliness
early
  earlier
  earliest
earmark
earn (money)
earner

earnest
earnestly
earnestness
earphone
earring
earth
earthed
earthenware
earthly
earthquake
earwig
ease
  eased
  easing
easel
easily
easiness
east
Easter

easterly
eastern
eastward
eastwards
easy
  easier
  easiest
easygoing
eat
  ate
  eaten
  eating
eatable
eater
eats
eaves
eavesdrop
  eavesdropped
  eavesdropping
  eavesdrops
eavesdropper
ebb
  ebbed
  ebbing
ebb-tide
ebonite
ebony
ebullience
ebullient
ebulliently
eccentric
eccentrically
eccentricity

eccentricities *pl*
ecclesiastic
ecclesiastical
ecclesiastically
echelon
echo
  echoes *pl*
  echoed
  echoes
  echoing
eclair
eclat
eclectic
eclecticism
eclipse
  eclipsed
  eclipsing
ecliptic
eclogue
ecological
ecologically
ecologist
ecology
  ecologies *pl*
economic
economical
economically
economise
  economised
  economising
economist
economize
  economized

economizing
economy
  economies *pl*
ecstasy
  ecstasies *pl*
ecstatic
ecstatically
ecumenical
ecumenically
eczema
eddy
  eddies *pl*
  eddied
  eddies
  eddying
edelweiss
edge
  edged
  edging
edgeways
edgily
edginess
edgy
  edgier
  edgiest
edibility
edible
edict
edification
  (instruction)
edifice (building)
edify
  edified

edifies
edifying
edit
  edited
  editing
edition (book)
editor
editorial
editorially
educability
educable
educatability
educatable
educate
  educated
  educating
education
educational
educationalist
educationally
educationist
educative
educator
educe (to develop,
  infer)
  educed
  educing
educible
eduction
eel
eerie (creepy)
  eerier
  eeriest

eerily
eeriness
efface
  effaced
  effacing
effaceable
effacement
effect (to accomplish)
effective (useful)
effectively
effectiveness
effectual (actual)
effeminacy
effeminate
effeminately
effervesce
  effervesced
  effervescing
effervescence
effervescent
effete
efficacious
efficaciously
efficacy
efficiency
efficient
efficiently
effigy
  effigies pl
efflorescence
efflorescent
effluent
effluvium

effluvia pl
efflux
effort
effortless
effortlessly
effusion
effusive
effusively
effusiveness
egalitarian
egg
  egged
  egging
eggy
ego
egocentric
egocentricity
egoism
egoist
egoistic
egoistically
egotism (conceit)
egotist
egotistic
egotistical
egotistically
egregious
egregiously
egregiousness
egress
eiderdown
Eiffel (tower)
eight

eighteen
eighteenth
eighth
eighthly
eightieth
eighty
  eighties pl
Eire
Eisteddfod
either
ejaculate
  ejaculated
  ejaculating
ejaculation
ejaculatory
eject
ejection
ejector
eke
  eked
  eking
elaborate
  elaborated
  elaborating
elaborately
elaborateness
elaboration
elapse
  elapsed
  elapsing
elastic
elastically
elasticity

elated
elation
elbow
  elbowed
  elbowing
elder
elderly
eldest
elect
election
electioneering
elective
elector
electoral
electorate
electric
electrical
electrically
electrician
electricity
electrification
electrified
electrify
  electrified
  electrifies
  electrifying
electrocardiogram
  (E.C.G.)
electrocardiograph
electrocardiography
electrocute
  electrocuted
  electrocuting

electrocution
electrode
electrodynamic
electrodynamically
electrolysis
electrolyte
electrolytic
electromagnet
electromagnetic
electrometer
electrometric
electromotive
electromotive force
  (E.M.F.)
election
electronic
electronically
electroplate
electroplating
electrostatic
electrotechnical
eleemosynary
  (charitable)
elegance
elegant
elegantly
elegiac
elegy
  elegies pl
element
elemental
elementarily
elementary

elephant
elephantine
elevate
  elevated
  elevating
elevation
elevator
eleven
eleventh
elf
  elves pl
elfin
elfish
elicit (to evoke)
  elicited
  eliciting
elide
  elided
  eliding
eligibility
eligible
eliminate
  eliminated
  eliminating
elimination
eliminator
elision
elite
elitism
elitist
elixir
Elizabethan
ellipse

elliptic
elliptical
elliptically
elm
elocution
elocutionist
elongate
  elongated
  elongating
elongation
elope
  eloped
  eloping
elopement
eloquence
eloquent
eloquently
else
elsewhere
elucidate
  elucidated
  elucidating
elucidation
elude (to evade)
  eluded
  eluding
elusion (evasion)
elusive
elusiveness
elver
Elysian
emaciate
  emaciated

  emaciating
emaciation
e-mail
emancipate
  emancipated
  emancipating
emancipation
emancipator
emasculate
  emasculated
  emasculating
emasculation
embalm
embalmer
embalmment
embankment
embargo
  embargoes *pl*
  embargoed
  embargoes
  embargoing
embark
embarkation
embarras de richesse
embarrass
embarrassed
embarrassment
embassy
  embassies *pl*
embattle
  embattled
  embattling
embed

embedded
embedding
embeds
embellish
embellishment
ember
embezzle
  embezzled
  embezzling
embezzlement
embezzler
embitter
  embittered
  embittering
embitterment
emblazon
  emblazoned
  emblazoning
emblem
emblematic
emblematically
embodiment
embody
  embodied
  embodies
  embodying
embolism
embonpoint
emboss
embossment
embrace
  embraced
  embracing

embrasure
embrocation
embroider
embroidered
embroidery
  embroideries *pl*
embroil
  embroiled
  embroiling
embroilment
embryo
embryologist
embryology
embryonic
emend (to remove
  errors)
  emended
  emending
emendation
emerald
emerge
  emerged
  emerging
emergence
emergency
  emergencies *pl*
emergent
emergently
emeritus
emersion
  (reappearance)
emery
emetic

emigrant
emigrate (to leave
  country)
  emigrated
  emigrating
emigration
émigré
  émigrés *pl*
eminence
eminent (famous)
eminently
emissary
  emissaries *pl*
emission
emit (to send out)
  emits
  emitted
  emitting
emitter
emollient (softening)
emolument (pay)
emotion
emotional
emotionally
emotive
empathise
  empathised
  empathising
empathize
  empathized
  empathizing
empathy
emperor

emphasis
  emphases *pl*
emphasise
  emphasised
  emphasising
emphasize
  emphasized
  emphasizing
emphatic
emphatically
emphysema (lung
  disease)
empire
empirical
  (experiment)
empirically
emplacement
employ
  employed
  employing
  employs
employability
employable
employee
employer
employment
emporium
  emporia,
    emporiums *pl*
empower
  empowered
  empowering
empress

empresses *pl*
emptily
emptiness
empty
  empties *pl*
  emptied
  empties
  emptying
  emptier
  emptiest
emu
  emus *pl*
emulate
  emulated
  emulating
emulation
emulative
emulator
emulsification
emulsifier
emulsify
  emulsified
  emulsifies
  emulsifying
emulsion
enable
  enabled
  enabling
enablement
enact
enactment
enamel
  enamelled

enamelling
enamels
  enameled *Am*
  enameling *Am*
enameler *Am*
enameller
enamor *Am*
enamored *Am*
enamour
enamoured
en bloc
encampment
encase
  encased
  encasing
enceinte
encephalitis
enchant
  enchanted
  enchanting
enchanter
enchantment
enchantress
encircle
  encircled
  encircling
encirclement
enclave
enclose
  enclosed
  enclosing
enclosure
encode

encoded
encoding
encompass
encore
  encored
  encoring
encounter
  encountered
  encountering
encourage
  encouraged
  encouraging
encouragement
encroach
encroachment
encumber
  encumbered
  encumbering
encumbrance
encyclical
encyclopedia,
    encyclopaedia
  encyclopedias,
    encyclopaedias *pl*
encyclopedic,
  encyclopaedic
end
  ended
  ending
endanger
  endangered
  endangering
endear

endeared
endearing
endearment
endeavor *Am*
endeavored
endeavoring
endeavour
endeavoured
endeavouring
endemic
endemically
endive
endless
endlessly
endocrine
endorse
endorsed
endorsing
endorsement
endorser
endow
endowed
endowing
endowment
endurable
endurance
endure
endured
enduring
enema
enemas *pl*
enemy
enemies *pl*

energetic
energetically
energise
energised
energising
energiser
energize
energized
energizing
energizer
energy
energies *pl*
enervate
enervated
enervating
enervation
en famille
enfeeble
enfeebled
enfeebling
enfeeblement
enforce
enforced
enforcing
enforceability
enforceable
enforcement
enfranchise
enfranchised
enfranchising
enfranchisement
engage
engaged

engaging
engagement
engender
engendered
engendering
engine
engineer
engineered
engineering
engorge
engorged
engorging
engrained
engrave
engraved
engraving
engraver
engross
engrossment
engulf
engulfed
engulfing
enhance
enhanced
enhancing
enhancement
enigma
enigmas *pl*
enigmatic
enigmatically
enjoin
enjoined
enjoining

enjoy
  enjoyed
  enjoying
  enjoys
enjoyable
enjoyably
enjoyment
enlarge
  enlarged
  enlarging
enlargeable
enlargement
enlarger
enlighten
  enlightened
  enlightening
enlightenment
enlist
  enlisted
  enlisting
enlistment
en masse
enmity
  enmities *pl*
ennoble
  ennobled
  ennobling
ennoblement
ennui (boredom)
enormity
  enormities *pl*
enormous
enormously

enough
en passant
enquire (to ask)
  enquired
  enquiring
enquiry
  enquiries *pl*
enrage
  enraged
  enraging
enrapture
  enraptured
  enrapturing
enrich
enrichment
enrol
  enrolled
  enrolling
  enrols
  enroled *Am*
  enroling *Am*
  enrollment *Am*
  enrolment
en route
ensconce
  ensconced
  ensconcing
ensemble
enshrine
  enshrined
  enshrining
ensign
enslave

enslaved
  enslaving
enslavement
ensue (to follow)
  ensued
  ensuing
ensure (to make sure)
  ensured
  ensuring
entail
  entailed
  entailing
entailment
entangle
  entangled
  entangling
entanglement
entente
enter
  entered
  entering
enteric
enteritis
enterprise
enterprising
entertain
  entertained
  entertaining
entertainer
entertainment
enthral
  enthralled
  enthralling

enthrals
enthrall *Am*
enthralls
enthrallment *Am*
enthralment
enthrone
enthroned
enthroning
enthronement
enthuse
enthused
enthusing
enthusiasm
enthusiast
enthusiastic
enthusiastically
entice
enticed
enticing
enticement
entire
entired
entiring
entirely
entirety
entitle
entitled
entitling
entitlement
entity
entities *pl*
entomb
entombed

entombing
entombment
entomological
entomologist
entomology
entourage
entrails
entrance
entranced
entrancing
entrancement
entrant
entrap
entrapped
entrapping
entraps
entreat
entreated
entreating
entreaty
entreaties *pl*
entrée
entrées *pl*
entrench
entrenchment
entrepôt
entrepreneur
entrepreneurial
entropy
entrust
entry
entries *pl*
entwine

entwined
entwining
enumerate
enumerated
enumerating
enumeration
enumerator
enunciate
enunciated
enunciating
enunciation
enunciator
envelop (to cover)
enveloped
enveloping
envelope (covering)
envelopment
envenom
envenomed
envenoming
enviable
envious
enviously
environ
environment
environmental
environmentally
envisage
envisaged
envisaging
envoy
envoys *pl*
envy

envied

envies

envying

enwrap

enwrapped

enwrapping

enwraps

enzyme

eolith (ancient flint)

epaulet *Am*

epaulette

ephemera (insect)

ephemerae *pl*

ephemeral (short-lived)

ephemerally

ephemeron (printed item)

ephemera *pl*

epic

epical

epically

epicene (both sexes)

epicenter *Am*

epicentre

epicure

epicurean

epicureanism

epicycle

epicyclic

epidemic

epidermal

epidermis

epidiascope

epigastric

epigastrium

epigastria *pl*

epiglottis

epigram (clever saying)

epigrammatic

epigraph (inscription)

epilepsy

epileptic

epilogue

Epiphany

episcopacy

episcopal

episcopalian

episcopate

episode

episodic

epistle

epistolary

epitaph (inscription on tomb)

epithet (adjective)

epitome

epitomes *pl*

epitomise

epitomised

epitomising

epitomize

epitomized

epitomizing

epoch

epochal

eponym

eponymous

epsilon

equability

equable

equably

equal

equalled

equalling

equals

equaled *Am*

equaling *Am*

equalise

equalised

equalising

equaliser

equality

equalities *pl*

equalize

equalized

equalizing

equalizer

equally

equanimity

equate

equated

equating

equation

equator

equatorial

equerry

equerries *pl*

equestrian
equestrianism
equidistant
equilateral
equilibrate
  equilibrated
  equilibrating
equilibration
equilibrium
  equilibria,
  equilibriums *pl*
equine
equinoctial
equinox
  equinoxes *pl*
equip
  equipped
  equipping
  equips
equipage
equipment
equipoise
equitable
equitably
equity
  equities *pl*
equivalence
equivalent
equivocal
equivocally
equivocate
  equivocated
  equivocating

equivocation
equivocator
era
  eras *pl*
eradicable
eradicate
  eradicated
  eradicating
eradication
erasable
erase
  erased
  erasing
eraser
erasure
ere (before)
erect
  erected
  erecting
erection
erector
erg (unit)
ergo (therefore)
ergonomics
ergotism (disease)
ermine
erode
  eroded
  eroding
erogenous
erosion
erosive
erotic

erotica
erotically
eroticism
erotism
err
  erred
  erring
  errs
errancy
errand (short journey)
errant (wandering)
errantry
errata
erratic
erratically
erroneous
erroneously
error
ersatz
erstwhile
eructate (to belch)
  eructated
  eructating
eructation
erudite (learned)
eruditely
erudition
erupt
  erupted
  erupting
eruption
eruptive
eruptively

erysipelas
escalade (to climb
    over)
  escaladed
  escalading
escalate (to increase)
  escalated
  escalating
escalation
escalator
escallop, scallop
    (shellfish)
escalope (slice of veal)
escapade
escape
  escaped
  escaping
escapement (of a
    clock)
escaper
escapism
escapologist
escargot (snail)
escarpment (of a hill)
eschatological
eschatology
eschew
  eschewed
  eschewing
escort
  escorted
  escorting
Eskimo

    Eskimos, Eskimo pl
esoteric
esoterical
esoterically
esotericism
espadrilles
espalier
especial
especially
Esperanto
espionage
esplanade
espousal
espouse
  espoused
  espousing
espresso
  espressos pl
esprit de corps
espy
  espied
  espies
  espying
Esquire, Esq.
essay (try)
  essays pl
  essayed
  essaying
  essays
essayist
essence
essential
essentially

establish
establishable
establishment
estate
esteem
  esteemed
esthete Am
esthetic Am
esthetically Am
estheticism Am
esthetics Am
estimable
estimate
  estimated
  estimating
estimation
estimator
estranged
estrangement
estuary
  estuaries pl
et cetera, etc.
etch
etcher
eternal
eternally
eternity
  eternities pl
ether
ethereal
ethereally
ethic
ethical

ethically
ethics
ethnic
ethnically
ethnological
ethnology
ethos
ethyl
ethylene
etiolate
  etiolated
  etiolating
etiolation
etiology
etiquette
etude
etymological
etymologically
etymologist
etymology
eucalyptus
  eucalypti,
  eucalyptuses *pl*
Eucharist
Euclid
Euclidean
eugenic
eugenically
eugenics
eulogise
  eulogised
  eulogising
eulogistic

eulogistically
eulogize
  eulogized
  eulogizing
eulogy
  eulogies *pl*
eunuch
euphemism
euphemistic
euphemistically
euphonious
euphony (pleasant
  sound)
  euphonies *pl*
euphoria
euphoric
euphuism (affected
  style of speech)
euphuistic
Eurasian
eureka
eurhythmics
Eurocrat
Eurodollar
Europe
European
eustachian
euthanasia
evacuate
  evacuated
  evacuating
evacuation
evacuee

evade
  evaded
  evading
evaluate
  evaluated
  evaluating
evaluation
evanesce
  evanesced
  evanescing
evanescent
evangelical
evangelise
  evangelised
  evangelising
evangelism
evangelist
evangelize
  evangelized
  evangelizing
evaporate
  evaporated
  evaporating
evaporation
evaporator
evasion
evasive
evasively
evasiveness
eve
even
  evened
  evening

evening (time of day)
evenly
evenness
event
eventful
eventfully
eventide
eventual
eventuality
  eventualities *pl*
eventually
eventuate
  eventuated
  eventuating
ever
everlasting
evermore
every
everybody
everyone
everywhere
evict
  evicted
  evicting
eviction
evidence
evident
evidently
evil
evilly
evince
  evinced
  evincing

eviscerate
  eviscerated
  eviscerating
evisceration
evocation
evocative
evoke
  evoked
  evoking
evolution
evolutionary
evolutionism
evolutionist
evolve
  evolved
  evolving
ewe
ewer
ex officio
exacerbate
  exacerbated
  exacerbating
exacerbation
exact
  exacted
  exacting
exactitude
exactly
exactness
exaggerate
  exaggerated
  exaggerating
exaggeration

exaggerator
exalt
  exalted
  exalting
exaltation
exam
examination
examine
  examined
  examining
examiner
example
exasperate
  exasperated
  exasperating
exasperation
excavate
  excavated
  excavating
excavation
excavator
exceed (surpass)
  exceeded
  exceeding
exceedingly
excel
  excelled
  excelling
  excels
excellence
Excellency
  Excellencies *pl*
excellent

excellently

except

  excepted

  excepting

exception

exceptional

exceptionally

excerpt

excess

  excesses *pl*

excessive

excessively

exchange

  exchanged

  exchanging

exchangeable

exchanger

exchequer

excisable

excise

  excised

  excising

excision

excitability

excitable

excitation

excite

  excited

  exciting

excitement

exciter

exclaim

  exclaimed

exclaiming

exclamation

exclamatory

exclude

  excluded

  excluding

exclusion

exclusive

exclusively

exclusiveness

exclusivity

excommunicate

  excommunicated

  excommunicating

excommunication

excrement

excrescence

excreta

excrete

  excreted

  excreting

excretion

excruciate

excruciating

excruciatingly

exculpate

  exculpated

  exculpating

exculpation

excursion

excusable

excusably

excuse

excused

excusing

execrable

execrably

execrate

  execrated

  execrating

execration

executant (performer)

execute

  executed

  executing

execution

executioner

executive

executor (of a Will)

executrix (female

  executor)

  executrices *pl*

exemplarily

exemplary

exemplification

exemplify

  exemplified

  exemplifies

  exemplifying

exempt

  exempted

  exempting

exemption

exercise (to keep fit)

  exercised

  exercising

exert
  exerted
  exerting
exertion
exeunt
exhalation
exhale
  exhaled
  exhaling
exhaust
  exhausted
  exhausting
exhaustible
exhaustion
exhaustive
exhaustively
exhibit
  exhibited
  exhibiting
exhibition
exhibitioner
exhibitionism
exhibitionist
exhibitor
exhilarant
exhilarate
  exhilarated
  exhilarating
exhilaration
exhort
  exhorted
  exhorting
exhortation

exhumation
exhume
  exhumed
  exhuming
exigency
  exigencies pl
exigent
exigently
exiguity
exiguous
exile
  exiled
  exiling
exist
  existed
  existing
existence
existent
existential
existentialism
exit
  exited
  exiting
exodus
  exoduses pl
exonerate
  exonerated
  exonerating
exoneration
exorbitance
exorbitant
exorbitantly
exorcise (to free

  from evil)
  exorcised
  exorcising
exorcism
exorcist
exorcize
  exorcized
  exorcizing
exotic
exotica
exotically
expand
expandable
expanse
expansible
expansion
expansive
expansively
expatiate (to talk at
    length)
  expatiated
  expatiating
expatriate
  expatriated
  expatriating
expatriation
expect
  expected
  expecting
expectancy
expectant
expectation
expectorant

expectorate
  expectorated
  expectorating
expectoration
expediency
  expediencies *pl*
expedient
expedite
  expedited
  expediting
expedition
expeditionary
expeditious
expeditiously
expel
  expelled
  expelling
  expels
expend
expendability
expendable
expenditure
expense
expensive
experience
  experienced
  experiencing
experiment
  experimented
  experimenting
experimental
experimentally
experimentation

experimenter
expert
expertise
expertly
expertness
expiate
  expiated
  expiating
expiation
expiration
expiratory
expire
  expired
  expiring
expiry
explain
  explained
  explaining
explainable
explanation
explanatory
expletive
explicable
explicate (to explain)
  explicated
  explicating
explicit
explicitly
explicitness
explode
  exploded
  exploding
exploit

exploited
exploiting
exploitation
exploiter
exploration
exploratory
explore
  explored
  exploring
explorer
explosion
explosive
explosively
exponent
exponential
export
  exported
  exporting
exportable
exportation
exporter
expose
  exposed
  exposing
exposé (detailed
  description)
exposition
expostulate
  expostulated
  expostulating
expostulation
exposure
expound

expounded
expounding
express
expressible
expression
expressionless
expressive
expressively
expressly
expropriate
  expropriated
  expropriating
expropriation
expropriator
expulsion
expunction
expunge
  expunged
  expunging
expurgate
  expurgated
  expurgating
expurgation
expurgatory
exquisite
exquisitely
extant
extemporaneous
extemporaneously
extempore
extemporisation
extemporise
  extemporised

extemporising
extemporization
extemporize
  extemporized
  extemporizing
extend
extendible
extensible
extension
extensive
extensively
extent
extenuate
  extenuated
  extenuating
extenuation
exterior
exterminate
  exterminated
  exterminating
extermination
exterminator
external
externally
extinct
extinction
extinguish
extinguisher
extirpate
  extirpated
  extirpating
extirpation
extirpator

extol
  extolled
  extolling
  extols
extort
extortion
extortionate
extortioner
extra
  extras *pl*
extract
  extracted
  extracting
extractable
extraction
extractive
extractor
extracurricular
extraditable
extradite
  extradited
  extraditing
extradition
extramarital
extramural
extraneous
extraneously
extraordinarily
extraordinary
extrapolate
  extrapolated
  extrapolating
extrapolation

extrasensory
extra-systole (heart-
beat)
extra-systolic
extraterrestrial
extraterritorial
extraterritoriality
extravagance
extravagant
extravagantly
extravaganza
extravaganzas *pl*
extreme
extremely
extremist
extremity
extremities *pl*
extricable
extricate
extricated
extricating
extrication
extrinsic
extrinsically
extroversion
extrovert
extrude
extruded
extruding
extruder
extrusion
exuberance
exuberant

exuberantly
exudation
exude
exuded
exuding
exult
exulted
exulting
exultant
exultation
eye
eyes *pl*
eyed
eyeing
eyeball
eyebrow
eyeful
eyelash
eyelashes *pl*
eyelid
eye-opener
eyepiece
eyesight
eyesore
eyewash
eyewitness
eyrie (eagle's nest)

fable
fabled
fabric
fabricate
  fabricated
  fabricating
fabrication
fabricator
fabulous
fabulously
facade
face
  faced
  facing
faceless
facet
faceted
facetious
facetiously

facetiousness
facia (panel)
facial
facially
facile
facilitate
  facilitated
  facilitating
facilitation
facility
  facilities *pl*
facsimile
fact
faction
factious
factitious
factor
  factored
  factoring

factorial
factorisation
factorise
  factorised
  factorising
factorization
factorize
  factorized
  factorizing
factory
  factories *pl*
factotum
  factotums *pl*
factual
factually
facultative (optional)
faculty
  faculties *pl*
fad
faddish
faddy
fade
  faded
  fading
faecal
faeces
fag
  fagged
  fagging
  fags
fag-end
faggot
fagot *Am*

Fahrenheit
faience
fail
　failed
　failing
　fails
failure
fain (gladly)
faint (weak)
fainter
faint-hearted
faintly
faintness
fair (clear; light-
　coloured; outdoor
　entertainment;
　satisfactory)
fairer
fair-haired
fairly
fairness
fairway
　fairways *pl*
fairy
　fairies *pl*
fairy tale
fait accompli
faith
faithful
faithfully
faithfulness
faithless
faithlessly

faithlessness
fake
　faked
　faking
faker (fraud)
fakir (Indian holy
　man)
falcon
falconer
falconry
fall
　fallen
　falling
　falls
fallacious
fallacy
　fallacies *pl*
fallibility
fallible
fallout
fallow
false
falsehood
falsely
falseness
falsetto
　falsettos *pl*
falsification
falsify
　falsified
　falsifies
　falsifying
falsity

falter
　faltered
　faltering
fame
familiar
familiarisation
familiarise
　familiarised
　familiarising
familiarity
familiarization
familiarize
　familiarized
　familiarizing
familiarly
family
　families *pl*
famine
famished
famous
famously
fan
　fanned
　fanning
　fans
fanatic
fanatically
fanaticism
fancier
fanciful
fancifully
fancy
　fancies *pl*

fancied
fancies
fancying
fancy-free
fanfare
fantasise
  fantasised
  fantasising
fantasize
  fantasized
  fantasizing
fantastic
fantastically
fantasy
  fantasies *pl*
far
  farther, further
  farthest, furthest
farad
faraway
farce
farceur
farcical
farcically
fare (money; food;
    to manage)
  fared
  faring
farewell
far-fetched
farinaceous
farm
farmer

farmhouse
farmyard
far-reached
far-reaching
farrier
farriery
far-seeing
far-sighted
farthing
fascia (band)
fascicle
fascinate
  fascinated
  fascinating
fascination
fascinator
Fascism
Fascist
Fascistic
fashion
  fashioned
  fashioning
fashionable
fashionably
fast
fasten
  fastened
  fastening
fastener
faster
fastidious
fastidiously
fastidiousness

fat
  fatter
  fattest
fatal
fatalism
fatalist
fatalistic
fatalistically
fatality
  fatalities *pl*
fatally
fat-head
fate
fateful
fatefully
father
  fathered
  fathering
father-in-law
  fathers-in-law *pl*
fatherland
fatherless
fatherly
fathom
fatigue
  fatigued
  fatiguing
fatness
fatten
  fattened
  fattening
fatuity
fatuous

fatuously
fatwa
  fatwas *pl*
faucet
fault
  faulted
  faulting
faultfinding
faultless
faulty
  faultier
  faultiest
faun (deity)
fauna (animals)
faux pas
favor *Am*
  favored
  favoring
favorable *Am*
favorably *Am*
favorite *Am*
favoritism *Am*
favour
  favoured
  favouring
favourable
favourably
favourite
favouritism
fawn (colour; deer; to
  flatter)
  fawned
  fawning

fax
  faxed
  faxing
fay
fealty
  fealties *pl*
fear
  feared
  fearing
fearful
fearfully
fearless
fearlessness
fearsome
feasibility
feasible
feasibly
feast
  feasted
  feasting
feat (achievement)
feather
  feathered
  feathering
featherbed
featherbedding
featherweight
feathery
feature
  featured
  featuring
featureless
febrile

February
fecal *Am*
feces *Am*
feckless
fecund
fecundity
fed (*from* feed)
federal
federalisation
federalise
  federalised
  federalising
federalism
federalist
federalization
federalize
  federalized
  federalizing
federally
federate
  federated
  federating
federation
fed-up
fee
feeble
feebler
feebly
feed
  fed
  feeding
  feeds
feedback

feel
  feeling
  feels
  felt
feeler
feelingly
feet (pl. of foot)
feign (to pretend)
feint (pretence)
felicitate
  felicitated
  felicitating
felicitation
felicitous
felicitously
felicity (happiness)
  felicities *pl*
feline
felinity
fell
fellow
fellowship
felon
felonious
felony
  felonies *pl*
felt
female
feminine
femininity
feminism
feminist
femme fatale

femmes fatales *pl*
femoral
femur (thigh bone)
fence
  fenced
  fencing
fencer
fend
  fended
  fending
fender
fennel
feral
ferment (to turn
    to alcohol)
  fermented
  fermenting
fermentation
fern
fernery
ferocious
ferociously
ferociousness
ferocity
ferret
  ferreted
  ferreting
ferric
ferrous
ferrule
ferry
  ferries *pl*
  ferried

ferries
  ferrying
fertile
fertilisation
fertilise
  fertilised
  fertilising
fertiliser
fertility
fertilization
fertilize
  fertilized
  fertilizing
fertilizer
fervency
fervent
fervently
fervid
fervor *Am*
fervour
festal
fester
  festered
  festering
festival
festive
festively
festivity
  festivities *pl*
festoon
feta, fetta (cheese)
fetal *Am*
fetch

fete (fair)
  feted
  feting
fête *Am*
  fêted
  fêting
fetid, foetid (smelly)
fetish
fetishism
fetlock
fetter (chain)
fettered
fettle
feud
feudal
feudalism
fever
fevered
feverish
feverishly
few
fez
  fezzes *pl*
fiancé *m*
  fiancés *pl*
fiancée *f*
  fiancées *pl*
fiasco
  fiascos *pl*
fiat
fib
  fibbed
  fibbing

fibs
fibber
fiber *Am*
fibre
fibroid
fibrositis
fibrous
fickle
fickleness
fickly
fiction
fictional
fictitious
fictitiously
fiddle
  fiddled
  fiddling
fiddler
fidelity
  fidelities *pl*
fidget
  fidgeted
  fidgeting
fidgety
field
fiend
fiendish
fiendishly
fierce
  fiercer
  fiercest
fiercely
fierceness

fierily
fieriness
fiery
  fierier
  fieriest
fiesta
  fiestas *pl*
fife
fifteen
fifteenth
fifth
fifthly
fiftieth
fifty
  fifties *pl*
fig
fight
  fighting
  fights
  fought
fighter
fig-leaf
figment
figurative
figuratively
figure
  figured
  figuring
figurehead
figurine
filament
filbert
filch

file (paper)
  filed
  filing
filial
filibuster
filigree
fill
filled
filler
fillet
  filleted
  filleting
fillip (stimulus)
filly (young horse)
  fillies *pl*
film
filter
  filtered
  filtering
filth
filthily
filthiness
filthy
  filthier
  filthiest
filtrate
filtration
fin
final (end)
finale (end in music)
finalise
  finalised
  finalising

finalist
finality
finalize
  finalized
  finalizing
finally
finance
  financed
  financing
financial
financially
financier
finch
  finches *pl*
find
  finding
  finds
  found
finder
fine
  fined
  fining
  finer
  finest
finely
fineness
finery
finesse (subtlety)
finger
  fingered
  fingering
fingernail
fingerprint

finical
finically
finicky
finis (end)
finish
finite
finitely
finny
fiord, fjord
fir (tree)
fire
  fired
  firing
firearm
fire brigade
fire engine
fire escape
fire extinguisher
firefly
  fireflies *pl*
fireplace
firework
firm
firmament
firmly
firmness
first
first aid
firstly
first-rate
firth
fiscal
fiscally

fish
  fish, fishes *pl*
fisher (catches fish)
fishery
  fisheries *pl*
fishily
fishmonger
fishy
fissile
fission
fissionable
fissure (crack)
fist
fisticuffs
fit
  fits
  fitted
  fitting
fitter
fittest
fitful
fitfully
fitness
five
fivefold
fivepence
fiver
fives (game)
fix
  fixes *pl*
fixation
fixative
fixedly

fixture
fizz
fizziness
fizzle
  fizzled
  fizzling
fizzy
  fizzier
  fizziest
fjord, fiord
flabbergast
  flabbergasted
  flabbergasting
flabbily
flabbiness
flabby
  flabbier
  flabbiest
flaccid
flaccidly
flag
  flagged
  flagging
  flags
flagellate (to flog)
  flagellated
  flagellating
flagellation
flageolet (bean)
flagon
flagrancy
flagrant
flagrantly

flail (stick for
  threshing)
  flailed
  flailing
flair (aptitude)
flake
  flaked
  flaking
flaky
  flakier
  flakiest
flambé
  flambéed
  flambéing
  flambés
flamboyance
flamboyant
flamboyantly
flame
  flamed
  flaming
flamenco
  flamencos *pl*
flamingo
  flamingos *pl*
flammable
flange
flank
flannel
flannelette
flap
  flapped
  flapping

flaps
flapper (girl)
flare (blaze)
  flared
  flaring
flash
flashy
  flashier
  flashiest
flask
flat
flatly
flatten
  flattened
  flattening
flatter
  flattered
  flattering
flatterer
flattery
flatulence
flatulent
flaunt
  flaunted
  flaunting
flautist
flavor *Am*
  flavored
  flavoring
flavorless *Am*
flavour
  flavoured
  flavouring

flavourless
flaw (fault)
flawless
flawlessly
flax
flaxen
flay
  flayed
  flaying
  flays
flea (insect)
fled (*from* flee)
fledgling
flee (to run away)
  fled
  fleeing
  flees
fleece
  fleeced
  fleecing
fleecy
  fleecier
  fleeciest
fleet
fleeting
flesh
fleshiness
fleshy
  fleshier
  fleshiest
fleur-de-lis
flew (*from* fly)
flex (to bend; cable)

flexibility
flexible
flick
flicker
  flickered
  flickering
flier, flyer
flight
flightiness
flighty
flimsily
flimsiness
flimsy
  flimsier
  flimsiest
flinch
fling
  flinging
  flings
  flung
flint
flippancy
flippant
flippantly
flipper
flirt
  flirted
  flirting
flirtation
flirtatious
flit
  flits
  flitted

flitting
float
  floated
  floating
flock (group)
floe (floating ice)
flog
  flogged
  flogging
  flogs
flood
  flooded
  flooding
floodgate
floodlight
  floodlighting
  floodlights
  floodlit
floor
  floored
  flooring
flop
  flopped
  flopping
  flops
floppy
flora
floral
florid
florist
floss
flossy
  flossier

flossiest
flotation
flotilla
  flotillas pl
flotsam
flounce
  flounced
  flouncing
flounder
  floundered
  floundering
flour (for bread)
flourish
floury
flout
  flouted
  flouting
flow
flower (of a plant)
  flowered
  flowering
flowery
flown (from fly)
flu (influenza)
fluctuate
  fluctuated
  fluctuating
fluctuation
flue (chimney)
fluency
fluent
fluently
fluff

fluffiness
fluffy
  fluffier
  fluffiest
fluid
fluidity
fluke
  fluked
  fluking
flummox
flummoxed
flung (from fling)
flunkey, flunky
  flunkeys, flunkies pl
fluoresce
  fluoresced
  fluorescing
fluorescence
fluorescent
fluoridation
fluoride
fluorine
flurry
  flurries pl
flush
fluster
  flustered
  flustering
flute
flutist
flutter
  fluttered
  fluttering

fluvial

flux

fly

flies *pl*

flew

flies

flown

flying

fly-by-night

flyer, flier

flyleaf

flyleaves *pl*

fly-post

fly-posting

flyweight

flywheel

foal

foam

fob

fobbed

fobbing

fobs

fo'c's'le, forecastle

focal

focus

foci, focuses *pl*

focused, focussed

focuses, focusses

focusing, focussing

fodder

foe

foes *pl*

foetal, fetal

foetid, fetid

foetus, fetus

foetuses, fetuses *pl*

fog

fogged

fogging

fogs

fogbound

fogey, fogy

fogeys, fogies *pl*

foggily

fogginess

foggy

foggier

foggiest

foghorn

foible

foil

foiled

foiling

foist

fold

foldaway

folder

foliage

folio

folios *pl*

folk

folklore

follicle

follicular

follow

followed

following

follower

followthrough

folly

follies *pl*

foment (to stir up)

fomented

fomenting

fomentation

fond

fondant

fonder

fondle

fondled

fondling

fondly

fondness

fondue

font

food

foodstuff

fool

fooled

fooling

foolery

foolhardiness

foolhardy

foolish

foolishly

foolproof

foolscap

foot

footed

footing

footage

football

footballer

footlight

footling

footnote

footsore

footstool

footwear

fop

foppish

forage

  foraged

  foraging

forager

foray

  forays *pl*

forbade (*from* forbid)

  (to abstain)

forbear

  forbearing

  forbears

  forbore

  forborne

forbearance

forbearing

forbears

forbid

  forbade

  forbidden

  forbidding

  forbids

forbore (*from* forbear)

forborne (*from* forbear)

force

  forced

  forcing

force majeure

forceful

forcefully

forcefulness

forceps

forcible

forcibly

ford

fore (before, in

  front of)

forearm

forebear (ancestor)

forebode

foreboding

forecast

forecaster

forecastle, fo'c's'le

foreclose

  foreclosed

  foreclosing

foreclosure

forecourt

forefather

forefinger

forefront

forego (to go before)

  foregoes

  foregoing

foregone

forewent

foreground

forehead

foreign

foreigner

foreignness

foreknowledge

forelock

foreman

  foremen *pl*

foremost

forenoon

forensic

forerunner

foresee

  foresaw

  foreseeing

  foreseen

  foresees

foreseeable

foreshadow

foreshore

foreshorten

  foreshortened

  foreshortening

foresight

foreskin

forest

forestall

forester

forestry

foretaste

foretell
foretelling
foretells
foretold
forethought
forever
forewarn
forewarned
forewarning
forewent (*from* forego)
forewoman
forewomen *pl*
foreword
forfeit
forfeited
forfeiting
forfeiture
forgave (*from* forgive)
forge
forged
forging
forger
forgery
forgeries *pl*
forget
forgets
forgetting
forgot
forgotten
forgetful
forgetfulness
forget-me-not
forgettable

forgivable
forgive
forgave
forgiven
forgives
forgiving
forgiveness
forgo (to give up)
forgoes
forgoing
forgone
forwent
forgot (*from* forget)
fork
fork-lift
forlorn
forlornly
form
formed
forming
formal
formalisation
formalise
formalised
formalising
formality
formalities *pl*
formalization
formalize
formalized
formalizing
formally (properly)
format

formats
formatted
formatting
formation
formative
former
formerly
Formica
formidable
formidably
formula
formulae, formulas *pl*
formulate
formulated
formulating
formulation
fornicate
fornicated
fornicating
fornication
fornicator
forsake
forsaken
forsakes
forsaking
forsook
forsooth
forsythia
forsythias *pl*
fort
forte (loud;
special skill)
forth (forward)

forthcoming
forthright
forthwith
fortieth
fortification
fortify
  fortified
  fortifies
  fortifying
fortissimo
  fortissimos,
    fortissimi *pl*
fortitude
fortress
  fortresses *pl*
fortuitous
fortuitously
fortuity
fortunate
fortunately
fortune
fortune-teller
fortune-telling
forty
  forties *pl*
forum
  forums, fora *pl*
forward
forwards
forwent (*from* forgo)
fossil
fossilisation
fossilise

fossilised
fossilising
fossilization
fossilize
  fossilized
  fossilizing
foster
  fostered
  fostering
fought (*from* fight)
foul (filthy; unfair)
  fouled
  fouling
fouler
foully
foul-mouthed
foulness
found (to establish)
  founded
  founding
foundation
founder
foundling
foundry
  foundries *pl*
fount
fountain
four
fourfold
four score
foursome
fourteen
fourteenth

fourth
fourthly
fowl (bird)
fox
foxhound
foyer
fracas
fraction
fractional
fractionally
fractious
fracture
  fractured
  fracturing
fragile
fragilely
fragility
fragment
fragmentary
fragmentation
fragrance
fragrant (sweet-
  smelling)
fragrantly
frail
frailer
frailty
  frailties *pl*
frame
  framed
  framing
frame-up
framework

franc (money)
Frances (female name)
franchise
Francis (male name)
frank (open-hearted)
frankfurter
frankincense
frankly
frankness
frantic
frantically
fraternal
fraternally
fraternisation
fraternise
  fraternised
  fraternising
fraternity
  fraternities *pl*
fraternization
fraternize
  fraternized
  fraternizing
Frau
fraud
fraudulence
fraudulent
fraudulently
fraught
Fräulein
fray
  frayed
  fraying

frays
freak
freakish
freckle
free
  freed
  freeing
  freer
  freest
free-for-all
freedom
freehold
freeholder
freelance
freelancing
freely
freemason
freemasonry
free-wheel
  free-wheeled
  free-wheeling
freeze
  freezes
  freezing
  froze
  frozen
freezer
freight (cargo)
freightage
freighter
French fries
frenetic
frenzied

frenzy
  frenzies *pl*
frequency
  frequencies *pl*
frequent
  frequented
  frequenting
frequently
fresco
  frescoes, frescos *pl*
fresh
freshen
  freshened
  freshening
fresher
freshly
freshman
  freshmen *pl*
freshness
fret
  frets
  fretted
  fretting
fretful
fretsaw
fretwork
Freudian
friability
friable
friar (monk)
friary
  friaries *pl*
fricassee

friction
frictional
Friday
  Fridays *pl*
fridge
fried
friend
friendlier
friendliness
friendly
friendship
frier, fryer (person or
  thing that fries)
fries (*from* fry)
Friesian
frieze
frigate
fright
frighten
  frightened
  frightening
frightful
frightfully
frightfulness
frigid
frigidity
frigidly
frill
fringe
  fringed
  fringing
fringe benefit
frippery

fripperies *pl*
Frisbee
frisk
friskiness
frisky
  friskier
  friskiest
fritter
  frittered
  frittering
frivolity
  frivolities *pl*
frivolous
frivolously
frizzle
  frizzled
  frizzling
frock
frog
frogman
  frogmen *pl*
frolic
  frolicked
  frolicking
  frolics
frolicsome
front
frontage
frontal
frontally
frontier
frontispiece
frost

frostbite
frostbitten
frostily
frosty
  frostier
  frostiest
froth
frothy
  frothier
  frothiest
froward
frowardness
frown
  frowned
  frowning
frowziness
frowzy
  frowzier
  frowzier
froze (*from* freeze)
frozen (*from* freeze)
frugal
frugality
frugally
fruit
fruiterer
fruitful
fruitfully
fruitfulness
fruitiness
fruition
fruitless
fruitlessly

fruity
  fruitier
  fruitiest
frump
frumpish
frustrate
  frustrated
  frustrating
frustration
fry
  fried
  fries
  frying
fryer, frier (person or
  thing that fries)
fuchsia (flower)
  fuchsias *pl*
fuddle
  fuddled
  fuddling
fudge
  fudged
  fudging
fuel
  fuelled
  fuelling
  fuels
  fueled *Am*
  fueling *Am*
fugal
fugitive
fugue
fulcrum

fulfil
  fulfilled
  fulfilling
  fulfils
fulfill *Am*
  fulfilled
  fulfilling
  fulfills
fulfillment *Am*
fulfilment
full
full-blooded
fully
fulminate
  fulminated
  fulminating
fulmination
fulsome
fulsomely
fulsomeness
fumble
  fumbled
  fumbling
fume
  fumed
  fuming
fumigate
  fumigated
  fumigating
fumigation
fumigator
fun
function

functioned
  functioning
functional
functionally
functionary
  functionaries *pl*
fund
  funded
  funding
fundamental
fundamentally
funeral
funerary
funereal (gloomy)
fungicidal
fungicide
fungoid
fungus
  fungi, funguses *pl*
funicular
funk
funky
  funkier
  funkiest
funnel
  funnelled
  funnelling
  funnels
  funneled *Am*
  funneling *Am*
funnily
funny
  funnier

funniest
fur (pelt)
  furred
  furring
  furs
furbelow
furbish
furbished
furious
furiously
furl
furled
furlong
furlough
furnace
furnish
furnisher
furniture
furor *Am*
furore
furred
furrier (fur dealer)
furrow
furry
  furrier
  furriest
further, farther
furtherance
furthered
furthering
furthermore
furthermost
furthest, farthest

furtive
furtively
furtiveness
fury
  furies *pl*
furze
fuse
  fused
  fusing
fuselage
fusible
fusilier
fusillade
fusion
fuss
fussily
fussiness
fussy
  fussier
  fussiest
fusty
futile
futilely
futility
future
futurism
futurist
futuristic
futurologist
futurology
fuzz
fuzzbox
fuzzily

fuzziness
fuzzy
  fuzzier
  fuzziest

gab
gabardine
gabble (talk)
  gabbled
  gabbling
gabbler
gable (roof)
gabled
gad
  gadded
  gadding
gadabout
gadfly
  gadflies *pl*
gadget
gadgetry
gads
Gaelic
gaff (hook)

gaffe (mistake)
gag
  gagged
  gagging
  gags
gaga
gage *Am*
  gaged
  gaging
gaggle
gaiety
gaily
gain
  gained
  gaining
gainer
gainful
gainfully
gainsay

gainsaid
gainsaying
gainsays
gait (walk)
gaiter
gaitered
gala
  galas *pl*
galactic
galah (bird)
galanty show
galaxy
  galaxies *pl*
gale
gall
gallant
gallantry
gall-bladder
galleon
gallery
  galleries *pl*
galley
  galleys *pl*
galling
gallivant
gallon
gallop (pace)
  galloped
  galloping
galloper
gallows
gallstone
galore

galosh, golosh
  galoshes, goloshes *pl*
galumph
galvanic
galvanisation
galvanise
  galvanised
  galvanising
galvanism
galvanization
galvanize
  galvanized
  galvanizing
galvanometer
gambit
gamble
  gambled
  gambling
gambler
gambol
  gambolled
  gambolling
  gambols
  gamboled *Am*
  gamboling *Am*
game
gamekeeper
gamely
gamesmanship
gamin (urchin) *m*
gamine (urchin) *f*
gaming room
gamma

gammon (ham)
gammy (lame)
  gammier
  gammiest
gamut
gamy
gander
gang
  ganged
  ganging
gangling
ganglion
  ganglia, ganglions *pl*
gangplank
gangrene
gangrenous
gangster
gangway
  gangways *pl*
gannet
gantry
  gantries *pl*
gaol, jail
  gaoled
  gaoling
  jailed
  jailing
gaoler, jailer, jailor
gap
gape
  gaped
  gaping
garage

garaged
garaging
garb
garbage
garble
  garbled
  garbling
garçon
  garçons *pl*
garden
  gardened
  gardening
gardener
gardenia
  gardenias *pl*
gardens
gargantuan
gargle
  gargled
  gargling
gargoyle
garish
garland
garlic
garlicky
garment
garner (to collect)
  garnered
  garnering
garnet (gem stone)
garnish
  garnished
garret (attic room)

arrison
garrisoned
garrisoning
arrote *Am*
garroted
garroting
:arrotte
garrotted
garrotting
:arrulity
:arrulous
:arrulously
:arter
:as
gases
gassed
gassing
:aseous
gash
gashed
gasket
gaslight
gasoline, gasolene
gasometer
gasp
gassiness
gassy
gassier
gassiest
gastric
gastritis
gastroenteritis
gastronome

gastronomic
gastronomical
gastronomy
gastropod
gastropods,
gastropoda *pl*
gate (entrance)
gateau
gateaus, gateaux *pl*
gateway
gateways *pl*
gather
gathered
gathering
gauche
gaucheness
gaucherie
gaudily
gaudiness
gaudy
gaudier
gaudiest
gauge
gauged
gauging
gaunt
gauntlet
gauss (unit of
magnetism)
gauze
gave (*from* give)
gavel
gavotte

gawkiness
gawky
gawkier
gawkiest
gay
gays *pl*
gayer
gayest
gaze (stare)
gazed
gazing
gazebo
gazebos, gazeboes *pl*
gazelle
gazette
gazetted
gazetting
gazetteer
gear
geared
gearing
gearbox
gearless
gecko
geckos *pl*
geek
geese (pl. of goose)
geezer
Geiger counter
geisha
geishas *pl*
gel (to turn to jelly)
gelled

gelling
gels
gelatine, gelatin
gelatinous
geld
gelding
gelid (very cold)
gelignite
gem
gendarme
gendarmerie,
  gendarmery
gender
gene
genealogical
genealogically
genealogist
genealogy
genera (*pl* of genus)
general
generalisation
generalise
  generalised
  generalising
generality
  generalities *pl*
generalization
generalize
  generalized
  generalizing
generally
generate
  generated

generating
generation
generative
generator
generic
generically
generosity
generous
generously
Genesis
genetic
genetically
genial
geniality
genially
genie, jinnee
  genies, genii, jinn *pl*
genital
genitive
genius
  geniuses *pl*
genocide
genome
genre
gent
  gents *pl*
genteel (well bred)
genteelism
genteelly
gentian (plant)
gentile (non-Jew)
gentility
gentle

gentler
gentlest
gentleman
  gentlemen *pl*
gentlemanly
gentleness
gentlewoman
  gentlewomen *pl*
gently
gentry
gents
genuflect
genuflection,
  genuflexion
genuine
genuinely
genuineness
genus (biological
  family)
  genera *pl*
Geoffrey
geographer
geographic
geographical
geographically
geography
geological
geologically
geologist
geology
geometric
geometrical
geometrically

eometrician
eometry
eophysical
eophysicist
eophysics
Georgian
cranium
geraniums *pl*
erbil, jerbil
eriatrician
eriatrics
erm
ermane
ermicidal
ermicide
erminate
germinated
germinating
germination
gerontocracy
gerontocracies *pl*
gerontology
gerrymander
gerund
gerundive
gestate
gestated
gestating
gestation
gesticulate
gesticulated
gesticulating
gesticulation

gesture
gestured
gesturing
get
gets
getting
got
gotten *Am*
getaway
geyser (hot spring)
ghastliness
ghastly
ghastlier
ghastliest
gherkin
ghetto
ghettos *pl*
ghost
ghostly
ghoul
ghoulish
giant
gibber (to speak
unclearly)
gibbered
gibbering
gibberish
gibbet
gibbon
gibbous
gibe (to mock)
gibed
gibing

giblets
giddily
giddiness
giddy
giddier
giddiest
gift
gift-wrap
gift-wrapped
gift-wrapping
gift-wraps
gig
gigabyte
gigantic
gigantically
giggle
giggled
giggling
giggler
gigolo
gigolos *pl*
gild (to cover
with gold)
gilded
gilding
gill
gilled
gillie, ghillie
gillyflower
gilt (gold)
gilt-edged
gimcrack
gimlet

gimmick
gimmickry
gimmicky
gin
ginger
gingerbread
gingerly
gingham
gingival
gingivitis
ginormous
gipsy, gypsy
  gipsies, gypsies *pl*
giraffe
gird
  girded
  girding
girder
girdle
girl
girlish
girlishness
giro
  giros *pl*
girt
girth
gist
give
  gave
  given
  gives
  giving
giver

gizmo
  gizmos *pl*
gizzard
glacé
glacial
glaciation
glacier
glad
gladden
  gladdened
  gladdening
gladder
glade
gladiator
gladiolus
  gladioli,
    gladioluses *pl*
gladsome
glamor *Am*
glamorisation
glamorise
  glamorised
  glamorising
glamorization
glamorize
  glamorized
  glamorizing
glamorous
glamorously
glamour
glance
  glanced
  glancing

gland
glandular
glare
  glared
  glaring
glass
  glasses *pl*
glasshouse
glassily
glassware
glassy
  glassier
  glassiest
glaucoma
glaucous
glaze
  glazed
  glazing
glazier
gleam
  gleamed
  gleaming
glean
  gleaned
  gleaning
gleaner
glebe
glee
gleeful
gleefully
glen
glengarry
glib

glibly
glibness
glide
  glided
  gliding
glider
glimmer
  glimmered
  glimmering
glimpse
  glimpsed
  glimpsing
glint
  glinted
  glinting
glisten
  glistened
  glistening
glitter
  glittered
  glittering
glitterati
gloaming
gloat
  gloated
  gloating
global
globally
globe
globe-trotter
globe-trotting
globular
globule

gloom
gloomily
gloominess
gloomy
  gloomier
  gloomiest
glorious
gloriously
glory
  glories *pl*
  gloried
  glories
  glorying
gloss
glossary
  glossaries *pl*
glossiness
glossy
  glossier
  glossiest
glottal
glottis
glove
glover
glow
glower
  glowered
  glowering
glow-worm
glucose
glue
  glued
  gluing

gluey
glum
  glummer
  glummest
glumly
glumness
glut
gluten
glutenous (having
  gluten)
glutinous (gluey)
glutted
glutton
gluttonous
gluttony
glycerin *Am*
glycerine
gnarled
gnash
gnat
gnaw (nibble)
  gnawed
  gnawing
  gnaws
gnocchi
gnome
gnu
go
  goes
  going
  gone
  went
goad

goaded
goading
goal
goalkeeper
goalless
goat
goatee
gob
gobble
  gobbled
  gobbling
gobbledegook,
  gobbledygook
go-between
goblet
goblin
gobsmacked
god
godchild
  godchildren *pl*
goddess
  goddesses *pl*
God-fearing
God-forsaken
godliness
godly
godparent
godsend
godspeed
Godsquad
goer
goggle
  goggled

goggling
goiter *Am*
goitre
goitrous
gold
golden
goldfinch
  goldfinches *pl*
goldilocks
goldsmith
golf
golf course
golfer
golf links
Goliath
golliwog
golosh, galosh
  goloshes, galoshes *pl*
gondola
  gondolas *pl*
gondolier
gone (*from* go)
goner
gong
gonorrhea *Am*
gonorrhoea
goo
good
goodbye
good-humored *Am*
good-humoured
good-looking
goodly

goodness
goodness' sake
goodnight
goodwill
goody
  goodies *pl*
gooey
googly
  googlies *pl*
goon
goose
  geese *pl*
gooseberry
  gooseberries *pl*
goose-flesh
goosestep
  goosestepped
  goosestepping
  goosesteps
gopher
gore
  gored
  goring
gorge
  gorged
  gorging
gorgeous
gorgeously
Gorgonzola
gorilla
  gorillas *pl*
gorse
gory

gorier
goriest
gosling
gospel
gospeler *Am*
gospeller
gossamer
gossip
  gossiped
  gossiping
gossiper
got (*from* get)
gotten (*from* get)
gouache
gouge
  gouged
  gouging
goulash
gourd
gourmand
gourmandism
gourmet
gout
gouty
govern
  governed
  governing
governable
governance
governess
government
governmental
governor

gown
grab
  grabbed
  grabbing
  grabs
grace
  graced
  gracing
graceful
gracefully
gracious
graciously
graciousness
gradation
grade
  graded
  grading
gradient
gradual
gradualism
gradually
graduate
  graduated
  graduating
graduation
graduator
graffiti
graft
  grafted
  grafting
grail
grain
gram, gramme

grammar
grammarian
grammatical
grammatically
gramophone
granary
  granaries *pl*
grand
Grand Prix
grandchild
  grandchildren *pl*
granddaughter
grandee
grandeur
grandfather
grandiloquence
grandiloquent
grandiloquently
grandiose
grandiosely
grandiosity
grandma
grandmother
grandpa
grandson
grange
granite
granny, grannie
  grannies *pl*
grant
granular
granularity
granulate

granulated

granulating

granulation

granule

grape

grapefruit

graph

graphic

graphical

graphically

graphite

graphologist

graphology

grapnel

grapple

grappled

grappling

grasp

grass

grasshopper

grassy

grate (fireplace; to scrape)

grated

grating

grateful

gratefully

grater (scraper)

graticule

gratification

gratify

gratified

gratifies

gratifying

gratin

gratis

gratitude

gratuitous

gratuitously

gratuity

gratuities *pl*

grave

graver

gravest

gravel

graveled *Am*

gravelled

gravelly

gravely *Am*

graveyard

gravitate

gravitated

gravitating

gravitation

gravitational

gravity

gravy

gray *Am*

grayed

graying

grays

grayer

grayest

grayish *Am*

grayling

grayness *Am*

graze

grazed

grazing

grease (oil)

greased

greasing

greaser

greasepaint

greasily

greasiness

greasy

greasier

greasiest

great

greater

greatest

greatly

greatness

grebe

greed

greedily

greediness

greedy

greedier

greediest

green

greener

greenest

greenback

greenery

greenfield

greengage

greengrocer

greenness

greet
 greeted
 greeting

gregarious

gregariousness

gremlin

grenade

grenadier

grew (*from* grow)

grey
 greyed
 greying
 greys
 greyer
 greyest

greyhound

greyish

greyness

grid

griddle

gridiron

grief

grievance

grieve
 grieved
 grieving

grievous

grievously

griffin, gryphon
 (fabulous beast)

griffon (dog; vulture)

grill (to cook)

grille (grating)

grilled

grill-room

grim
 grimmer
 grimmest

grimace
 grimaced
 grimacing

grime

griminess

grimly

grimness

grimy
 grimier
 grimiest

grin
 grinned
 grinning
 grins

grind

grinder

grip
 gripped
 gripping
 grips

gripe
 griped
 griping

grippe (influenza)

grisly

grist

gristle

gristly

grit
 grits
 gritted
 gritting

gritty

grizzle
 grizzled
 grizzling

grizzly

grizzly bear

groan
 groaned
 groaning

groats

grocer

grocery
 groceries *pl*

grog

grogginess

groggy
 groggier
 groggiest

groin (body)

grommet, grummet

groom

groove

groovy
 groovier
 grooviest

grope
 groped
 groping

gross
grosser
grossly
grossness
grotesque
grotesquely
grotesqueness
grotto
  grottoes *pl*
grouchy
ground
groundless
groundlessly
group
grouse
  groused
  grousing
grouser
grout
grove
grovel
  grovelled
  grovelling
  grovels
  groveled *Am*
  groveling *Am*
groveler *Am*
groveller
grow
  grew
  growing
  grown
growbag

grower
growl
grown-up
growth
groyne (breakwater)
grub
grubbily
grubbiness
grubby
  grubbier
  grubbiest
grudge
  grudged
  grudging
grudgingly
gruel
grueling *Am*
gruelling
gruesome
gruesomely
gruesomeness
gruff
gruffly
gruffness
grumble
  grumbled
  grumbling
grumbler
grummet, grommet
grumpily
grumpiness
grumpy
  grumpier

grumpiest
grunt
gruyère
gryphon, griffin
guano
guarantee
  guaranteed
  guaranteeing
  guarantees
guarantor
guaranty
guard
guardian
guardianship
guard-room
guava
  guavas *pl*
gubernatorial
Guernsey
guerrilla, guerilla
  (fighter)
  guerrillas, guerillas *pl*
guess
guesswork
guest
guffaw
guffawing
guidance
guide
  guided
  guiding
guild (society)
guilder (Dutch money)

Guildhall
guile
guileless
guillotine
  guillotined
  guillotining
guilt (emotion)
guiltily
guiltiness
guilty
  guiltier
  guiltiest
guinea
guinea-pig
guise
guitar
guitarist
gulf
Gulf Stream
gull
gulled
gullet
gullibility
gullible
gully
  gullies *pl*
gulp
  gulped
  gulping
gum
  gummed
  gumming
  gums

gumboil
gumminess
gummy
  gummier
  gummiest
gumption
gun
  gunned
  gunning
  guns
gunnel, gunwale
gunner
gunnery
gunpowder
gurgle
  gurgled
  gurgling
Gurkha
  Gurkhas *pl*
guru
gush
gusset
gust
  gusted
  gusting
gusto
gusty
gut
  guts
  gutted
  gutting
guts
gutsy

gutsier
gutsiest
gutter
guttering
guttersnipe
guttural
gutturally
guy
Guy Fawkes
guzzle
  guzzled
  guzzling
guzzler
gybe (in sailing)
  gybed
  gybing
gym
gymkhana
  gymkhanas *pl*
gymnasium
  gymnasiums,
  gymnasia *pl*
gymnast
gymnastic
gynaecological
gynaecologist
gynaecology
gynecological *Am*
gynecologist *Am*
gynecology *Am*
gypsum
gypsy, gipsy
  gypsies, gipsies *pl*

gyrate
  gyrated
  gyrating
gyration
gyratory
gyroscope
gyroscopic

H

habeas corpus
haberdasher
haberdashery
  haberdasheries *pl*
habit
habitable
habitat
habitation
habit-forming
habitual
habitually
habituate
  habituated
  habituating
habituation
habitude
habitué
hack
hacked-off

hackle
hackney
hackneyed
hacksaw
had (*from* have)
haddock
Hades
hadn't (had not)
haematologist
haematology
haematoma
  haematomas *pl*
haemoglobin
haemophilia
haemophiliac
haemorrhage
  haemorrhaged
  haemorrhaging
haemorrhoids

hag
haggard
haggis
haggle
  haggled
  haggling
haggler
haiku
hail (frozen rain;
    to greet)
  hailed
  hailing
hailer
hair (*eg* on head)
hairbreadth
hairiness
hairless
hairpiece
hairpin
hairy
  hairier
  hairiest
hair's breadth
hake
halcyon
hale (robust)
half
  halves *pl*
half-caste
half-hearted
halfway
halibut
halitosis

hall
hallelujah, halleluiah,
  alleluia
hallmark
hallmarked
hallo, hello, hullo
hallow (make sacred)
Halloween,
  Hallowe'en
hallowed
hallucinate
  hallucinated
  hallucinating
hallucination
hallucinatory
hallucinogen
halo (circle of light)
  haloes, halos pl
halt
halter
haltingly
halve
  halves pl
  halved
  halving
halyard, halliard
ham
hamburger
hamlet
hammer
  hammered
  hammering
hammock

hamper
  hampered
  hampering
hamster
hamstring
  hamstringing
  hamstrings
  hamstrung
hand
  handed
  handing
handcuff
  handcuffed
  handcuffing
handcuffs
handful
  handfuls pl
handicap
  handicapped
  handicapping
  handicaps
handicraft
handily
handiness
handiwork
handkerchief
handkerchiefs,
  handkerchieves pl
handle
  handled
  handling
handlebar
handler

handmade (article)
handmaid (girl)
hand-me-down
handout
handsome
handsomely
handsomeness
handwriting
handwritten
handy
  handier
  handiest
handyman
  handymen pl
hang
  hanging
  hangs
  hanged (criminal)
  hung
hangar (for aircraft)
hanger (for clothes)
hanger-on
hang-gliding
hangman
hangover
hang-up
hank
hanker
  hankered
  hankering
hanky, hankie
hanky-panky
hansom (cab)

haphazard
hapless
happen
  happened
  happening
happily
happiness
happy
  happier
  happiest
happy-go-lucky
harangue
  harangued
  haranguing
harass
harassed
harassment
harbinger
harbor *Am*
  harbored
  harboring
harborage *Am*
harbour
  harboured
  harbouring
harbourage
hard
harden
  hardened
  hardening
hardener
harder
hard-headed

hard-hearted
hardily (boldly)
hardly (barely)
hardness
hardship
hardware
hardy
  hardier
  hardiest
hare (animal; to run)
  hared
  haring
harebell
hare-brained
harelip
harem
haricot
hark
harken
harlequin
harlequinade
harlot
harlotry
harm
harmful
harmfully
harmless
harmlessly
harmlessness
harmonic
harmonica
  harmonicas *pl*
harmonically

harmonious
harmoniously
harmonisation
harmonise
  harmonised
  harmonising
harmonium
  harmoniums *pl*
harmonization
harmonize
  harmonized
  harmonizing
harmony
  harmonies *pl*
harness
harp
  harped
  harping
harpist
harpoon
  harpooned
  harpooning
harpooner
harpsichord
harpy
  harpies *pl*
harrier
harrow
harrowing
harry
  harried
  harries
  harrying

harsh
harshly
harshness
hart (deer)
hartebeest
harum-scarum
harvest
  harvested
  harvesting
harvester
has (*from* have)
has-been
hash
hashish, hasheesh
hasn't (has not)
hasp
hassle
  hassled
  hassling
hassock
haste
hasten
  hastened
  hastening
hastily
hasty
  hastier
  hastiest
hat
hatch
hatchback
hatchery
  hatcheries *pl*

hatchet
hatchway
  hatchways *pl*
hate
  hated
  hating
hateful
hatred
hatter
haughtily
haughtiness
haughty
  haughtier
  haughtiest
haul (to carry)
  hauled
  hauling
haulage
haulier
haunch
haunt
  haunted
  haunting
hausfrau
haute cuisine
hauteur
Havana
have
  had
  has
  having
haven
haven't (have not)

haver
  havered
  havering
haversack
havoc
hawk
hawkish
hawser
hawthorn
hay
hay fever
haymaker
hayrick
haystack
hazard
hazardous
hazardously
haze
hazel
hazily
haziness
hazy
  hazier
  haziest
head
  headed
  heading
headache
headachy
header
headless
headline
  headlined

headlining
headlong
headmaster
headmistress
headquarters
headshrinker
headstrong
headway
heal (health)
  healed
  healing
healer
health
healthily
healthy
  healthier
  healthiest
heap
  heaped
  heaping
hear
  heard
  hearing
  hears
hearer
hearken
  hearkened
  hearkening
hearsay
hearse
heart (body)
heartbreaking
heartbroken

heartbrokenly
hearten
  heartened
  heartening
hearth
heartiness
heartfelt
heartless
heartlessly
heart-rending
hearty
  heartier
  heartiest
heat
heater
heath
heathen
heathenism
heather
heatstroke
heatwave
heave
  heaved
  heaving
heaven
heavenly
heavily
heaviness
heavy
  heavier
  heaviest
heavyweight
hebdomadal

Hebraic
Hebrew
hecatomb
heckle
  heckled
  heckling
heckler
hectare (unit of area)
hectic
hectically
hectogram
hectoliter *Am*
hectolitre
hector (to bully)
  hectored
  hectoring
he'd (he would)
hedge
  hedged
  hedging
hedgehog
hedger
hedgerow
hedonism
hedonist
heed
  heeded
  heeding
heedful
heedless
heel (of foot)
heftily
heftiness

hefty
 heftier
 heftiest
hegemony
 hegemonies *pl*
heifer
height
heighten
 heightened
 heightening
heinous
heir
heir apparent
heiress
heirloom
held (*from* hold)
hele (to put plant
 in earth)
helical
helicopter
heliograph
heliotrope
heliport
helium
helix
 helices *pl*
hell
he'll (he will)
hellish
hellishly
hello, hallo, hullo
helm
helmet

helmsman
 helmsmen *pl*
helot
helotry
help
 helped
 helping
helper
helpful
helpfully
helpfulness
helpless
helplessly
helplessness
helpmate
helter-skelter
hem
 hemmed
 hemming
 hems
hematologist *Am*
hematology *Am*
hematoma *Am*
 hematomas *pl*
hemiplegia
hemiplegic
hemisphere
hemispherical
hemlock
hemoglobin *Am*
hemophilia *Am*
hemophiliac *Am*
hemorrhage *Am*

hemorrhaged
 hemorrhaging
hemorrhoids *Am*
hemp
hempen
hemstitch
hen
hen-coop
hence
henceforth
henchman
 henchmen *pl*
henna
hennaed
henpecked
hepatitis
heptagon
heptarchy
 heptarchies *pl*
her
herald
heraldic
heraldry
herb
herbaceous
herbage
herbal
herbalist
herbicide
herbivore
herbivorous
herculean
herd (of animals)

herdsman
  herdsmen *pl*
here (place)
hereabout
hereafter
hereby
hereditarily
hereditary
heredity
herein
hereof
heresy
  heresies *pl*
heretic
hereto
heretofore
hereunder
herewith
heritable
heritage
hermaphrodite
hermaphroditic
hermetic
hermetically
hermit
hermitage
hernia
  hernias *pl*
hero
  heroes *pl*
heroic
heroically
heroin (drug)

heroine (brave
  woman)
heroism
heron
herpes
herring
herringbone
hers
herself
he's (he is)
hesitancy
hesitant
hesitantly
hesitate
  hesitated
  hesitating
hesitation
hessian
heterodox
heterodoxy
heterodyne
heterogeneity
heterogeneous
heterosexual
heuristic
heuristically
hew (cut)
  hewed
  hewing
  hewn
  hews
hexagon
hexagonal

heyday
  heydays *pl*
hiatus
  hiatuses *pl*
hibernate
  hibernated
  hibernating
hibernation
hibernator
hiccup, hiccough
  hiccuped,
    hiccoughed
  hiccuping,
    hiccoughing
hide
  hid
  hidden
  hides
  hiding
hideaway
  hideaways *pl*
hidebound
hide-out
hideous
hideously
hierarch
hierarchy
  hierarchies *pl*
hieroglyph
hieroglyphic
hi-fi
  hi-fis *pl*
higgledy-piggledy

highfalutin,
  highfaluting
highland
highlander
highlight
  highlighted
  highlighting
highly
Highness
highway
  highways pl
highwayman
  highwaymen pl
hijack
hijacked
hijacker
hike
  hiked
  hiking
hiker
hilarious
hilarity
hill
hillock
hilly
hilt
him (he)
himself
hind
hinder
  hindered
  hindering

Hindi
hindmost, hindermost
hindrance
hindsight
Hindu
  Hindus pl
hinge
  hinged
  hinging
hint
  hinted
  hinting
hinterland
hip
hipped
hippo
  hippos pl
hippodrome
hippopotamus
  hippopotamuses,
    hippopotami pl
hippy, hippie
  hippies pl
hire
  hired
  hiring
hire purchase
hireling
hirsute
his
hiss
  hissed
  hisses

hissing
histamine
histology
historian
historic
historical
historically
history
  histories pl
histrionic
histrionically
hit
  hits
  hitting
hitch
hitch-hike
  hitch-hiked
  hitch-hiking
hitch-hiker
hi-tech
hither
hitherto
hitter
hive
  hived
  hiving
hoar (grey)
hoard (to store)
hoarder
hoarding
hoariness
hoarse (husky)
hoarsely

hoarseness
hoarser
hoary
hoax
  hoaxes *pl*
hoaxer
hobble
  hobbled
  hobbling
hobbledehoy
  hobbledehoys *pl*
hobby
  hobbies *pl*
hobby-horse
hobgoblin
hobnail
hobnob
  hobnobbed
  hobnobbing
  hobnobs
hobo
  hobos, hoboes *pl*
hock
hockey
hocus
  hocused, hocussed
  hocuses, hocusses
  hocusing, hocussing
hocus-pocus
hod
hodgepodge
hoe (tool)
  hoed

  hoeing
hoedown
hog
  hogged
  hogging
  hogs
hoggish
hogmanay
  hogmanays *pl*
hogshead
hogwash
hoi polloi
hoist
hold
  held
  holding
  holds
holdall
holder
holdup
hole (opening)
  holed
  holing
holey
holiday
  holidays *pl*
  holidayed
  holidaying
  holidays
holiness
hollandaise
hollow
  hollowed

  hollowing
holly (tree)
  hollies *pl*
hollyhock
holocaust
hologram
holograph
holster
holy (sacred)
  holier
  holiest
Holy Ghost
homage
home
  homed
  homing
home-coming
homeless
homeliness
homely
  homelier
  homeliest
home-made
homeopath *Am*
homeopathic *Am*
homeopathy *Am*
homesick
homesickness
homespun
homestead
homeward
homewards
homework

191

homicidal
homicide
homily
  homilies *pl*
homoeopath
homoeopathic
homoeopathy
homogeneity
homogeneous (of
  same type)
homogenise
  homogenised
  homogenising
homogenize
  homogenized
  homogenizing
homogenous (of
  same descent)
homologous
homonym
homonymic
homophobia
homophobic
homophone
homo sapiens
homosexual
homosexuality
hone
  honed
  honing
honest
honestly
honesty

honey
honeycomb
honeydew
honeyed
honeymoon
honeymooner
honeysuckle
honor *Am*
  honored
  honoring
honorable *Am*
honorably *Am*
honorarium
  honorariums,
  honoraria *pl*
honorary
honorific
honour
  honoured
  honouring
honourable
honourably
hood
hooded
hoodlum
  hoodlums *pl*
hoodwink
hoodwinked
hoof
  hooves, hoofs *pl*
  hoofed
  hoofing
  hoofs

hookah
  hookahs *pl*
hookey
hooligan
hooliganism
hoop
hoop-la
hooray
  hoorays *pl*
hoot
  hooted
  hooting
hooter
Hoover
hoover
  hoovered
  hoovering
hop
  hopped
  hopping
  hops
hope
  hoped
  hoping
hopeful
hopefully
hopelessly
hopelessness
hopper
hopscotch
horde (crowd)
horizon
horizontal

horizontally

hormone

horn

horned

hornet

hornpipe

horoscope

horrendous

horrible

horribly

horrid

horrific

horrifically

horrify

  horrified

  horrifies

  horrifying

horror

hors d'oeuvre

  hors d'oeuvres *pl*

horse (animal)

horseback

horsehair

horsepower

horseradish

horseshoe

horsewhip

  horsewhipped

  horsewhipping

  horsewhips

horsy

horticultural

horticulture

horticulturist

hosanna

  hosannas *pl*

hose

  hosed

  hosing

hosiery

hospice

hospitable

hospitably

hospital

hospitalisation

hospitalise

  hospitalised

  hospitalising

hospitality

hospitalization

hospitalize

  hospitalized

  hospitalizing

host

  hosted

  hosting

hostage

hostel

hostelry

  hostelries *pl*

hostess

hostile

hostilely

hostility

  hostilities *pl*

hot

hotter

hottest

hotchpotch, hotchpot

hotel

hotelier

hotheaded

hotly

hound

hour (tie)

houri

  houris *pl*

hourly

house

  housed

  housing

housebreaker

houseful

household

householder

housekeeper

housekeeping

housemaster

housewife

  housewives *pl*

housework

hove

hovel

hover

  hovered

  hovering

hovercraft

how

however

howitzer
howl
howler
howsoever
hoyden
hub
hubbub
huddle
  huddled
  huddling
hue (colour; outcry)
huff
huffily
huffy
hug
  hugged
  hugging
  hugs
huge
hugely
Huguenot
hulk
hulking
hull
hullabaloo
  hullabaloos *pl*
hullo, hallo, hello
hum
  hummed
  humming
  hums
human
humane (kind)

humanely
humaneness
humanism
humanist
humanistic
humanitarian
humanitarianism
humanity
  humanities *pl*
humanly
humble
humbleness
humbly
humbug
humdrum
humeral
humerus (arm-bone)
humid
humidifier
humidify
  humidified
  humidifies
  humidifying
humidity
humiliate
  humiliated
  humiliating
humiliation
humility
humming-bird
hummock (mound)
humor *Am*
  humored

humoring
humoresque
humorist
humorous
humorously
humour
  humoured
  humouring
hump
humpback
humus (of soil)
hunch
hunchback
hundred
hundredfold
hundredth
hundredweight
hung (*from* hang)
hunger
  hungered
  hungering
hungrily
hungry
  hungrier
  hungriest
hunk
hunt
hunter
huntress
huntsman
  huntsmen *pl*
hurdle
  hurdled

hurdling
hurdy-gurdy
  hurdy-gurdies *pl*
hurl
  hurled
  hurling
hurly-burly
hurrah, hurray
hurricane
hurriedly
hurry
  hurried
  hurries
  hurrying
hurt
hurtle
  hurtled
  hurtling
husband
husbandry
hush
husk
huskily
huskiness
husky
  huskies *pl*
hussar
hussy
  hussies *pl*
hustings
hustle
  hustled
  hustling

hustler
hut
hutch
hutment
hyacinth
hybrid
hydra
  hydras *pl*
hydrangea
  hydrangeas *pl*
hydrant
hydrate
  hydrated
  hydrating
hydration
hydraulic
hydraulically
hydrocarbon
hydrocephalic
hydrocephalus
hydrochloric
hydrodynamic
hydroelectric
hydrofoil
hydrogen
hydrology
hydrolysis
hydrolytic
hydrometer
hydrometric
hydrometry
hydropath
hydropathic

hydrophobia
hydroplane
hydroponics
hydrostatic
hydrotherapeutic
hydrotherapy
hydroxide
hyena, hyaena
  hyenas, hyaenas *pl*
hygiene
hygienic
hygienically
hygienist
hygrometer
hygrometric
hygroscope
hygroscopic
hymen
hymeneal
hymn (song)
hymnal
hype
  hyped
  hyping
hyperbola (curve)
  hyperbolas *pl*
hyperbole
  (exaggeration)
hyperbolic
hyperbolical
hypercritical (over-
  critical)
hyperglycaemia

(excess sugar)
hyperglycemia (excess sugar) Am
hypermarket
hypersensitive
hypertension
hypertensive
hyperthyroidism
hyphen
hyphenated
hypnosis
hypnotic
hypnotise
  hypnotised
  hypnotising
hypnotism
hypnotist
hypnotize
  hypnotized
  hypnotizing
hypoallergenic
hypochondria
hypochondriac
hypocrisy
hypocrite
hypocritical
hypocritically
hypodermic
hypodermically
hypoglycaemia (sugar deficiency
hypoglycaemic
hypoglycemia Am

hypoglycemic Am
hypotenuse
hypothermia
hypothesis
  hypotheses pl
hypothetical
hypothetically
hysterectomy
  hysterectomies pl
hysteresis
hysteria
hysterical
hysterically
hysterics

I
ibex
  ibexes *pl*
ibis
  ibises *pl*
ice
  iced
  icing
iceberg
ice cap
icebreaker
ice cream
icehockey
ichthyologist
ichthyology
icicle
icing
icily
icon

iconoclasm
iconoclast
icy
  icier
  iciest
I'd (I would)
idea
  ideas *pl*
idealisation
idealise
  idealised
  idealising
idealism
idealist
idealization
idealize
  idealized
  idealizing
ideally

idée fixe
idem
identical
identically
identifiable
identification
identify
  identified
  identifies
  identifying
identikit
identity
  identities *pl*
ideological
ideologically
ideology
  ideologies *pl*
idiocy
idiom
idiomatic
idiomatically
idiosyncrasy
  idiosyncrasies *pl*
idiosyncratic
idiosyncratically
idiot
idiotic
idiotically
idle (lazy)
  idled
  idling
idleness
idler

idly
idol (image)
idolater
idolatrous
idolatry
idolisation
idolise
  idolised
  idolising
idolization
idolize
  idolized
  idolizing
idyll (poem)
idyllic
igloo
  igloos pl
igneous
ignitable
ignite
  ignited
  igniting
igniter
ignition
ignoble
ignobly
ignominious
ignominiously
ignominy
  ignominies pl
ignoramus
  ignoramuses pl
ignorance

ignorant
ignorantly
ignore
  ignored
  ignoring
I'll (I will)
ilk
ill
ill-advised
ill-assorted
ill-bred
ill-defined
illegal
illegality
  illegalities pl
illegally
illegibility
illegible
illegibly
illegitimacy
illegitimate
illegitimately
ill-fated
ill-gotten
illicit (unlawful)
illicitly
illimitable
illiteracy
illiterate
  (ill-mannered)
illness
illogical
illogicality

  illogicalities pl
illogically
ill-treated
illuminate
  illuminated
  illuminating
illumination
illusion (deception)
illusionist
illusive (unreal)
illusory
illustrate
  illustrated
  illustrating
illustration
illustrative
illustrator
illustrious
illustriously
illustriousness
I'm (I am)
image
imagery
imaginable
imaginary
imagination
imaginative
imaginatively
imagine
  imagined
  imagining
imam
imbalance

imbecile

imbecility

imbibe

  imbibed

  imbibing

imbroglio

  imbroglios *pl*

imbue

  imbued

  imbuing

imitate

  imitated

  imitating

imitation

imitative

imitator

immaculacy

immaculate

immaculately

immanence

immanency

immanent (inherent)

immaterial

immaterially

immature

immaturely

immaturity

immeasurable

immeasurably

immediacy

immediate

immediately

immemorial

immense

immensely

immensity

immerse

  immersed

  immersing

immersion

immigrant

immigrate (to come
  as settler)

  immigrated

  immigrating

immigration

immigrator

imminence

imminent (happening
  soon)

imminently

immiscible

immobile

immobilisation

immobilise

  immobilised

  immobilising

immobility

immobilization

immobilize

  immobilized

  immobilizing

immoderate

immoderately

immodest

immodestly

immodesty

immoral

immorality

immorally

immortal

immortalisation

immortalise

  immortalised

  immortalising

immortality

immortalization

immortalize

  immortalized

  immortalizing

immortally

immovable

immovably

immune

immunisation

immunise

  immunised

  immunising

immunity

immunization

immunize

  immunized

  immunizing

immunodeficiency

immunology

immure

  immured

  immuring

immutability

immutable
immutably
imp
impact
impair
  impaired
  impairing
impairment
impale
  impaled
  impaling
impalpable
impalpably
impart
impartial
impartiality
impartially
impassable (*eg* road)
impasse
impassioned
impassive
impassively
impassivity
impatience
impatient
impatiently
impeach
impeachable
impeachment
impeccability
impeccable
impeccably
impecuniosity

impecunious
impedance
impede
  impeded
  impeding
impediment
impedimenta
impel
  impelled
  impelling
  impels
impeller
impend
impending
impenetrability
impenetrable
impenitence
impenitent
impenitently
imperative
imperatively
imperceptible
imperceptibly
imperfect
imperfection
imperfectly
imperial
imperialism
imperialist
imperialistic
imperil
  imperilled
  imperilling

  imperils
  imperiled *Am*
  imperiling *Am*
imperilment
imperious
imperiously
imperiousness
imperishable
imperishably
impermeability
impermeable
impermissible
impersonal
impersonally
impersonate
  impersonated
  impersonating
impersonation
impersonator
impertinence
impertinent
impertinently
imperturbability
imperturbable
imperturbably
impervious
imperviousness
impetigo
impetuosity
impetuous
impetuously
impetus
  impetuses *pl*

impiety
impinge
  impinged
  impinging
impingement
impious
impish
impishly
impishness
implacability
implacable
implacably
implant
implantation
implausibility
implausible
implausibly
implement
implementation
implicate
  implicated
  implicating
implication
implicit
implicitly
implode
  imploded
  imploding
implore
  implored
  imploring
implosion
implosive

imply
  implied
  implies
  implying
impolite
impolitely
impoliteness
impolitic
impoliticly
imponderability
imponderable
import
  imported
  importing
importance
important
importantly
importation
importunate
importunately
importune
  importuned
  importuning
importunity
impose
  imposed
  imposing
imposition
impossibility
impossible
impossibly
impost
impostor

imposture
impotence
impotent
impotently
impound
impoverish
impoverishment
impracticability
impracticable
impracticably
impractical
imprecate
  imprecated
  imprecating
imprecation
imprecise
imprecisely
imprecision
impregnability
impregnable
impregnably
impregnate
  impregnated
  impregnating
impregnation
impresario
  impresarios pl
impress
impressed
impression
impressionable
impressionism
impressive

impressively
impressiveness
imprest (money
  advanced)
imprimatur
imprint
imprison
imprisonment
improbability
improbable
improbably
impromptu
improper
improperly
impropriety
  improprieties *pl*
improvable
improve
  improved
  improving
improvement
improver
improvidence
improvident
improvidently
improvisation
improvise
  improvised
  improvising
improviser
imprudence
imprudent
imprudently

impugn
  impugned
  impugning
impulse
impulsive
impulsively
impunity
impure
impurity
  impurities *pl*
imputable
imputation
impute
  imputed
  imputing
inability
in absentia
inaccessibility
inaccessible
inaccuracy
  inaccuracies *pl*
inaccurate
inaccurately
inaction
inactive
inactively
inactivity
inadequacy
  inadequacies *pl*
inadequate
inadequately
inadmissibility
inadmissible

inadmissibly
inadvertence
inadvertent
inadvertently
inadvisability
inadvisable
inadvisably
inalienability
inalienable
inane
inanely
inanimate
inanity
  inanities *pl*
inapplicable
inappreciable
inappreciably
inappropriate
inappropriately
inappropriateness
inapt (not fitting)
inaptitude
inaptly
inaptness
inarticulate
inarticulately
inarticulateness
inartistic
inartistically
inasmuch
inattention
inattentive
inattentively

inaudibility
inaudible
inaudibly
inaugural
inaugurate
  inaugurated
  inaugurating
inauguration
inaugurator
inauguratory
inauspicious
inauspiciously
inborn
inbreed
  inbred
  inbreeding
  inbreeds
incalculability
incalculable
incalculably
incandescence
incandescent
incantation
incapability
incapable
incapably
incapacitate
  incapacitated
  incapacitating
incapacitation
incapacity
incarcerate
  incarcerated

  incarcerating
incarceration
incarnate
incarnation
incautious
incautiously
incendiarism
incendiary
  incendiaries *pl*
incense (perfume; to
  anger)
  incensed
  incensing
incentive
inception
incertitude
incessant
incessantly
incest
incestuous
incestuously
inch
incidence
incident
incidental
incidentally
incinerate
  incinerated
  incinerating
incineration
incinerator
incipient
incise

incision
incisive
incisively
incisor
incitation
incite (to urge)
  incited
  inciting
incitement
inciter
incivility
  incivilities *pl*
inclemency
  inclemencies *eg*
inclement
inclemently
inclination
incline
  inclined
  inclining
include
  included
  including
inclusion
inclusive
inclusively
incognito
incoherence
incoherent
incoherently
incombustibility
incombustible
income

incomer
incoming
incommensurable
incommensurate
incommode
  incommoded
  incommoding
incommodious
incommunicado
incomparable
incomparably
incompatibility
incompatible
incompetence
incompetent
incompetently
incomplete
incompletely
incompleteness
incomprehensibility
incomprehensible
incomprehensibly
incompressibility
incompressible
inconceivable
inconceivably
inconclusive
inconclusively
incongruity
  incongruities *pl*
incongruous
incongruously
inconsequent

inconsequential
inconsequently
inconsiderable
inconsiderably
inconsiderate
inconsiderately
inconsistency
  inconsistencies *pl*
inconsistent
inconsistently
inconsolable
inconspicuous
inconspicuously
inconspicuousness
inconstancy
inconstant
incontestable
incontestably
incontinence
incontinent
incontrovertible
incontrovertibly
inconvenience
inconvenient
inconveniently
inconvertibility
inconvertible
incorporate
  incorporated
  incorporating
incorporation
incorrect
incorrectly

incorrectness
incorrigibility
incorrigible
incorrigibly
incorruptibility
incorruptible
increase
  increased
  increasing
increasingly
incredibility
incredible
incredibly
incredulity
incredulous
increment
incriminate
  incriminated
  incriminating
incrimination
incriminatory
incubate
  incubated
  incubating
incubation
incubator
incubus
  incubuses, incubi *pl*
inculcate
  inculcated
  inculcating
inculcation
inculpate

inculpated
inculpating
inculpation
incumbency
  incumbencies *pl*
incumbent
incur
  incurred
  incurring
  incurs
incurability
incurable
incurably
incurious
incursion
incursive
indebted
indebtedness
indecency
  indecencies *pl*
indecent
indecently
indecipherable
indecision
indecisive
indecisively
indeclinable
indecorous
indecorously
indecorousness
indecorum
indeed
indefatigability

indefatigable
indefatigably
indefensible
indefensibly
indefinable
indefinite
indefinitely
indelible
indelibly
indelicacy
  indelicacies *pl*
indelicate
indelicately
indemnification
indemnify
  indemnified
  indemnifies
  indemnifying
indemnity
  indemnities *pl*
indent
indentation
indented
indenture
independence
independent
independently
indescribable
indescribably
indestructibility
indestructible
indestructibly
indeterminable

indeterminate
indeterminately
index
  indexes, indices *pl*
indexation
indicate
  indicated
  indicating
indication
indicative
indicator
indict (to accuse)
indictable
indictment
indifference
indifferent
indifferently
indigence
indigenous
indigent
indigestibility
indigestible
indigestion
indignant
indignantly
indignation
indignity
  indignities *pl*
indigo
indirect
indirectly
indiscernible
indiscipline

indiscreet
indiscreetly
indiscretion
indiscriminate
indiscriminately
indispensability
indispensable
indispensably
indisposed
indisposition
indisputable
indisputably
indistinct
indistinguishable
indite (to write)
  indited
  inditing
individual
individualisation
individualise
  individualised
  individualising
individualism
individualist
individualistic
individuality
individualization
individualize
  individualized
  individualizing
individually
indivisible
indivisibility

indivisibly
indoctrinate
  indoctrinated
  indoctrinating
indoctrination
indolence
indolent
indolently
indomitable
indomitably
indoor
indoors
indubitable
indubitably
induce
  induced
  inducing
inducement
induct
inductance
induction
inductive
inductively
indulge
  indulged
  indulging
indulgence
indulgent
indulgently
industrial
industrialisation
industrialise
  industrialised

industrialising
industrialist
industrialization
industrialize
  industrialized
  industrializing
industrially
industrious
industriously
industry
  industries pl
inebriated
inebriation
inedibility
inedible
ineducable
ineffable
ineffably
ineffective
ineffectively
ineffectiveness
ineffectual
ineffectually
inefficiency
  inefficiencies pl
inefficient
inefficiently
inelastic
inelastically
inelasticity
inelegancy
inelegant
inelegantly

ineligibility
ineligible
inept
ineptitude
ineptly
inequality
  inequalities pl
inequitable
inequitably
ineradicable
ineradicably
inert
inertia
inertly
inertness
inescapable
inescapably
inessential
inestimable
inestimably
inevitability
inevitable
inevitably
inexact
inexactitude
inexcusable
inexcusably
inexhaustible
inexhaustibly
inexorable
inexorably
inexpediency
inexpedient

inexpediently
inexpensive
inexpensively
inexperience
inexplicable
inexplicably
inexpressible
inexpressibly
inextinguishable
inextricable
inextricably
infallibility
infallible
infallibly
infamous
infamously
infamy
infancy
infant
infanticide
infantile
infantry
infantryman
  infantrymen pl
infatuated
infatuation
infect
  infected
  infecting
infection
infectious
infectiousness
infelicitous

infelicitously
infelicity
  infelicities pl
infer
  inferred
  inferring
  infers
inference
inferential
inferior
inferiority
infernal
infernally
inferno
  infernos pl
infertile
infertility
infest
infestation
infidel
infidelity
  infidelities pl
infighting
infiltrate
  infiltrated
  infiltrating
infiltration
infiltrator
infinite
infinitely
infinitesimal
infinitesimally
infinitival

infinitive
infinitude
infinity
infirm
infirmary
  infirmaries pl
infirmity
  infirmities pl
inflame
  inflamed
  inflaming
inflammable
inflammation
inflammatory
inflatable
inflate
  inflated
  inflating
inflation
inflationary
inflect
inflection
inflexibility
inflexible
inflexibly
inflexion
inflict
infliction
influence
  influenced
  influencing
influential
influentially

influenza
influx
  influxes pl
inform
  informed
  informing
informal
informality
informally
informant
information
informative
informer
infra dig
infraction
infra-red
infrastructure
infrequency
infrequent
infrequently
infringe
  infringed
  infringing
infringement
infuriate
  infuriated
  infuriating
infuse
  infused
  infusing
infusion
ingenious (clever)
ingeniously

ingénue
ingenuity
ingenuous (naive)
ingenuously
ingenuousness
ingest
ingestion
inglorious
ingloriously
ingoing
ingot
ingrain
  ingrained
  ingraining
ingratiate
  ingratiated
  ingratiating
ingratitude
ingredient
ingress
ingrowing
ingrown
inhabit
  inhabited
  inhabiting
inhabitable
inhabitant
inhalant
inhalation
inhale
  inhaled
  inhaling
inherence

inherent
inheritance
inheritor
inhibit
  inhibited
  inhibiting
inhibition
inhibitory
inhospitable
inhospitably
inhuman (barbarous)
inhumane (cruel)
inhumanely
inhumanity
  inhumanities *pl*
inhumanly
inimical
inimitable
inimitably
iniquitous
iniquitously
iniquity
  iniquities *pl*
initial
  initialled
  initialling
  initials
  initialed *Am*
  initialing *Am*
initially
initiate
  initiated
  initiating

initiation
initiative
initiator
inject
injection
injudicious
injudiciously
injunction
injure
  injured
  injuring
injurious
injuriously
injury
  injuries *pl*
injustice
ink
inkling
inky
  inkier
  inkiest
inlaid
inland
in-law
inlay
  inlaid
  inlaying
  inlays
inlet
inmate
in memoriam
inmost
inn (hostelry)

innards
innate
innately
inner
innermost
innings
innkeeper
innocence
innocent
innocently
innocuous
innocuously
innovate
  innovated
  innovating
innovation
innovator
innuendo
  innuendoes,
  innuendos *pl*
innumerable
innumerably
inoculate
  inoculated
  inoculating
inoculation
inoffensive
inoffensively
inoffensiveness
inoperable
inoperative
inoperativeness
inopportune

inopportunely
inordinate
inordinately
inorganic
input
  inputs
  inputted
  inputting
inquest
inquire (to
    investigate)
  inquired
  inquiring
inquiry (investigation)
  inquiries *pl*
inquisition
inquisitive
inquisitively
inquisitiveness
inquisitor
inquisitorial
inroad
inrush
insalubrious
insalubrity
insane
insanely
insanitariness
insanitary
insanity
insatiable
insatiably
inscribe

inscribed
  inscribing
inscription
inscrutability
inscrutable
inscrutably
insect
insecticide
insecure
insecurely
insecurity
inseminate
  inseminated
  inseminating
insemination
insensate
insensibility
insensible
insensibly
insensitive
insensitively
insensitivity
inseparable
inseparably
insert
insertion
inset
  insets
  insetting
inshore
inside
insider
insidious

insidiously
insidiousness
insight
  (understanding)
insignia
insignificance
insignificant
insignificantly
insincere
insincerely
insincerity
insinuate
  insinuated
  insinuating
insinuation
insinuator
insipid
insipidly
insipidness
insist
insistence
insistent
insistently
insobriety
insolence
insolent
insolently
insolubility
insoluble
insolubly
insolvency
insolvent
insomnia

insomniac
insouciance
insouciant
inspect
inspection
inspector
inspectorate
inspiration
inspire
  inspired
  inspiring
instability
install
installation
installment *Am*
instalment
instance
instant
instantaneous
instantaneously
instantly
instead
instep
instigate
  instigated
  instigating
instigation
instigator
instil
  instilled
  instilling
  instils
instill *Am*

instilled
instilling
instills
instinct
instinctive
instinctively
institute
  instituted
  instituting
institution
institutional
institutionalise
  institutionalised
  institutionalising
institutionalize
  institutionalized
  institutionalizing
instruct
instruction
instructional
instructive
instructor
instrument
instrumental
instrumentalist
instrumentality
instrumentation
insubordinate
insubordinately
insubordination
insubstantial
insufferable
insufferably

insufficiency
insufficient
insufficiently
insular
insularity
insulate
  insulated
  insulating
insulation
insulator
insulin
insult
insuperable
insuperably
insupportable
insurability
insurable
insurance
insure (protect
    financially)
  insured
  insuring
insurer
insurgence
insurgency
insurgent
insurmountable
insurmountably
insurrection
insurrectionary
intact
intake
intangible

intangibly
integer
integral
integrally
integrate
  integrated
  integrating
integration
integrity
intellect
intellectual
intellectualise
  intellectualised
  intellectualising
intellectualism
intellectualize
  intellectualized
  intellectualizing
intellectually
intelligence
intelligent
intelligently
intelligentsia
  intelligentsias *pl*
intelligible
intelligibly
intemperance
intemperate
intemperately
intend
intense
intensely
intensification

intensify
  intensified
  intensifies
  intensifying
intensity
  intensities *pl*
intensive
intensively
intent (purpose;
  earnest)
intention
intentional
intentionally
intently
inter (bury)
  interred
  interring
  inters
inter alia
interact
interaction
interbreed
  interbred
  interbreeding
  interbreeds
intercalary
intercalate (to insert)
  intercalated
  intercalating
intercalation
intercede
  interceded
  interceding

intercept
interception
interceptor
intercession
interchange
  interchanged
  interchanging
interchangeable
intercom.
intercommunicate
  intercommunicated
  intercommunicating
intercommunication
interconnect
interconnection
intercontinental
intercourse
interdenominational
interdepartmental
interdependence
interdependent
interdependently
interdict
interdiction
interdisciplinary
interest
interested
interesting
interface
  interfaced
  interfacing
interfere
  interfered

interfering
interference
interim
interior
interiorly
interject
interjection
interlace
  interlaced
  interlacing
interleave
  interleaved
  interleaving
interline
  interlined
  interlining
interlock
interlope
  interloped
  interloping
interloper
interlude
intermarriage
intermarry
  intermarried
  intermarries
  intermarrying
intermediary
  intermediaries *pl*
intermediate
intermediately
interment (burial)
intermezzo

intermezzos,
  intermezzi *pl*
interminable
interminably
intermingle
  intermingled
  intermingling
intermission
intermittent
intermittently
intern (to confine)
  interned
  interning
intern, interne
  (doctor)
internal
internally
international
internationalisation
internationalise
  internationalised
  internationalising
internationalism
internationalization
internationalize
  internationalized
  internationalizing
internationally
internecine
internee
Internet
internment
  (confinement)

interpellate (to ask
  questions)
interpellated
interpellating
interpellation
  (interrogation)
interplanetary
Interpol
interpolate (to insert)
interpolated
interpolating
interpolation
  (insertion)
interpose
interposed
interposing
interposition
interpret
interpreted
interpreting
interpretation
interpreter
interracial
interregnum
  interregnums,
    interregna *pl*
interrelate
interrelated
interrelating
interrelation
interrogate
interrogated
interrogating

interrogation
interrogative
interrogator
interrupt
  interrupted
  interrupting
interrupter
interruption
intersect
  intersected
  intersecting
intersection
intersperse
  interspersed
  interspersing
interspersion
interstellar
interstice
interstitial
interval
intervene
  intervened
  intervening
intervention
interview
  interviewed
  interviewing
interviewee
interviewer
interweave
  interweaves
  interweaving
  interwove

interwoven
intestacy
intestate
intestinal
intestine
intimacy
intimate
  intimated
  intimating
intimately
intimation
intimidate
  intimidated
  intimidating
intimidation
intolerable
intolerably
intolerance
intolerant
intolerantly
intonation
intone
  intoned
  intoning
intoxicant
intoxicate
  intoxicated
  intoxicating
intoxication
intractability
intractable
intractably
intramuscular

intransigence
intransigent
intransigently
intransitive
intrauterine
intravenous
intrepid
intrepidity
intrepidly
intricacy
  intricacies *pl*
intricate
intricately
intrigue
  intrigued
  intriguing
intrinsic
intrinsically
introduce
  introduced
  introducing
introduction
introductory
introspection
introspective
introversion
introvert
intrude
  intruded
  intruding
intruder
intrusion
intrusive

intuition
intuitive
intuitively
inundate
  inundated
  inundating
inundation
inure
  inured
  inuring
invade
  invaded
  invading
invader
invalid
invalidate
  invalidated
  invalidating
invalidation
invalidism
invaluable (precious)
invariable
invariably
invasion
invective
inveigh (to abuse)
  inveighed
  inveighing
inveigle (to entice)
  inveigled
  inveigling
invent
  invented

inventing
invention
inventive
inventiveness
inventor
inventory
  inventories pl
inverse
inversely
inversion
invert
  inverted
  inverting
invertebrate
inverter
invest
  invested
  investing
investigate
  investigated
  investigating
investigation
investigator
investiture
investment
investor
inveteracy
inveterate
inveterately
invidious (causing
    offence)
invidiously
invidiousness

invigilate
  invigilated
  invigilating
invigilation
invigilator
invigorate
  invigorated
  invigorating
invigoration
invincibility
invincible
invincibly
inviolable (sacred)
inviolate (unbroken)
invisibility
invisible
invisibly
invitation
invite
  invited
  inviting
invocation
invoice
  invoiced
  invoicing
invoke
  invoked
  invoking
involuntarily
involuntary
involution
involve
  involved

involving

involvement

invulnerability

invulnerable

inward

inwardly

inwardness

inwards

iodide

iodine

ion (atom)

ionic

ionisation

ionise

  ionised

  ionising

ionization

ionize

  ionized

  ionizing

ionosphere

iota

  iotas *pl*

ipecacuanha

  ipecacuanhas *pl*

ipso facto

irascibility

irascible

irascibly

irate

irately

ire (anger)

ireful

iridescence

iridescent

iris

  irises *pl*

irk

  irked

  irking

irksome

iron (metal)

ironic

ironical

ironically

ironmonger

ironmongery

irony

  ironies *pl*

irradiate

  irradiated

  irradiating

irradiation

irrational

irrationality

irrationally

irreconcilability

irreconcilable

irreconcilably

irrecoverable

irrecoverably

irredeemable

irredeemably

irreducible

irreducibly

irrefutable

irrefutably

irregular

irregularity

  irregularities *pl*

irregularly

irrelevance

irrelevant

irrelevantly

irreligious

irremediable

irremediably

irremissible

irremovable

irremovably

irreparable

irreparably

irreplaceable

irrepressible

irrepressibly

irreproachable

irreproachably

irresistible

irresistibly

irresolute

irresolutely

irrespective

irrespectively

irresponsibility

irresponsible

irresponsibly

irretrievable

irretrievably

irreverence

rreverent
rreverently
rreversibility
rreversible
rreversibly
rrevocability
rrevocable
rrevocably
irrigate
  irrigated
  irrigating
irrigation
irrigator
irritability
irritable
irritably
irritant
irritate
  irritated
  irritating
irritation
irrupt (to break in)
  irrupted
  irrupting
irruption
irruptive
isinglass
island
islander
isle (island)
islet
isn't (is not)
isobar

isochronous
isolate
  isolated
  isolating
isolation
isometric
isometrically
isosceles
isotherm
isothermal
isotope
issuance
issue
  issued
  issuing
isthmus
  isthmuses, isthmi *pl*
italic
italicise
  italicised
  italicising
italicize
  italicized
  italicizing
itch
  itched
  itching
itchy
  itchier
  itchiest
item
itemise
  itemised

  itemising
itemize
  itemized
  itemizing
iterate
  iterated
  iterating
iteration
iterative
itinerant
itinerary
  itineraries *pl*
it's (it is)
its
itself
I've (I have)
ivory
  ivories *pl*
ivy
  ivies *pl*

jab
  jabbed
  jabbing
  jabs
jabber
  jabbered
  jabbering
jack
jackal
jackanapes
jackass
jackdaw
jacket
jackhammer
jack-in-the-box
  jack-in-the-boxes *pl*

jackknife
  jackknives *pl*
  jackknifed
  jackknifes
  jackknifing
jackpot
Jacobean (of James I's
  time)
Jacobin (French
  revolutionary)
Jacobinic
Jacobinical
Jacobite (loyal to
  James II)
jade
  jaded

  jading
jag
jagged
jaguar
jail, gaol
jailer, gaoler, jailor
jalopy
  jalopies *pl*
jam (sweet spread; to
  be stuck)
  jammed
  jamming
  jams
jamb (of door)
jamboree
jammy
  jammier
  jammiest
jangle
  jangled
  jangling
janitor
japan (to varnish)
  japanned
  japanning
  japans
japonica
  japonicas *pl*
jar
  jarred
  jarring
  jars
jardinière

argon
jasmine, jasmin
jasper
jaundice
jaundiced
jaunt
jauntily
jauntiness
jaunty
  jauntier
  jauntiest
javelin
jaw
jawbone
jay
  jays *pl*
jaywalk
  jaywalked
  jaywalking
jaywalker
jazz
jazzy
  jazzier
  jazziest
jealous
jealously
jealousy
jeans (trousers)
jeep
jeer
  jeered
  jeering
jejune

jellied
jelly
  jellies *pl*
jemmy
  jemmies *pl*
jeopardise
  jeopardised
  jeopardising
jeopardize
  jeopardized
  jeopardizing
jeopardy
jerk
jerkily
jerkin
jerkiness
jerky
  jerkier
  jerkiest
jeroboam
jerry-builder
jerry-building
jerry-built
jersey
  jerseys *pl*
jest
jester
jet
  jets
  jetted
  jetting
jet-propelled
jetsam

jettison
  jettisoned
  jettisoning
jetty
  jetties *pl*
Jew
jewel (cut gem)
jeweled *Am*
jeweler *Am*
jewelled
jeweller
jewellery
jewelry *Am*
Jewish
Jewry
jib
  jibbed
  jibbing
  jibs
jibe
  jibed
  jibing
jiffy
  jiffies *pl*
jig
jiggered
jigsaw
jilt
  jilted
  jilting
jingle
  jingled
  jingling

jingo
  jingoes *pl*
jingoism
jinx
  jinxes *pl*
jitters
jittery
jive
  jived
  jiving
job
jobber
jobbing
jobless
jockey
  jockeys *pl*
jocose (playful)
jocosely
jocosity
jocular
jocularity
jocularly
jocund
jocundity
jocundly
jodhpurs
joey
  joeys *pl*
jog
  jogged
  jogging
  jogs
joggle

joggled
joggling
joie de vivre
join
  joined
  joining
joiner
joinery
joint
jointer
jointly
jointure
joist
joke
  joked
  joking
joker
jokingly
jollification
jollify
  jollified
  jollifies
  jollifying
jollily
jollity
jolly
  jollier
  jolliest
jolt
  jolted
  jolting
jonquil
josser

jostle
  jostled
  jostling
jot
  jots
  jotted
  jotting
joule (unit of energy)
journal
journalese
journalism
journalist
journey
  journeys *pl*
  journeyed
  journeying
  journeys
jovial
joviality
jovially
jowl
joy
  joys *pl*
joyful
joyfully
joyless
joyous
joyously
joyride
joyriding
jubilant
jubilantly
jubilation

bilee
daism
dder
juddered
juddering
dge
judged
judging
dgement, judgment
dicature
dicial
dicially
diciary
  judiciaries *pl*
dicious
diciously
do
g
jugged
jugging
jugs
ggernaut
ggle
juggled
juggling
ggler
gular
ice
uiced
uicing
icily
iciness
icy

juicier
juiciest
jujitsu
jujube
jukebox
julep
julienne
jumble
  jumbled
  jumbling
jumbo
jump
  jumped
  jumping
jumper
jumpily
jumpiness
jumpy
  jumpier
  jumpiest
junction
juncture
jungle
junior
juniper
junk
junket
  junketed
  junketing
junta
  juntas *pl*
juridical
jurisdiction

jurisdictional
jurisprudence
jurisprudent
jurist
juror
jury
  juries *pl*
juryman
  jurymen *pl*
just
justice
justiciary
  justiciaries *pl*
justifiable
justifiably
justification
justify
  justified
  justifies
  justifying
justly
jut
  juts
  jutted
  jutting
jute
juvenile
juxtapose
  juxtaposed
  juxtaposing
juxtaposition

K

kale (cabbage)	keenness	kerchief
kaleidoscope	keep	kerchiefs *pl*
kaleidoscopic	keeping	kernel (centre)
kalends, calends	keeps	kerosene, kerosine
kamikaze	kept	kestrel
kangaroo	keeper	ketch
kangaroos *pl*	keepsake	ketchup
kaolin	keg	kettle
kapok	kelp	kettledrum
karate	kempt	key (lock)
katabolism, catabolism	ken	keys *pl*
kayak	kennel	keyed
kebab	kennelled	keying
kedgeree	kennelling	keyboard
keel	kennels	keyhole
keen	kenneled *Am*	keynote
keener	kenneling *Am*	khaki
keenest	kerb (road edge)	khan (Oriental title)
keenly	kerbstone	kibbutz
		kibbutzim *pl*
		kibbutznik
		kibosh
		kick
		kick-off
		kid
		kidded
		kidding
		kids
		kidnap
		kidnapped
		kidnapping
		kidnaps
		kidnaped *Am*

kidnaping *Am*

kidnaper *Am*

kidnapper

kidney

  kidneys *pl*

kids

kill

killer

kiln

kilo

  kilos *pl*

kilocycle

kilogram, kilogramme

kilohertz

kiloliter *Am*

kilolitre

kilometer *Am*

kilometre

kiloton

kilotonne (metric)

kilowatt

kilt

kimono

  kimonos *pl*

kin

kind

kindergarten

  kindergartens *pl*

kind-hearted

kindle

  kindled

  kindling

kindliness

kindly

kindness

kindred

kinetic

king

kingdom

kink

kinky

kinsfolk

kinship

kinsman

  kinsmen *pl*

kinswoman

  kinswomen *pl*

kiosk

kipper

kippered

kirk

kiss

kit

  kits

  kitted

  kitting

kitchen

kitchenette

kite

kith

kitten

kittenish

kitty (fund of money)

klaxon

kleptomania

kleptomaniac

knack

knacker

knackered

knackering

knapsack

knave

knavery

knavish

knead (to mix dough)

knee

  kneed

  kneeing

kneecap

kneel

  kneeled

  kneeling

knell (sound of bell)

knelt

knew (from know)

knickerbockers

knickers

knick-knack

knife

  knives *pl*

  knifed

  knifes

  knifing

knight (chivalric)

  knighted

  knighting

knight-errant

knight-errantry

knighthood

knightly (chivalrous)
knit (handicraft)
  knits
  knitted
  knitting
knitter
knob (*eg* on a door)
knobby
knock
knocker
knock-kneed
knoll (small hill)
knot (*eg* in string
  knots
  knotted
  knotting
knout (to flog)
  knouted
  knouting
know (have the
  knowledge)
  knew
  knowing
  known
  knows
know-how, knowhow
  (expertise)
knowledge
knowledgeable
knowledgeably
knuckle
  knuckled
  knuckling

koala
  koalas *pl*
koala bear
Kodak
kohlrabi
kookaburra
Koran
kosher
kowtow
Krishna
krona (Swedish
  money)
  kronor *pl*
krone (currency)
  kroner *pl*
kudos
kumquat
kung-fu

laager (encampment)
label
  labelled
  labelling
  labels
  labeled *Am*
  labeling *Am*
labial (of the lips)
labor *Am*
  labored
  laboring
laboratory
  laboratories *pl*
laborious
laboriously
labour
  laboured
  labouring
laburnum

laburnums *pl*
labyrinth
labyrinthine
lace
  laced
  lacing
lacerate (to tear)
  lacerated
  lacerating
laceration
lachrymal
lachrymose
lack
lackadaisical
lackadaisically
lackey
  lackeys *pl*
lackluster *Am*
lacklustre

laconic
laconically
lacquer (varnish)
  lacquered
  lacquering
lacrosse
lactation
lactic
lad
ladder
laddie
laden
lading
ladle
  ladled
  ladling
lady
  ladies *pl*
ladylike
ladyship
lag
  lagged
  lagging
  lags
lager (beer)
laggard
lagoon
laid (*from* lay)
lain (*from* lie)
lair (den)
laird
laissez-faire
laity

lake
lama (priest)
lamb (young sheep)
lambast, lambaste
  lambasted
  lambasting
  lambasts, lambastes
lambda
  lambdas *pl*
lambent
lambkin
lambskin
lame
lamely
lameness
lament
lamentable
lamentably
lamentation
lamina
  laminae *pl*
laminated
lamination
lamp
lamplight
lampoon
  lampooned
  lampooning
lampooner
lamprey
  lampreys *pl*
lance
  lanced

lancing
lancer (soldier)
lancers (dance)
lancet
land
landfall
landfill
landlady
  landladies *pl*
landlocked
landlord
landlubber
landmark
landowner
landscape
  landscaped
  landscaping
landslide
lane (track; road)
language
languid
languidly
languidness
languish
languor
languorous
lank
lankiness
lanky
  lankier
  lankiest
lanolin
lantern

lanyard
lap
  lapped
  lapping
  laps
lapdog
lapel
lapidary
  lapidaries *pl*
lapis lazuli
lapse
  lapsed
  lapsing
larboard
larceny
  larcenies *pl*
larch
lard
larder
large
largely
largess, largesse
larghetto
  larghettos *pl*
largish
largo
  largos *pl*
lark
larva
  larvae *pl*
larval
laryngeal
laryngitis

arynx
  larynges *pl*
ascivious
asciviously
asciviousness
ase (act as a laser)
  lased
  lasing
aser
ash
ass
assie
assitude
asso
  lassos, lassoes *pl*
  lassoed
  lassoes
  lassoing
ast
lastly
latch
latchkey
late
  later
  latest
lately
latency
latent
lateral
laterally
latex
lath (strip of wood)
lathe (machine)

lather
  lathered
  lathering
latitude
latrine
latter
latter-day
latterly
lattice
laud (to praise)
laudable
laudably
laudanum
laugh
laughable
laughing stock
laughter
launch
launched
launder
  laundered
  laundering
launderette
laundress *f*
laundry
  laundries *pl*
laureate
laurel
laurel wreath
lava (*from* volcano)
lavatory
  lavatories *pl*
lavender

laver (kind of
  seaweed)
lavish
lavishly
lavishness
law (rule)
law-abiding
lawful
lawfully
lawfulness
lawless
lawlessly
lawlessness
lawn
lawn-mower
lawsuit
lawyer
lax
laxative
laxity
laxly
lay
  laid
  laying
  lays
lay-by
  lay-bys *pl*
layer
  layered
  layering
layette
layman
  laymen *pl*

lay-off
laze
  lazed
  lazing
lazily
laziness
lazy
  lazier
  laziest
lea (meadow)
leach (filter)
lead (to go first;
    metal)
  leading
  leads
  led
leaded
leaden
leader
leadership
leaf (on tree)
  leaves pl
  leafed
  leafing
  leafs
leafage
leafiness
leafless
leaflet
leafy
  leafier
  leafiest
league

leak (hole in pipe)
leakage
leaky
  leakier
  leakiest
lean
  leaned
  leaning
  leans
  leant
leaner
leanness
lean-to
  lean-tos pl
leap
  leaped
  leaping
  leapt
leapfrog
  leapfrogged
  leapfrogging
  leapfrogs
leapyear
learn
  learned
  learning
  learns
  learnt
lease
  leased
  leasing
leasehold
leash

least
leastways
leastwise
leather
leatherette
leathery
leave (to depart)
  leaves
  leaving
  left
leaven
leavened
lecher
lecherous
lechery
lectern
lecture
  lectured
  lecturing
lecturer
led (from lead)
ledge
ledger (book)
lee (shelter)
leech (worm)
leek (vegetable)
leer
  leered
  leering
leery
leeward
leeway
left

left wing
left-handed
leftward
left-winger
leg
  legged
  legging
  legs
legacy
  legacies *pl*
legal
legalisation
legalise
  legalised
  legalising
legality
legalization
legalize
  legalized
  legalizing
legally
legate
legation
legato
  legatos *pl*
legend
legendary
leger (stand)
legerdemain
leggings
leggy
legibility
legible

legibly
legion
legionnaire
legionary
  legionaries *pl*
legislate
  legislated
  legislating
legislation
legislator (law maker)
legislature (legal
  assembly)
legitimacy
legitimate
legitimately
legitimation
legitimatise
  legitimatised
  legitimatising
legitimatize
  legitimatized
  legitimatizing
legitimise
  legitimised
  legitimising
legitimize
  legitimized
  legitimizing
legume
leguminous
Leicester
leisure

leisurely
leitmotiv, leitmotif
lemming
lemon
lemonade
lend
  lending
  lends
  lent
lender
length
lengthen
  lengthened
  lengthening
lengthily
lengthways
lengthwise
lengthy
lenience
leniency
lenient
leniently
lens
lent (*from* lend)
Lent
Lenten
lentil
leonine
leopard
leotard
leper
leprechaun
leprosy

leprous
lesbian
lèse-majesté
lesion
less
lessee
lessen (to reduce)
  lessened
  lessening
lesser
lesson (study)
lessor (granter of lease)
let
lethal
lethally
lethargic
lethargically
lethargy
let's (let us)
lettable
letter
  lettered
  lettering
letterhead
lettuce
leucocyte
leukaemia
  leukaemias *pl*
leukemia *Am*
  leukemias *pl*
level
  levelled
  levelling

levels
leveled *Am*
leveling *Am*
leveler *Am*
level-headed
leveller
lever
  levered
  levering
leverage
leviathan
Levis (jeans)
levitate
  levitated
  levitating
levitation
levity (humour)
levy (payment)
  levies *pl*
  levied
  levies
  levying
lewd
lewdly
lewdness
lexicographer
lexicography
lexicon
liability
  liabilities *pl*
liable
liaise
  liaised

liaising
liaison
liar (person who lies)
libation
libel
  libelled
  libelling
  libels
  libeled *Am*
  libeling *Am*
libeler *Am*
libeller
libellous
libelous *Am*
liberal (generous)
Liberal (politics)
liberality
liberally
liberate
  liberated
  liberating
liberation
liberator
libertine (licentious
  person)
liberty
  liberties *pl*
libidinal
libidinous
libido
  libidos *pl*
librarian
library

libraries *pl*

libretto

  librettos, libretti *pl*

lice (*pl* of louse)

licence (permission)

license (to grant
   permission;
   permission *Am*)

  licensed

  licensing

licensee

licenser

licentiate

licentious

licentiousness

lichen

lick

licorice, liquorice

lid

lidded

lido

  lidos *pl*

lie (horizontal)

  lain

  lay

  lies

  lying

lie (to fib)

  lied

  lies

  lying

lied (German song)

  lieder *pl*

lien (right to property)

lieu (instead of)

lieutenancy

lieutenant

life

  lives *pl*

lifebuoy

lifeguard

lifeless

lifelessly

lifelike

lifelong

life-size

life-sized

lift

lift-off

ligament

ligature

light

  lights

  lighted

  lighting

  lit

lighten

  lightened

  lightening

light-hearted

light-heartedly

lighthouse

lightly

lightness

lightning (in
  thunderstorm)

lightweight

lignite

like

  liked

  liking

likeable, likable

likelihood

likely

liken

  likened

  likening

likeness

likewise

lilac

lilliputian

lilt

lily

  lilies *pl*

lily-livered

limb

limber

  limbered

  limbering

limbless

limbo

  limbos *pl*

lime

limelight

limerick

limit

  limited

  limiting

limitation

limousine
limp
limpet
limpid
limpness
linchpin
linctus
  linctuses *pl*
line
  lined
  lining
lineage
lineal
lineament
linear
linearity
linen
linen draper
liner
linger
  lingered
  lingering
lingerie
lingo
  lingoes *pl*
lingua franca
  lingua francas *pl*
lingual
linguist
linguistic
liniment
link
linkage

links (golf)
linnet
lino
linocut
linoleum
linotype
linseed
lint
lintel
lion
lioness
  lionesses *pl*
lion-hearted
lionisation
lionise
  lionised
  lionising
lionization
lionize
  lionized
  lionizing
lip
lipped
lip-read
lip-reader
lip-reading
lipstick
liquefaction
liquefiable
liquefy
  liquefied
  liquefies
  liquefying

liquescent
liqueur (strong, sweet
  alcohol)
liquid
liquidate
  liquidated
  liquidating
liquidation
liquidator
liquidise
  liquidised
  liquidising
liquidity
liquidize
  liquidized
  liquidizing
liquor (liquid)
liquorice, licorice
lira (Italian money)
  lire, liras *pl*
lisle
lisp
lissom, lissome (agile)
list
listen
  listened
  listening
listener
listeria
lit (*from* light)
litany
  litanies *pl*
liter *Am*

literacy
literal (exact)
literally
literary (learned)
literate
literature
lithe
lithograph
lithography
litigant
litigate
  litigated
  litigating
litigation
litigious
litmus
litmus paper
litre (measure)
litter (rubbish)
  littered
  littering
little
littoral (near the sea)
liturgical
liturgy
  liturgies pl
live
  lived
  living
liveable
livelihood
liveliness
lively

livelier
liveliest
liven (to cheer up)
  livened
  livening
liver
liverish
livery (costume)
  liveries pl
livestock
livid
lizard
llama (animal)
load
loaf
  loaves pl
  loafed
  loafing
  loafs
loafer
loam
loamy
loan
  loaned
  loaning
loath, loth (unwilling)
loathe (to hate)
  loathed
  loathing
loathsome
lob
  lobbed
  lobbing

lobs
lobby
  lobbies pl
  lobbied
  lobbies
  lobbying
lobe (of the ear)
lobster
local (nearby)
locale (locality of
  events)
localisation
localise
  localised
  localising
locality
  localities pl
localization
localize
  localized
  localizing
locally
locate
  located
  locating
location
locative (grammar)
loch (lake)
lock (hair, in door,
  on canal)
locker
locket
lockjaw

lockout
  lockouts *pl*
locksmith
locomotion
locomotive
locum
  locums *pl*
locum tenens
  (substitute)
locus
  loci *pl*
locust
lode (of metal ore)
lodge
  lodged
  lodging
lodgement, lodgment
lodger
loft
loftily
loftiness
lofty
  loftier
  loftiest
log
  logged
  logging
  logs
loganberry
  loganberries *pl*
logarithm
logarithmic
logarithmically

log-book
loggerheads
loggia
  loggias *pl*
logic
logical
logically
logician
logistics
logo, logotype
loin
loiter
  loitered
  loitering
loiterer
loll
lollipop
lone
lonelier
loneliness
lonely
lonesome
long
longer
longevity
longitude
longitudinal
longitudinally
long-suffering
longways
longwise
loo (lavatory)
loofah

look
looker-on
  lookers-on *pl*
loom
  loomed
  looming
loop
  looped
  looping
loophole
loose
  loosed
  loosing
loose-leaf
loosely
loosen
  loosened
  loosening
looseness
loot (plunder)
looter
lop
  lopped
  lopping
  lops
lope (to run)
  loped
  loping
lopsided
loquacious
loquaciously
loquaciousness
loquacity

lord
Lord Mayor
lordship
lordly
lore (tradition)
lorgnette
lorry
 lorries *pl*
lose
 loses
 losing
 lost
loser
loss
lost
lot
loth, loath (unwilling)
Lothario
 Lotharios *pl*
lotion
lottery
 lotteries *pl*
lotus
 lotuses *pl*
loud
loudly
loud-mouthed
loudness
loudspeaker
lounge
 lounged
 lounging
lour

loured
 louring
louse
 lice *pl*
lousy
lout
loutish
louver *Am*
louvre
love
 loved
 loving
loveable, lovable
lovelier
loveliness
lovelorn
lovely
lover
low
 lowed
 lowing
lower
lower
 lowered
 lowering
lowliness
lowly
lowness
loyal
loyalism
loyalist
loyally
loyalty

loyalties *pl*
lozenge
lubricant
lubricate
 lubricated
 lubricating
lubrication
lucid
lucidity
lucidly
luck
luckily
lucky
 luckier
 luckiest
lucrative
lucratively
lucre
ludicrous
ludicrously
ludicrousness
luff
lug
 lugged
 lugging
 lugs
luggage
lugger
lugubrious
lugubriously
lukewarm
lull
lullaby

lullabies *pl*
lumbago
lumbar (part of the
  body)
lumber (timber;
  rubbish)
lumberjack
lumber-room
lumen
luminary
  luminaries *pl*
luminescence
luminescent
luminosity
luminous
lump
lumpiness
lumpy
  lumpier
  lumpiest
lunacy
  lunacies *pl*
lunar
lunatic
lunch
luncheon
lung
lunge
  lunged
  lunging
lungfish
lurch
lure

lured
luring
lurid
luridly
lurk
luscious
lusciousness
lush
lust
luster *Am*
lustful
lustily
lustiness
lustre
lustrous
lusty
  lustier
  lustiest
lute (musical
  instrument)
Lutheran
luxuriance
luxuriant
luxuriate
  luxuriated
  luxuriating
luxurious
luxuriously
luxury
  luxuries *pl*
lychee
Lycra
lying (*from* lie)

lymph
lymphatic
lynx
  lynxes *pl*
lyre (harp)
lyric
lyrical
lyrically
lyricism
lyrics

ma'am (Madame)
macabre
macadam
macadamise
  macadamised
  macadamising
macadamize
  macadamized
  macadamizing
macaroni
macaroon
macaw
mace
mace-bearer
macerate
  macerated
  macerating
maceration
Mach (speed ratio)

machiavellian
machination
machine
  machined
  machining
machinery
machinist
mackerel
mackintosh
macramé
macrobiotic
macrocosm
macroscopic
macula (spot on skin)
  maculae pl
mad
  madder
  maddest
madam

Madame
  Mesdames pl
madden
maddening
madder (plant or red
  dye)
madding
made (from make)
Madeira
Mademoiselle
  Mesdemoiselles pl
madly
madman
  madmen pl
madness
Madonna
madrigal
maelstrom
maestro
  maestros, maestri pl
Mafia
magazine
magenta
maggot
maggoty
magic
magical
magically
magician
magisterial
magisterially
magistracy
  magistracies pl

magistral
magistrate
magistrature
magnanimity
magnanimous
magnanimously
magnate (great man)
magnesia
magnesium
magnet
magnetic
magnetically
magnetisable
magnetisation
magnetise
  magnetised
  magnetising
magnetism
magnetizable
magnetization
magnetize
  magnetized
  magnetizing
magneto
  magnetos pl
magnification
magnificence
magnificent
magnificently
magnifier
magnify
  magnified
  magnifies

magnifying
magnitude
magnolia
  magnolias pl
magnum
  magnums pl
magnum opus
  magna opera pl
magpie
maharajah, maharaja
  maharajahs,
    maharajas pl
maharani, maharanee
  maharanis,
    maharanees pl
mah-jong
mahogany
maid
maiden
maidenly
mail (letters; armour)
mailbox
maim
  maimed
  maiming
main (principal)
mainly
maintain
  maintained
  maintaining
maintenance
maisonette
maitre d'hotel

maize (corn)
majestic
majestically
majesty
  majesties pl
majolica
major
major-domo
  major-domos pl
majority
  majorities pl
make
made
makes
making
make-up
maker
makeshift
makeweight
maladjusted
maladjustment
maladministration
maladroit
maladroitness
malady
  maladies pl
malaise
malapropism
malapropos
malaria
malcontent
male (masculine)
malediction

malefaction
malefactor
malevolence
malevolent
malformation
malfunction
malice
malice aforethought
malicious
maliciously
malign
  maligned
  maligning
malignancy
malignant (very bad)
maligner
malignity
malinger
  malingered
  malingering
malingerer
mall (shady walk)
mallard
malleability
malleable
mallet
mallow
malnutrition
malodorous
malpractice
malt
maltreat
  maltreated

  maltreating
maltreatment
mamma, mama
mammal
mammalian
mammary
mammogram
mammon
mammography
mammoth
man
  men pl
  manned
  manning
  mans
manacle
manage
  managed
  managing
manageable
management
manager
managerial
managing
mandarin
mandatary (person)
mandate
  mandated
  mandating
mandatory
  (compulsory)
mandible
mandolin (musical

  instrument)
mandoline (vegetable
  slicer)
mandrake
mandrel (part of lathe)
mandrill (baboon)
mane (of horse)
manège
maneuver Am
maneuverable Am
maneuverability Am
maneuvering Am
manful
manfully
manganese
mange
mangel-wurzel
manger
mangle
  mangled
  mangling
mango
  mangoes, mangos pl
mangrove
mangy
manhandle
  manhandled
  manhandling
manhole
manhood
mania
  manias pl
maniac

maniacal
manic
manicure
  manicured
  manicuring
manicurist
manifest
manifestation
manifesto
  manifestos,
    manifestoes *pl*
manifold
manikin (little
  man)
mankind
manliness
manly
manna (miraculous
  food)
mannequin (model)
manner
mannered
mannerism
mannerly
manoeuvrability
manoeuvrable
manoeuvre
  manoeuvred
  manoeuvring
manometer
manor (estate)
manorial
manse

mansion
manslaughter
mantel (shelf)
mantelpiece
mantle (cloak)
manual
manually
manufacture
  manufactured
  manufacturing
manufacturer
manure
manuscript
many
map
  mapped
  mapping
  maps
maple
mar
  marred
  marring
  mars
marathon
maraud
  marauded
  marauding
marauder
marble
marcasite
march
marcher
marchioness

Mardi Gras
mare (horse)
margarine
margin
marginal
marginally
marguerite
marigold
marijuana, marihuana
marina (harbour)
  marinas *pl*
marinade
  marinaded
  marinading
marinate
  marinated
  marinating
marine
mariner
marionette
marital
maritime
marjoram
mark
marked
markedly
marker
market
marketability
marketable
marketeer
marketing
marksman

marl
marlinspike,
  marlinespike
marmalade
marmoreal
marmoset
marmot
maroon
  marooned
  marooning
marquee (large tent)
marquetry
marquis, marquess
marriage
marriageable
marrow
marry
  married
  marries
  marrying
marsh
marshal
  marshalled
  marshalling
  marshals
  marshaled *Am*
  marshaling *Am*
marshmallow
marsupial
mart (market place)
marten (weasel)
martial
martially

Martian
martin (bird)
martinet
martyr
martyrdom
marvel
  marvelled
  marvelling
  marvels
  marveled *Am*
  marveling *Am*
marvellous
marvellously
marvelous *Am*
marvelously *Am*
Marxism
Marxist
marzipan
mascara
mascot
masculine
masculinity
mash
mask (face cover)
masochism
masochist
mason
masonic
masonry
masque
  (entertainment)
masquerade
  masqueraded

masquerading
mass
massacre
  massacred
  massacring
massage
  massaged
  massaging
masseur *m*
masseuse *f*
massif (mountain
  tops)
massive (very
  large)
massively
massiveness
mast
mastectomy
  mastectomies *pl*
master
  mastered
  mastering
masterful
masterfully
masterpiece
mastery
masthead
masticate
  masticated
  masticating
mastication
mastiff
  mastiffs *pl*

mastoid
masturbate
　masturbated
　masturbating
masturbation
mat (rug)
　mats
　matted
　matting
matador
match
matchless
matchmaker
mate
　mated
　mating
material
materialisation
materialise
　materialised
　materialising
materialism
materialist
materialization
materialize
　materialized
　materializing
materially
maternal
maternally
maternity
matey
math (mathematics)

Am
mathematical
mathematician
mathematics
maths
matinee
matins
matriarch
matriarchal
matriarchy
　matriarchies *pl*
matriculate
　matriculated
　matriculating
matriculation
matrimonial
matrimony
matrix
　matrices, matrixes *pl*
matron
matt (dull surface)
matter
　mattered
　mattering
matter-of-fact
mattock
mattress
maturation
mature
　matured
　maturing
　maturely
maturity

maudlin
maul
　mauled
　mauling
mausoleum
　mausoleums *pl*
mauve
maverick
mawkish
mawkishness
maxim
　maxims *pl*
maximal
maximisation
maximise
　maximised
　maximising
maximization
maximize
　maximized
　maximizing
maximum
　maximums,
　　maxima *pl*
may
May (month)
maybe
mayday (distress
　signal)
May Day (May 1st)
mayhem
mayn't (may not)
mayonnaise

mayor (council
  official)
mayoral
mayoralty
maypole
maze (tangle of paths)
mazurka
  mazurkas *pl*
mead
meadow
meager *Am*
meagerly *Am*
meagerness *Am*
meagre
meagrely
meagreness
meal
  mealier
  mealiest
mealtime
mealy
mealy-mouthed
mean (to signify;
  average; thrifty)
  meaning
  means
  meant
meander
  meandered
  meandering
meaningful
meaningfully
meaningless

meanly
meanness
means
means test
meant (*from* mean)
meantime
meanwhile
measles
measly
measurable
measurableness
measure
  measured
  measuring
measurement
meat (food)
meatless
mechanic
mechanical
mechanically
mechanician
mechanisation
mechanise
  mechanised
  mechanising
mechanism
mechanization
mechanize
  mechanized
  mechanizing
medal (*eg* for bravery)
medallion
medallist

medalist *Am*
meddle (to interfere)
  meddled
  meddling
meddler (person who
  meddles)
meddlesome
media (*eg* newspapers)
mediaeval, medieval
medial
medially
median
mediate
  mediated
  mediating
mediation
mediator
medic (doctor)
medical
medically
medicament
Medicare
medicate
  medicated
  medicating
medication
medicinal
medicinally
medicine
medieval, mediaeval
mediocre
mediocrity
  mediocrities *pl*

meditate
  meditated
  meditating
meditation
meditator
Mediterranean
medium (*eg* art)
  media *pl*
medium (spiritualist)
  mediums *pl*
medlar (fruit)
medley
  medleys *pl*
meek
meekly
meekness
meet (contact)
  meeting
  meets
  met
megahertz
megalith
megalithic
megalomania
megalomaniac
megaphone
megastar
megastore
megaton, megatonne
megavolt
megawatt
megohm
melancholia

melancholias *pl*
melancholic
melancholy
mélange
melanoma
  melanomas *pl*
melee *Am*
  melees *pl*
mêlée
  mêlées *pl*
meliorate
  meliorated
  meliorating
melioration
mellifluous
mellow
melodic
melodically
melodious
melodrama
  melodramas *pl*
melodramatic
melodramatically
melody
  melodies *pl*
melon
melt
member
membership
membrane
membranous,
  membraneous
memento

mementoes,
  mementos *pl*
memo
  memos *pl*
memoir
memorabilia
memorable
memorably
memorandum
  memoranda,
  memorandums *pl*
memorial
memorise
  memorised
  memorising
memorize
  memorized
  memorizing
memory
  memories *pl*
memsahib
men (*pl* of man)
menace
  menaced
  menacing
ménage
menagerie
mend
mendacious
mendaciously
mendacity
mendicant
mendicity

menhir
menial
menially
meningitis
menopausal
menopause
menstrual
menstruate
  menstruated
  menstruating
menstruation
mensuration
mental
mentality
mentally
menthol
mention
mentor (adviser)
menu
  menus *pl*
mercantile
mercenary
  mercenaries *pl*
mercerise
  mercerised
  mercerising
mercerize
  mercerized
  mercerizing
merchandise
merchant
merciful
mercifully

merciless
mercilessly
mercurial
mercury
mercy
  mercies *pl*
mere
merely
merest
meretricious
merge
  merged
  merging
merger
meridian
meridional
meringue
merit
  merited
  meriting
meritocracy
  meritocracies *pl*
meritorious
meritoriously
mermaid
merrier
merrily
merriment
merry
Mesdames (*pl* of
  Madame)
Mesdemoiselles (*pl* of
  Mademoiselle)

mesh
mesmerise
  mesmerised
  mesmerising
mesmerism
mesmerize
  mesmerized
  mesmerizing
mess
message
messenger
Messiah
Messianic
Messieurs (*pl* of
  Monsieur)
messily
messiness
Messrs (Messieurs)
messy
  messier
  messiest
met (*from* meet)
metabolic
metabolism
metal (*eg* silver)
metaled *Am*
metalled
metallic
metallurgical
metallurgist
metallurgy
metamorphose
  metamorphosed

metamorphosing
metamorphosis
  metamorphoses *pl*
metaphor
metaphorical
metaphorically
metaphysical
metaphysically
metaphysics
mete (to apportion)
  meted
  meting
meteor
meteoric
meteorically
meteorite
meteoroid
meteorological
meteorologist
meteorology
meter (to measure,
  eg gas)
  metered
  metering
meter (measurement)
  Am
methane
methedrine
method
methodical
methodically
methodology
methyl

methylated
meticulous
meticulously
meticulousness
metiér
metre (measure of
  length)
metric
metricate
  metricated
  metricating
metrication
metricise
  metricised
  metricising
metricize
  metricized
  metricizing
metronome
metropolis
metropolitan
mettle (temperament)
mews (stables)
mezza voce (softly)
mezzanine
mezzo forte
mezzo-soprano
  mezzo-sopranos *pl*
mezzotint
miaow, miaou
miasma
  miasmata, miasmas *pl*
miasmal

mica
mice (*pl* of mouse)
mickle, muckle (large
  amount)
microbe
microbial
microbiologist
microbiology
microcosm
microfiche
micrometer
microphone
microscope
microscopic
microscopy
microtome
microwave
micturition
midday
midden
middle
middleman
  middlemen *pl*
middleweight
middling
midge
midget
midi (skirt length)
midinette
midnight
midriff
midshipman
  midshipmen *pl*

midst
midsummer
midway
Midwest
Midwesterner
midwife
 midwives *pl*
midwifery
mien (appearance)
miffed
might
mightily
mightiness
mighty
 mightier
 mightiest
mignonette
migraine
migrant
migrate
 migrated
 migrating
migration
migrator
mikado
 mikados *pl*
mike
 miked
 miking
mil (millilitre)
milch-cow
mild
milder

mildew
mildewy
mildly
mildness
mile
mileage
milieu
 milieus, milieux *pl*
militancy
militant
militarily
militarisation
militarise
 militarised
 militarising
militarism
militarist
militarization
militarize
 militarized
 militarizing
military
militate
 militated
 militating
militia
 militias *pl*
milk
milker
milkiness
milkmaid
milksop
milky

milkier
milkiest
mill (grind)
mille-feuille
millennium
 millenniums,
  millennia *pl*
millipede
miller
millet
milliard
milligram,
 milligramme
milliliter *Am*
millilitre
millimeter *Am*
millimetre
milliner
millinery
million
millionaire
millionairess *f*
millionth
millipede
millivolt
milliwatt
millstone
mime
 mimed
 miming
mimic
 mimicked
 mimicking

mimics
mimicker
mimicry
mimosa
  mimosas *pl*
minaret
minatory
mince
  minced
  mincing
mincemeat
mincepie
mincer
mind (brain; to object)
minder
mindful
mindless
mine
  mined
  mining
miner (person who mines)
mineral
mineralogist
mineralogy
minestrone
mingle
  mingled
  mingling
mingy (stingy)
miniature
minibus

minicab
minim
minimal
minimally
minimise
  minimised
  minimising
minimize
  minimized
  minimizing
minimum
  minimums, minima *pl*
mining
minion
miniskirt
minister
  ministered
  ministering
ministerial
ministrant
ministration
ministry
  ministries *pl*
mink
minnow
minor (smaller; juvenile)
minority
  minorities *pl*
minstrel
mint
mint sauce

minuet
minus
  minuses *pl*
minuscule
minute
  minuted
  minuting
minutely
minuteness
minutes (notes of meeting)
minutiae
minx
miracle
miraculous
miraculously
mirage
mire
mirror
  mirrored
  mirroring
mirth
mirthful
miry
misadventure
misalliance
misanthrope
misanthropic
misanthropy
misapplication
misapply
  misapplied
  misapplies

misapplying
misapprehend
misapprehension
misappropriate
  misappropriated
  misappropriating
misappropriation
misbehave
  misbehaved
  misbehaving
misbehavior *Am*
misbehaviour
miscalculate
  miscalculated
  miscalculating
miscalculation
miscarriage
miscarry
  miscarried
  miscarries
  miscarrying
miscast
miscegenation
miscellaneous
miscellany
  miscellanies *pl*
mischance
mischief
mischievous
mischievously
miscible
misconceive
  misconceived

misconceiving
misconception
misconduct
misconstruction
misconstrue
  misconstrued
  misconstruing
miscount
miscreant
misdeed
misdemeanor *Am*
misdemeanour
mise en scène
  mises en scène *pl*
miser
miserable
miserably
miserliness
miserly
misery
  miseries *pl*
misfire
  misfired
  misfiring
misfit
misfortune
misgiving
misgovern
misgovernment
misguidance
misguide
  misguided
  misguiding

mishandle
  mishandled
  mishandling
mishap
mishmash
misinform
misinterpret
  misinterpreted
  misinterpreting
  misinterpretation
misjudge
  misjudged
  misjudging
misjudgement,
  misjudgment
mislay
  mislaid
  mislaying
  mislays
mislead
  misleading
  misleads
  misled
mismanage
  mismanaged
  mismanaging
mismanagement
mismatch
misnomer
misogynist
misogyny
misplace
  misplaced

misplacing
misplacement
misprint
mispronounce
  mispronounced
  mispronouncing
mispronunciation
misquotation
misquote
  misquoted
  misquoting
misread
  misreading
misrepresent
misrepresentation
misrule
miss
  misses *pl*
Miss
  Misses *pl*
missal (book of prayer)
misshapen
missile
missing
mission
missionary
  missionaries *pl*
Mississippi
missive
misspell
  misspelled
  misspelling
  misspells

misspelt
misspend
  misspending
  misspends
  misspent
misstate
  misstated
  misstating
misstatement
mist (fog)
mistake
  mistaken
  mistakes
  mistaking
  mistook
mistakenly
Mister, Mr
  Messrs *pl*
mistily
mistime
  mistimed
  mistiming
mistiness
mistletoe
mistral
mistranslate
  mistranslated
  mistranslating
mistranslation
mistress
mistrust
mistrustful
misty

mistier
mistiest
misunderstand
  misunderstanding
  misunderstands
  misunderstood
misuse
  misused
  misusing
mite (small insect)
miter *Am*
mitigate
  mitigated
  mitigating
mitigation
mitre
mitten
mix
  mixed
  mixing
mixer
mixture
mizen, mizzen (sail)
mnemonic
moan
  moaned
  moaning
moaner
moat (ditch)
moated
mob
  mobbed
  mobbing

mobs
mobile
mobilisation
mobilise
  mobilised
  mobilising
mobility
mobilization
mobilize
  mobilized
  mobilizing
moccasin
Mocha (coffee)
mock
mockery
mock-heroic
modal
mode
model
  modelled
  modelling
  models
  modeled *Am*
  modeling *Am*
moderate
  moderated
  moderating
moderately
moderation
moderator
modern
modernisation
modernise

  modernised
  modernising
modernism
modernity
modernization
modernize
  modernized
  modernizing
modest
modestly
modesty
modicum
modifiable
modification
modify
  modified
  modifies
  modifying
modish
modular
modulate
  modulated
  modulating
modulation
modulator
module (unit of
  measurement)
modulus
  moduli *pl*
modus operandi
  modi operandi *pl*
mogul
mohair

Mohammed,
  Muhammad
Mohammedan,
  Muhammadan
moiety
moist
moisten
  moistened
  moistening
moistness
moisture
moisturise
  moisturised
  moisturising
moisturize
  moisturized
  moisturizing
molar
molasses
mold *Am*
  molded
  molding
molder *Am*
  moldered
  moldering
moldiness *Am*
moldy *Am*
  moldier
  moldiest
mole
molecular
molecule
molehill

moleskin
molest
molestation
mollify
  mollified
  mollifies
  mollifying
mollusc
mollusk *Am*
mollycoddle
  mollycoddled
  mollycoddling
Molotov cocktail
molt *Am*
molten
molybdenum
moment
momentarily
momentary
momentous
momentum
monachal (like a
  monk)
monachism
monarch
monarchical
monarchy
  monarchies *pl*
monastery
  monasteries *pl*
monastic
monasticism
Monday

monetarism
monetarist
monetary
money
  moneys, monies *pl*
moneyless
Mongol
Mongolian
mongolism
mongoose
  mongooses *pl*
mongrel
monitor
  monitored
  monitoring
monk
monkey
  monkeys *pl*
monochromatic
monochrome
monocle
monogamist
monogamous
monogamy
monogram
monograph
monolith
monolithic
monologue
monomania
monomaniac
monoplane
monopolisation

monopolise
  monopolised
  monopolising
monopolist
monopolistic
monopolization
monopolize
  monopolized
  monopolizing
monopoly
  monopolies *pl*
monorail
monosyllabic
monosyllable
monotheism
monotonous
monotonously
monotony
monotype
monoxide
Monseigneur
Monsieur
  Messieurs *pl*
monsoon
monster
monstrosity
  monstrosities *pl*
monstrous
montage
month
monthly
monument
monumental

monumentally

moo
- moos *pl*
- mooed
- mooing
- moos

mooch

mood

moodily

moodiness

moody
- moodier
- moodiest

moon
- mooned
- mooning

moonless

moonlight

moonlighting

moonlit

moonshine

moor (to tether; heath)
- moored
- mooring

moorage

moose

moot (undecided)

moot point

mop (to wipe)
- mopped
- mopping
- mops

mope (to feel sad)
- moping
- moped

moped (motorbike)

moppet

moral

morale (state of mind)

moralise
- moralised
- moralising

morality

moralize
- moralized
- moralizing

morally

morass

moratorium
- moratoriums, moratoria *pl*

morbid

morbidity

morbidness

mordant

more (extra)

moreover

morganatic

morganatically

morgue

moribund

morn (morning)

morning

Morocco

moron

moronic

morose

morosely

moroseness

Morpheus

morphia

morphine

morphological

morphology
- morphologies *pl*

morris dancer

Moroccan

morrow

Morse (code)

morsel

mortal

mortality

mortally

mortar

mortar board

mortgage
- mortgaged
- mortgaging

mortgagee

mortgagor

mortification

mortify
- mortified
- mortifies
- mortifying

mortise, mortice

mortuary
- mortuaries *pl*

mosaic
Moslem, Muslim
mosque
mosquito
  mosquitoes *pl*
moss
mossy
  mossier
  mossiest
most
mostly
mote (speck)
motel
motet
moth
moth-eaten
mother
  mothered
  mothering
mother tongue
mother-in-law
  mothers-in-law *pl*
mothering
motherless
motherly
motif
  motifs *pl*
motion
motionless
motivate
  motivated
  motivating
motivation

motive
motley
motor
  motored
  motoring
motorboat
motorise
  motorised
  motorising
motorist
motorize
  motorized
  motorizing
motorway
  motorways *pl*
mottled
motto
  mottoes *pl*
moujik, muzhik
  (Russian peasant)
mould
  moulded
  moulding
moulder
  mouldered
  mouldering
mouldiness
mouldy
  mouldier
  mouldiest
moult
mound
mount

mountain
mountaineer
mountainous
mountebank
mourn (to grieve)
mourner
mournful
mournfully
mourning (for the
  dead)
mouse
  mice *pl*
mouser
moussaka
mousse (fruit cream)
moustache
mousy
mouth
mouthed
mouthful
  mouthfuls *pl*
mouthpiece
movable, moveable
move
  moved
  moving
movement
movie
mow
  mowed
  mowing
  mown
mower

Mr
Mrs
much
mucilage
mucilaginous
muck
muckle, mickle (large
  amount)
mucky
mucous (slimy)
mucus (phlegm)
mud
muddle
  muddled
  muddling
muddle-headed
muddler
muddy
  muddied
  muddies
  muddying
  muddier
  muddiest
mudslinging
muff
muffin
muffle
  muffled
  muffling
mufti
mug
  mugged
  mugging

  mugs
mugger
muggy
  muggier
  muggiest
mugwump
mulatto
  mulattos,
    mulattoes pl
mulberry
  mulberries pl
mulch
mulct
mule
muleteer
mulish
mulligatawny
mullion
multifarious
multiform
multilateral
multilaterally
multiple
multiplex
multiplication
multiplicity
multiplier
multiply
  multiplied
  multiplies
  multiplying
multiracial
multitude

multitudinous
mum (silent)
mumble
  mumbled
  mumbling
mumbo-jumbo
mummery
mummified
mummy
  mummies pl
munch
mundane
municipal
municipality
  municipalities pl
munificence
munificent
munition
mural
murder
  murdered
  murdering
murderer
murderess
murderous
murderously
murk
murkily
murkiness
murky
  murkier
  murkiest
murmur

murmured
murmuring
murrain
muscat
muscatel
muscle (body)
  muscled
  muscling
muscular
muse (to think)
  mused
  musing
museum
  museums *pl*
mush
mushroom
mushy
  mushier
  mushiest
music
musical
musically
musician
musk
musket
musketry
Muslim, Moslem
muslin
musquash
mussel (mollusc)
must
mustache *Am*
mustang

mustard
muster
  mustered
  mustering
mustn't (must not)
musty
mustiness
mutability
mutable
mutant
mutation
mute
mutely
mutilate
  mutilated
  mutilating
mutilation
mutilator
mutineer
mutinous
mutiny
  mutinies *pl*
  mutinied
  mutinies
  mutinying
mutter
  muttered
  muttering
mutton
mutual
mutually
Muzak
muzhik

muzzily
muzziness
muzzle
  muzzled
  muzzling
muzzy
my
mycelium
  mycelia *pl*
mycology
myelitis
myocarditis
myocardium
  myocardia *pl*
myopia
myopic
myriad
myrmidon
myrrh
myrtle
myself
mysterious
mysteriously
mystery
  mysteries *pl*
mystic
mystical
mysticism
mystification
mystify
  mystified
  mystifies
  mystifying

mystique
myth
mythical
mythological
mythologist
mythology
   mythologies *pl*
myxomatosis

nab
  nabbed
  nabbing
  nabs
nabob
nadir
nag
  nagged
  nagging
  nags
nagger
naiad
nail
naive
naiveté, naivety
naked
nakedly
nakedness
namby-pamby

name
  named
  naming
nameable
name-dropper
nameless
namely
namesake
nanny
  nannies *pl*
nap
  napped
  napping
  naps
napalm
nape (of neck)
naphtha
  naphthas *pl*
naphthalene

napkin
nappy
  nappies *pl*
narcissism
narcissus
  narcissus, narcissi,
    narcissuses *pl*
narcosis
narcotic
narrate
  narrated
  narrating
narration
narrative
narrator
narrow
narrower
narrowly
narrow-minded
narrowness
nasal
nasally
nascency
nascent
nastily
nastiness
nasturtium
  nasturtiums *pl*
nasty
  nastier
  nastiest
natal
natality

natation
nation
national
nationalisation
nationalise
  nationalised
  nationalising
nationalism
nationalist
nationalistic
nationality
  nationalities *pl*
nationalization
nationalize
  nationalized
  nationalizing
nationally
native
nativity
NATO, N.A.T.O.
natter
  nattered
  nattering
natterer
natty
  nattier
  nattiest
natural
naturalisation
naturalise
  naturalised
  naturalising
naturalism

naturalist
naturalistic
naturalization
naturalize
  naturalized
  naturalizing
naturally
nature
naught (nothing)
naughtily
naughtiness
naughty
  naughtier
  naughtiest
nausea
nauseate
  nauseated
  nauseating
nauseous
nautical
nautilus
  nautiluses, nautili *pl*
naval (of ships; navy)
nave (of church)
navel (umbilicus)
navigability
navigable
navigate
  navigated
  navigating
navigation
navigator
navvy (labourer)

navvies *pl*
navy (ships)
  navies *pl*
nay (no)
N.B. (nota bene)
né (born) *m*
neap (of the tide)
near
  neared
  nearing
nearby
nearer
nearly
nearness
near-sighted
neat
  neater
  neatest
neatly
neatness
nebula
  nebulae, nebulas *pl*
nebulosity
nebulous
necessarily
necessary
necessitate
  necessitated
  necessitating
necessitous
necessity
  necessities *pl*
neck

neckerchief
necklace
necktie
necromancy
necrosis
nectar
nectarine
née *f*
need (to require)
needful
needle
  needled
  needling
needless
needlessly
needlework
needy
  needier
  neediest
neep (turnip)
ne'er
ne'er-do-well
nefarious
nefariously
negate
  negated
  negating
negation
negative
negatively
neglect
neglectful
negligee, negligé

negligence
negligent
negligently
negligible
negligibly
negotiable
negotiate
  negotiated
  negotiating
negotiation
negotiator
Negress *f*
  Negresses *pl*
Negro
  Negroes *pl*
Negroid
neigh (horse's cry)
neighbor *Am*
neighborhood *Am*
neighboring *Am*
neighborliness *Am*
neighborly *Am*
neighbour
neighbourhood
neighbouring
neighbourliness
neighbourly
neighing
neither
Nemesis
neoclassical
neolithic
neologism

neology
neon
neophyte
nephew
nephritic
nephritis
nepotism
nerve
  nerved
  nerving
nerve-racking
nervous
nervously
nervousness
nervy
  nervier
  nerviest
nest
nestle
  nestled
  nestling
net
  nets
  netted
  netting
net, nett (weight
  or price)
nether (lower)
nettle
network
neural
neuralgia
neurasthenia

neurasthenic
neuritis
neurological
neurologist
neurology
neurosis
  neuroses *pl*
neurotic
neuter
  neutered
  neutering
neutral
neutralisation
neutralise
  neutralised
  neutralising
neutrality
neutralization
neutralize
  neutralized
  neutralizing
neutron
never
nevermore
nevertheless
new
newborn
newcomer
newel
newfangled
new-laid
newly
newness

news
newsagent
newspaper
newsworthy
newt
next
nib
nibble
  nibbled
  nibbling
nice
nicely
niceness
nicety
  niceties *pl*
niche
nick
nickel
nickname
  nicknamed
  nicknaming
nicotine
niece
niggard
niggardly
niggle
  niggled
  niggling
nigh
night (end of day)
nightclub
nightdress
nightdress

nightfall
nightingale
nightlife
nightlight
nightly
nightmare
nightmarish
night porter
night shift
night-time
night watchman
nihilism
nihilistic
nil
nimble
nimbler
nimbly
nimbus
  nimbi, nimbuses *pl*
nimby
  nimbys *pl*
nincompoop
nine
nineteen
nineteenth
ninetieth
ninety
  nineties *pl*
ninny
  ninnies *pl*
ninth
ninthly
nip

nipped
nipping
nips
nipper
nipple
nirvana
nisi
nit (insect)
niter *Am*
nit-picking
nitrate
nitre
nitric
nitrite
nitrogen
nitroglycerine,
  nitroglycerin
nitrous
nitty-gritty
no (negative)
  noes *pl*
nitwit
no one
nob
Nobel prize
nobility
noble
nobleman
  noblemen *pl*
nobler
noblesse oblige
nobly
nobody

nobodies *pl*
nocturnal
nocturnally
nocturne
nod
  nodded
  nodding
  nods
nodal
noddle (head)
node
nodular
nodule (lump)
Noel
noggin (mug)
nogging (brickwork)
nohow (by no means)
noise
noiseless
noiselessly
noisily
noisiness
noisome
noisy
  noisier
  noisiest
nom de plume
nomad
nomadic
nomenclature
nominal
nominally
nominate

nominated
nominating
nomination
nominative
  (grammar)
nominator
nominee
nonage
nonagenarian
nonce
nonce-work
nonchalance
nonchalant
nonchalantly
non-combatant
non-commissioned
non-committally
non compos mentis
non-conductor
nonconformist
non-contributory
non-cooperation
non-cooperative
nondescript
none
none the less,
  nonetheless
nonentity
  nonentities *pl*
non-essential
nonesuch, nonsuch
nonetheless
non-existent

nonflammable

nonpareil

nonplussed

nonsense

nonsensical

nonsensically

non sequitur
  non sequiturs *pl*

nonsuch, nonesuch

noodle

nook

noon

noose

norm

normal

normalisation

normalise
  normalised
  normalising

normality

normalization

normalize
  normalized
  normalizing

normally

north

northerly

northern

northward

northwards

nose
  nosed
  nosing

nosegay
  nosegays *pl*

nosey, nosy
  nosier
  nosiest

nosiness

nostalgia

nostalgic

nostril

nostrum
  nostrums *pl*

nosy, nosey
  nosier
  nosiest

notability
  notabilities *pl*

notable

notably

notary
  notaries *pl*

notation

notch

note
  noted
  noting

noteworthiness

noteworthy

nothing

notice
  noticed
  noticing

noticeable

noticeably

notifiable

notification

notify
  notified
  notifies
  notifying

notion

notional

notionally

notoriety

notorious

notoriously

notwithstanding

nougat

nought (zero)

noun

nourish

nourishment

nouveau riche
  nouveaux riches *pl*

nouvelle cuisine

novel

novelette

novelist

novelty
  novelties *pl*

novice

noviciate

now

nowadays

nowhere

nowise

noxious

nozzle
nuance
nubile
nubility
nuclear
nucleus
  nuclei *pl*
nude
nudge
  nudged
  nudging
nudism
nudist
nudity
nugatory
nugget
nuisance
null
nullification
nullify
  nullified
  nullifies
  nullifying
numb
number
  numbered
  numbering
numbness
numeral
numerator
numerical
numerically
numerous

numismatic
numismatist
numskull
nun
nuncio
  nuncios *pl*
nunnery
  nunneries *pl*
nuptial
nurse
  nursed
  nursing
nurseling
nursemaid
nursery
  nurseries *pl*
nurseryman
  nurserymen *pl*
nurture
  nurtured
  nurturing
nut
nutcracker
nutmeg
nutrient
nutriment
nutrition
nutritious
nutritive
nutty
  nuttier
  nuttiest
nuzzle

  nuzzled
  nuzzling
nylon
nymph
nymphomania
nymphomaniac

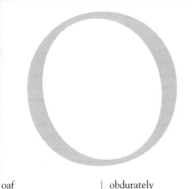

oaf
  oafs *pl*
oafish
oak
oaken
oakum
oar (of boat)
oasis
  oases *pl*
oast
oast house
oat
oath
oatmeal
obbligato
  obbligatos,
    obbligati *pl*
obduracy
obdurate

obdurately
obedience
obedient
obediently
obeisance
obelisk
obese
obesity
obey
  obeyed
  obeying
  obeys
obituary
  obituaries *pl*
object
objection
objectionable
objective
objectively

objectivity
objector
objet d'art
  objets d'art *pl*
oblation
obligation
obligatory
oblige
  obliged
  obliging
oblique
obliquely
obliquity
obliterate
  obliterated
  obliterating
obliteration
oblivion
oblivious
oblong
obloquy
  obloquies *pl*
obnoxious
obnoxiousness
oboe
  oboes *pl*
oboist
obscene
obscenely
obscenity
  obscenities *pl*
obscure
  obscured

obscuring
obscurely
obscurity
  obscurities *pl*
obsequious
obsequiously
obsequiousness
observable
observance
observant
observation
observatory
  observatories *pl*
observe
  observed
  observing
observer
obsess
obsessed
obsession
obsessive
obsolescence
obsolescent
obsolete
obstacle
obstetric
obstetrician
obstetrics
obstinacy
obstinate
obstinately
obstreperous
obstreperously

obstreperousness
obstruct
obstruction
obstructive
obstructively
obtain
  obtained
  obtaining
obtainable
obtrude
  obtruded
  obtruding
obtruder
obtrusion
obtrusive
obtuse
obtusely
obtuseness
obverse
obviate
  obviated
  obviating
obvious
obviously
occasion
occasional
occasionally
occident (west)
occidental
occlude
  occluded
  occluding
occlusion

occult
occultation
occupancy
occupant
occupation
occupational
occupier
occupy
  occupied
  occupies
  occupying
occur
  occurred
  occurring
  occurs
occurrence
ocean
oceanic
ocelot
ocher *Am*
ochre
o'clock
octagon
octagonal
octane
octave
octavo
  octavos *pl*
octet
October
octogenarian
octopus
  octopuses *pl*

octoroon
ocular
oculist
odd
odder
oddity
　oddities *pl*
oddly
oddment
odds
odds-on
ode
odious
odiously
odiousness
odium
odor *Am*
odoriferous
odorless *Am*
odorous
odour (smell)
odourless
oedema
　oedemas,
　　oedemata *pl*
oesophageal
oesophagus
off
offal
offence
offend
offender
offense *Am*

offensive
offensively
offensiveness
offer
　offered
　offering
offertory
offhand
offhanded
offhandedly
offhandedness
office
officer
official
officialese
officially
officiate
　officiated
　officiating
officious
officiously
officiousness
offing
off-licence
off-peak
offprint
offset
　offsets
　offsetting
offshoot
offside
offspring
oft

often
oftener
ogle
　ogled
　ogling
ogre
ogress
ohm
ohmic
ohmmeter
Ohm's Law
oil
　oiled
　oiling
oily
ointment
OK, O.K., okay
old
old maid
olden
older
old-fashioned
old-maidish
oleaginous
oleander
olfaction
olfactory
oligarch
oligarchy
　oligarchies *pl*
oligopoly
　oligopolies *pl*
olive

Olympia
Olympian
Olympic
ombudsman
omega
omelet *Am*
omelette
omen
omicron
ominous
ominously
omission
omit (leave out)
  omits
  omitted
  omitting
omnibus
  omnibuses *pl*
omnipotence
omniscience
omniscient
omnivorous
once
once-over
oncoming
one
oneness
onerous
onerousness
oneself
one-up
one-upmanship
ongoing

onion
on-line, online
onlooker
only
onomatopoeia
onomatopoeic
onrush
onset
onslaught
onus
onward, onwards
onyx
oolite
oolitic
ooze
  oozed
  oozing
opacity
opal
opalescence
opalescent
opaque
opaquely
opaqueness
open
  opened
  opening
open-and-shut
open-ended
opener
openly
openness
opera

operas *pl*
operability
operable
operate
  operated
  operating
operatic
operatically
operation
operational
operationally
operative
operator
operetta
  operettas *pl*
ophthalmia
ophthalmic
ophthalmologist
ophthalmology
opiate (drug)
opine
  opined
  opining
opinion
opinionated
opium
opossum
  opossums *pl*
opponent
opportune
opportunely
opportuneness
opportunism

pportunist
pportunity
 opportunities *pl*
ppose
 opposed
 opposing
pposer
pposite
pposition
ppress
ppression
ppressive
ppressively
ppressor
pprobrious
pprobrium
pt
ptative
ptic
ptical
ptically
ptician
ptimisation
ptimise
 optimised
 optimising
ptimism
ptimist
ptimistic
ptimistically
ptimization
ptimize
 optimized

optimizing
optimum
 optima, optimums *pl*
option
optional
optionally
opulence
opulent
opus
 opuses, opera *pl*
oracle
oracular
oral (by mouth)
orally
orange
orangeade
orang-utan,
 orang-utang
orate
 orated
 orating
oration
orator
oratorio (sacred
 opera)
 oratorios *pl*
oratory
 oratories *pl*
orb
orbit
 orbited
 orbiting
orbital

orchard
orchestra
 orchestras *pl*
orchestrate
 orchestrated
 orchestrating
orchestration
orchestrator
orchid
ordain
 ordained
 ordaining
ordeal
order
 ordered
 ordering
orderliness
orderly
ordinal
ordinance (decree)
ordinarily
ordinary
ordinate
ordination
ordnance (military
 stores)
Ordnance Survey
ordure
ore (mineral)
oregano
organ
organic
organically

organisation
organise
  organised
  organising
organiser
organism
organist
organization
organize
  organized
  organizing
organizer
orgasm
orgiastic
orgy
  orgies *pl*
oriel
orient
oriental
orientally
orientate
  orientated
  orientating
orientation
orifice
origami
origin
original
originality
originally
originate
  originated
  originating

originator
orison
ormolu
ornament
ornamental
ornamentation
ornate
ornately
ornithologist
ornithology
orotund
orphan
orphanage
orphaned
orrery
  orreries *pl*
orthodontics
orthodontist
orthodox
orthodoxy
  orthodoxies *pl*
orthographic
orthography
orthopaedic
orthopedic *Am*
ortolan
oscillate
  oscillated
  oscillating
oscillation
oscillator
oscillatory
oscillogram

oscillograph
oscilloscope
osculate
  osculated
  osculating
osculation
osier
osmosis
osprey
  ospreys *pl*
osseous
ossification
ossify
  ossified
  ossifies
  ossifying
ossuary
  ossuaries *pl*
ostensible
ostensibly
ostensive
ostensively
ostentation
ostentatious
ostentatiously
osteoarthritis
osteology
osteopath
osteopathic
osteopathy
ostler
ostracise
  ostracised

ostracising
ostracism
ostracize
  ostracized
  ostracizing
ostrich
  ostriches *pl*
other
otherwise
otiose
otitis
otter
ottoman
oubliette
ought
oughtn't (ought not)
ounce
our
ours
ourself
  ourselves *pl*
out
  outed
  outing
outage
outbid
  outbidding
  outbids
outboard
outbound
outbreak
outburst
outcast

outclass
outclassed
outcome
outcry
  outcries *pl*
outdo
  outdid
  outdoes
  outdoing
  outdone
outdoors
outer
outermost
outfit
outfitter
outfitting
outflank
outflanked
outgoing
outgrow
  outgrew
  outgrowing
  outgrown
  outgrows
outgrowth
outlandish
outlast
outlaw
outlawry
outlay
  outlays *pl*
outlet
outline

outlined
outlining
outlive
  outlived
  outliving
outlook
outlying
outmaneuver *Am*
  outmaneuvered
  outmaneuvering
outmanoeuvre
  outmanoeuvred
  outmanoeuvring
outmoded
outmost
outnumber
  outnumbered
  outnumbering
out-patient
outpost
outpouring
output
  outputs
  outputted
  outputting
outrage
  outraged
  outraging
outrageous
outrageously
outran (*from* outrun)
outreach
outrider

outrigger
outright
outrun
  outran
  outrunning
  outruns
outset
outshine
  outshines
  outshining
  outshone
outside
outsider
outsized
outskirts
outsourcing
outspoken
outspokenness
outstanding
outstation
outstay
  outstayed
  outstaying
  outstays
outstretched
outstrip
  outstripped
  outstripping
  outstrips
outvote
  outvoted
  outvoting
outward

outward-bound
outwardly
outweigh
outwit
  outwits
  outwitted
  outwitting
outworn
ova
oval
ovary
  ovaries *pl*
ovation
oven
over
overact
overall
overarm
overate (*from* to overeat)
overawe
  overawed
  overawing
overbalance
  overbalanced
  overbalancing
overbear
  overbearing
overboard
overburden
  overburdened
  overburdening
overcame (*from*

overcome)
overcast
overcharge
  overcharged
  overcharging
overcoat
overcome
  overcame
  overcomes
  overcoming
overconfident
overcrowded
overdo
  overdid
  overdoes
  overdoing
  overdone
overdose
  overdosed
  overdosing
overdraft
overdraw
  overdrawing
  overdrawn
  overdraws
  overdrew
overdress
  overdressed
overdrive
overdue
overeat
  overate
  overeaten

overeating
overeats
overflow
  overflowed
  overflowing
  overflown
  overflows
overground
overgrow
  overgrew
  overgrowing
  overgrown
  overgrows
overgrowth
overhand
  overhanding
overhaul
overhead
overhear
  overhears
  overhearing
  overheard
overheat
  overheated
  overheating
overhang
  overhanging
  overhangs
  overhung
over-indulgence
overjoyed
overland
overlap

overlapped
  overlapping
  overlaps
overlay
  overlaid
  overlaying
  overlays
overleaf
overload
  overloaded
  overloading
overlook
overnight
overpay
  overpaid
  overpaying
  overpays
overpopulated
overpower
  overpowered
  overpowering
overran (*from*
  overrun)
overrate
  overrated
  overrating
overreact
overreach
override
  overridden
  overrides
  overriding
  overrode

overripe
overrule
  overruled
  overruling
overrun
  overran
  overrunning
  overruns
overseas (abroad)
oversee (supervise)
  oversaw
  overseeing
  overseen
  oversees
overseer
over-sexed
overshadow
  overshadowed
overshoot
overshot
oversight
over-simplification
over-simplify
  over-simplified
  over-simplifies
  over-simplifying
oversleep
  oversleeping
  oversleeps
  overslept
overspend
  overspending
  overspends

overspent
overstate
  overstated
  overstating
overstatement
overstay
  overstayed
  overstaying
  overstays
overstep
  overstepped
  overstepping
  oversteps
oversubscribed
overt
overtake
  overtakes
  overtaking
  overtook
overtax
overtaxing
over-the-counter
overthrow
  overthrew
  overthrowing
  overthrown
  overthrows
overtime
overtired
overtly
overtone
overtook (*from*
  overtake)

overture
overturn
overweening
overweight
overwhelm
overwork
overwrought
oviduct
oviparous
ovoid
ovulate
  ovulated
  ovulating
ovulation
ovum (egg cell)
  ova *pl*
owe
  owed
  owing
owl
own
  owned
  owning
owner
ox
  oxen *pl*
oxalic
oxalic acid
oxide
oxidisation
oxidise
  oxidised
  oxidising

oxidization
oxidize
  oxidized
  oxidizing
oxtail
oxtongue
oxyacetylene
oxygen
oxygenate
  oxygenated
  oxygenating
oxygenation
oxymoron
  oxymorons *pl*
oyster
ozone

pace
  paced
  pacing
pachyderm
pachydermatous
pacifiable
Pacific
pacific (peaceful)
pacifically
pacification
pacifier
pacifism
pacifist
pacify
  pacified
  pacifies
  pacifying
pack
package

packaged
  packaging
packed
packet (parcel)
packhorse
pact (treaty)
pad
  padded
  padding
  pads
paddle
  paddled
  paddling
paddler
paddock
padlock
padlocked
padre
paean

paediatrician
paediatrics
paedophile
pagan
paganism
page
  paged
  paging
pageant
pageantry
  pageantries pl
pagination
pagoda
  pagodas pl
paid (from pay)
paid-up
pail (bucket)
paillasse
pain (discomfort)
pained
painful
painfully
painless
painlessly
painstaking
paint
painter
pair (couple)
  paired
  pairing
paisley
pal (friend)
palace

palaeographic
palaeography
Palaeolithic
palaeontology
Palaeozoic
palatable (tasting
    good)
palate (of mouth)
palatial
palaver
    palavered
    palavering
pale (whitish; stake
    or post)
    paled
    paling
palely
paleness
paleographic Am
paleography
Paleolithic Am
palette (artist's)
palindrome
palisade
pall
palladium
pall-bearer
palled
pallet (tool; mattress)
palliasse
palliate
    palliated
    palliating

palliation
palliative
pallid (pale)
palling
pallor
pally
palpitation
palm
palmist
palmistry
palomino
    palominos pl
palpable
palpably
palpate
    palpated
    palpating
palpation
palpitate
    palpitated
    palpitating
palsied
palsy
paltriness
paltry
    paltrier
    paltriest
pamper
    pampered
    pampering
pamphlet
pamphleteer
pan

panned
panning
pans
Pan (god of nature)
panacea
panache
pancake
panchromatic
pancreas
panda (animal)
    pandas pl
pandemic
pandemonium
pander (to indulge)
    pandered
    pandering
pane (glass)
panegyric
panel
    panelled
    panelling
    panels
    paneled Am
    paneling Am
panelist Am
panellist
pang
panic
    panicked
    panicking
    panics
panicky
panic-stricken

pannier
panoply
  panoplies *pl*
panorama
  panoramas *pl*
panoramic
panoramically
pansy
  pansies *pl*
pant
pantaloon
pantechnicon
pantheism
pantheistic
Pantheon
panther
pantile
pantomime
pantry
  pantries *pl*
pants
papacy
  papacies *pl*
papal
paparazzi
paper
  papered
  papering
paperback
paperclip
paperweight
papier mâché
papist

papistry
paprika
papyrus
  papyri *pl*
par
parable
parabola
  parabolas *pl*
parabolic
parabolically
parachute
  parachuted
  parachuting
parachutist
parade
  paraded
  parading
paradise
paradox
  paradoxes *pl*
paradoxical
paradoxically
paraffin
paragliding
paragon
paragraph
parakeet
parallax
parallel
  paralleled,
    parallelled
  paralleling,
    parallelling

  parallels
parallelepiped
parallelism
parallelogram
paralyse
  paralysed
  paralysing
paralysis
paralytic
paralyze *Am*
  paralyzed
  paralyzing
parameter
paramilitary
  paramilitaries *pl*
paramount
paramour
paranoia
paranoiac
paranoid
parapet
paraphernalia
paraphrase
  paraphrased
  paraphrasing
paraplegia
paraplegic
parasite
parasitic
parasol
paratrooper
paratroops
paratyphoid

parboil
  parboiled
  parboiling
parcel
  parcelled
  parcelling
  parcels
  parceled *Am*
  parceling *Am*
parched
parchment
pardon
  pardoned
  pardoning
pardonable
pare (to cut)
  pared
  paring
paregoric
parent
parentage
parental
parentally
parenthesis
  parentheses *pl*
parenthetic
par excellence
pariah
parish
parishioner
Parisian *m*
Parisienne *f*
parity

  parities *pl*
park
parka
  parkas *pl*
parlance
parley
  parleyed
  parleying
  parleys
parliament
parliamentarian
parliamentary
parlor *Am*
parlour
parlous
Parmesan
parochial
parochialism
parochially
parodist
parody
  parodies *pl*
  parodied
  parodies
  parodying
parole
paroxysm
paroxysmal
parquet
parquetry
parricidal
parricide
parrot

parry
  parried
  parries
  parrying
parse
  parsed
  parsing
parsimonious
parsimony
parsley
parsnip
parson
parsonage
part
partake
  partaken
  partaking
  partook
partaker
parterre
parthenogenesis
parthenogenetic
parthenogenetically
Parthenon
partial
partiality
partially
participant
participate
  participated
  participating
participation
participator

participial
participle
particle
particular
particularise
  particularised
  particularising
particularity
  particularities *pl*
particularize
  particularized
  particularizing
particularly
partisan
partition
  partitioned
  partitioning
partly
partner
  partnered
  partnering
partnership
partook
partridge
part-time
parturient
parturition
party
  parties *pl*
  partied
  parties
  partying
parvenu

parvenus *pl*
parvenue *f*
  parvenues *pl*
paschal (of Easter)
pass
passable
passably
passage
passé
passed
passenger
passer-by
  passers-by *pl*
passim
passion
passionate
passionately
passive
passively
passiveness
passivity
passport
password
past
pasta
paste
  pasted
  pasting
pasteboard
pastel (picture)
pasteurisation
pasteurise
  pasteurised

pasteurising
pasteurization
pasteurize
  pasteurized
  pasteurizing
pastille (lozenge)
pastime
pastor (minister)
pastoral
pastorate
pastry
  pastries *pl*
pasturage
pasture (grazing land)
pasty (pie; paste-like)
  pasties *pl*
pat
  pats
  patted
  patting
patch
patched
patchwork
patchy
pate (head)
pâté
pâté de foie gras
patent
patentable
patentee
patently
paterfamilias
paternal

paternalistic
paternally
paternity
paternoster
path
pathetic
pathetically
pathless
pathogenic
pathological
pathologically
pathologist
pathology
pathos
pathway
patience
patient
patiently
patina
  patinas *pl*
patio
  patios *pl*
patisserie
  patisseries *pl*
patois
patriarch
patriarchal
patriarchy
  patriarchies *pl*
patrician
patricide
patrimonial
patrimony

patrimonies *pl*
patriot
patriotic
patriotically
patriotism
patrol
  patrolled
  patrolling
  patrols
patron
patronage
patroness
patronise
  patronised
  patronising
patroniser
patronize
  patronized
  patronizing
patronizer
patronymic
patten (kind of shoe)
patter
  pattered
  pattering
pattern (design)
patterned
patty
  patties *pl*
paucity
paunch
paunchy
pauper

pauperism
pause
  paused
  pausing
pave
  paved
  paving
pavement
pavilion
pavior, paviour
pavlova
  pavlovas *pl*
paw (animal's foot)
  pawed
  pawing
pawn
pawnbroker
pay
  paid
  paying
  pays
payable
payee
payer
paymaster
payment
pay-off
payphone
payroll
pea
  peas *pl*
peace
peaceable

peaceably
peaceful
peacefully
peacefulness
peach
peacock
peahen
peak
  peaked
  peaking
peak-load
peaky
peal (of bells)
  pealed
  pealing
peanut
pear (fruit)
pearl
pearly
  pearlies pl
peasant
peasantry
peasepudding
peat
pebble
pebbly
peccadillo
  peccadilloes,
    peccadillos pl
peccant (sinning)
peck
peckish
pectoral

peculation
peculator
peculiar
peculiarity
  peculiarities pl
peculiarly
pecuniary
pedagogue (teacher)
pedagogy
pedal (of bicycle)
  pedalled
  pedalling
  pedals
  pedaled Am
  pedaling Am
pedant
pedantic
pedantry
peddle (to sell trifles)
  peddled
  peddling
peddler
pedestal
pedestrian
pediatrician Am
pediatrics Am
pedicure
pedigree
pediment
pedlar (hawker)
pedometer
peek (to peep)
  peeked

peeking
peel (to remove skin)
  peeled
  peeling
peep
  peeped
  peeping
peer (look)
  peered
  peering
peerage
peeress
peerless
peeved
peevish
peevishness
peewit, pewit
peg
  pegged
  pegging
  pegs
pejorative
pejoratively
Pekinese
pelagic
pelican
pellet
pell-mell
pellucid (clear)
pelmet
pelt
pelvic
pelvis

pen
  penned
  penning
  pens
penal
penalisation
penalise
  penalised
  penalising
penalization
penalize
  penalized
  penalizing
penalty
  penalties *pl*
penance
pence
penchant
pencil
  pencilled
  pencilling
  pencils
  penciled *Am*
  penciling *Am*
pendant (hanging
  jewel)
pendent (hanging)
pending
pendulous (drooping)
pendulum
  pendulums *pl*
penetrability
penetrable

penetrate
  penetrated
  penetrating
penetration
penetrative
penfriend
penguin
penicillin
peninsula
  peninsulas *pl*
peninsular (of a
  peninsula)
penis
  penises *pl*
penitence
penitent
penitential
penitentiary
  penitentiaries *pl*
penknife
  penknives *pl*
pennant
penniless
pennilessness
pennon
penny
  pennies, pence *pl*
penology
pension
pensionable
pensioner
pensive
pensively

pensiveness
pentagon
pentagonal
pentameter
Pentateuch
pentathlon
penultimate
penultimately
penumbra
  penumbrae,
    penumbras *pl*
penurious
penury
peon
peony (plant)
  peonies *pl*
people
  peopled
  peopling
pep
  pepped
  pepping
  peps
pepper
  peppered
  peppering
peppercorn
peppermint
peppery
pepsin
peptic
Pepys
Pepysian

peradventure
perambulate
  perambulated
  perambulating
perambulation
perambulator
per annum
per capita
perceivable
perceive
  perceived
  perceiving
per cent
percentage
perceptible
perceptibly
perception
perceptive
perch
perchance
percipience
percipient
percolate
  percolated
  percolating
percolation
percolator
percuss
percussion
percussive
perdition
peregrinate
  peregrinated

peregrinating
peregrination
peregrine
peremptorily
peremptoriness
peremptory
perennial
perennially
perfect
perfection
perfectionist
perfidious
perfidy
perforate
  perforated
  perforating
perforation
perforator
perforce
perform
performance
performer
perfume
  perfumed
  perfuming
perfumery
  perfumeries *pl*
perfunctorily
perfunctoriness
perfunctory
pergola
  pergolas *pl*
perhaps

pericardial
pericardium
  pericardia *pl*
peril
perilous
perilously
perimeter
period
periodic
periodical
periodically
periodicity
peripatetic
peripheral
periphery
periphrasis
periscope
perish
perishable
peritoneum
  peritonea,
    peritoneums *pl*
peritonitis
periwinkle
perjure
  perjured
  perjuring
perjurer
perjurious
perjury
perk
perkiness
perky

perm
permafrost
permalloy
permanence
permanency
permanent
permanently
permanganate
permeability
permeable
permeate
  permeated
  permeating
permeation
permissible
permission
permissive
permissiveness
permit
  permits
  permitted
  permitting
permutation
pernicious
perniciously
perniciousness
pernickety
perorate
  perorated
  perorating
peroration
peroxide
perpendicular

perpendicularity
perpendicularly
perpetrate
  perpetrated
  perpetrating
perpetrator
perpetual
perpetually
perpetuate
  perpetuated
  perpetuating
perpetuity
perplex
perplexity
perquisite
per se
persecute
  persecuted
  persecuting
persecution
persecutor
perseverance
persevere
  persevered
  persevering
persiflage
persimmon
persist
persistence
persistency
persistent
persistently
person

persona grata
persona non grata
personable
personage
personal
personality
  personalities *pl*
personally
personate
  personated
  personating
personation
personator
personification
personify
  personified
  personifies
  personifying
personnel (staff)
perspective
perspicacious
perspicacity
perspicuity
perspicuous
perspiration
perspire
  perspired
  perspiring
persuadable
persuade
  persuaded
  persuading
persuader

persuasion
persuasive
persuasively
pert
pertain
pertinacious
pertinaciously
pertinacity
pertinence
pertinent
pertly
pertness
perturb
perturbation
peruke
perusal
peruse
  perused
  perusing
pervade
  pervaded
  pervading
pervasion
pervasive
pervasively
perverse
perversely
perversion
perversity
pervert
perverter
perverted
pervious

peseta (Spanish money)
peso (S. American money)
pessary
  pessaries *pl*
pessimism
pessimist
pessimistic
pessimistically
pest
pester
  pestered
  pestering
pesterer
pesticide
pestiferous
pestilence
pestilent
pestilential
pestle
pet
  pets
  petted
  petting
petal
petaled *Am*
petalled
petard
peter
  petered
  petering
petite

petit four
  petit fours *pl*
petition
petitioner
petit mal
petit point
petrel (sea bird)
petrification
petrify
  petrified
  petrifies
  petrifying
petrol
petroleum
petticoat
pettifog
  pettifogged
  pettifogging
  pettifogs
pettifogger
pettifoggery
pettily
pettiness
pettish
petty
  pettier
  pettiest
petulance
petulant
petulantly
pew
pewit, peewit
pewter

pfennig (German
  money)
phagocyte
phalanx
  phalanges,
    phalanxes *pl*
phallic
phallus
  phalluses *pl*
phantasm
phantasmagoria
phantasmal
phantasmic
phantom
pharisaic
Pharisee
pharmaceutical
pharmacist
pharmacologist
pharmacology
pharmacopoeia
pharmacy
  pharmacies *pl*
pharyngeal
pharyngitis
pharynx
  pharynxes *pl*
phase
  phased
  phasing
pheasant
phenacetin
phenobarbital

phenobarbitone
phenol (type of
  benzene)
phenomenal
phenomenally
phenomenon
  phenomena *pl*
phenyl (formed from
  benzene)
phial, vial
philander
philanderer
philanthropic
philanthropically
philanthropist
philanthropy
philatelist
philately
philharmonic
philistine
philistinism
philologist
philology
philosopher
philosophical
philosophically
philosophy
  philosophies *pl*
philter *Am*
philtre (love potion)
phlebitis
phlegm
phlegmatic

phlegmatically
phlox
phobia
  phobias *pl*
phoenix
  phoenixes *pl*
phone (telephone)
  phoned
  phoning
phonetic
phonetically
phoney (sham)
  phoneys *pl*
phonograph
phosgene
phosphate
phosphorescence
phosphorescent
phosphoric
phosphorus
photocopier
photocopy
  photocopies *pl*
  photocopied
  photocopies
  photocopying
photogenic
photograph
photographer
photography
photometer
photometric
photometry

photostat
photosynthesis
phrase
  phrased
  phrasing
phraseology
phrenetic, frenetic
phrenologist
phrenology
phthisical
phthisis
phylactery
  phylacteries *pl*
phylloxera
phylum
  phyla *pl*
physical
physically
physician
physicist
physics
physiognomist
physiognomy
physiological
physiologically
physiologist
physiotherapist
physiotherapy
physique
pianissimo
pianist
piano
  pianos *pl*

pianoforte
pianola
  pianolas *pl*
piaster *Am*
piastre (Turkish
  money)
piazza
  piazzas *pl*
picador
picaresque
Piccadilly
piccalilli
  piccalillis *pl*
piccolo
  piccolos *pl*
pick
pick-a-back,
  piggyback
pickax *Am*
pickaxe
picker
picket
  picketed
  picketing
pickle
  pickled
  pickling
pickpocket
  pickpocketed
  pickpocketing
picnic
  picnicked
  picnicking

  picnics
picnicker
picric
pictorial
pictorially
picture
  pictured
  picturing
picturesque
picturesquely
picturesqueness
piddle
  piddled
  piddling
pidgin English
pie
piebald
piece
  pieced
  piecing
pièce de résistance
piecemeal
piece-work
piecing
pied-à-terre
pier (on coast)
pierce
  pierced
  piercing
pier-head
pierrette
pierrot
pietism

pietist
piety
piezoelectric
piezoelectricity
piffle
piffling
pig
pigeon
pigeon-hole
  pigeon-holed
  pigeon-holing
pigeon-toed
piggery
  piggeries *pl*
piggish
piggyback,
   pick-a-back
pigheaded
pigheadedness
pig-iron
piglet
pigment
pigmentation
pigsty
  pigsties *pl*
pike
pikestaff
pilaff, pilaf
pilchard
pile
  piled
  piling
pile-up

pilfer
  pilfered
  pilfering
pilferage
pilferer
pilgrim
pilgrimage
pill
pillage
  pillaged
  pillaging
pillager
pillar
pillar box
  pillar boxes *pl*
pillion
pillory
  pilloried
  pillories
  pillorying
pillow
pilot
  piloted
  piloting
pilotage
pimpernel
pimple
pimply
pin
  pinned
  pinning
  pins
pinafore

pince-nez
pincers
pinch
pinched
pinch-hit
  pinch-hits
  pinch-hitting
pinch-hitter
pincushion
pine
  pined
  pining
pineapple
ping-pong
pinhead
pinion
  pinioned
  pinioning
pin-up
  pin-ups *pl*
pink
pinnace
pinnacle
pinpoint
pinstripe
pint
pioneer
  pioneered
  pioneering
pious
piously
pip
  pipped

pipping
pips
pipe
 piped
 piping
piper
pipette
pippin
pipsqueak
piquancy
piquant
pique
 piqued
 piquing
piquet (card game)
piracy
pirate
piratical
pirating
pirouette
 pirouetted
 pirouetting
piscatorial
piscina (fish pond)
piscine (bathing pool)
pistachio
 pistachios pl
pistil (of flower)
pistol (firearm)
piston
pit
 pits
 pitted

 pitting
pitch
pitcher (jug)
piteous
piteously
pitfall
pith
pithily
pithiness
pithy
pitiable
pitiful
pitifully pitiless
pitilessly
pittance
pituitary
pity
 pities pl
 pitied
 pities
 pitying
pivot
 pivoted
 pivoting
pivotal
pixy, pixie
 pixies pl
pizza
 pizzas pl
pizzeria
 pizzerias pl
pizzicato
 pizzicatos pl

placability
placable
placard
placate
 placated
 placating
placation
place
 placed
 placing
placebo
 placebos pl
placement
placenta
 placentas pl
placid
placidity
placidly
placket
plagiarise
 plagiarised
 plagiarising
plagiarism
plagiarist
plagiarize
 plagiarized
 plagiarizing
plague
 plagued
 plaguing
plaice (fish)
plaid
plain

plainclothes
plainer
plainly
plainness
plainsong
plain-spoken
plaint
plaintiff (prosecutor)
plaintive (sad)
plaintively
plaintiveness
plait (of hair)
  plan
  planned
  planning
  plans
planchette
plane
  planed
  planing
planet
planetarium
  planetaria,
    planetariums pl
planetary
plank
plankton
planner
plant
plantain
plantation
planter
plaque

plasma
plaster
  plastered
  plastering
plasterer
plastic
plastically
plasticine
plasticity
plate
  plated
  plating
plateau
  plateaus, plateaux pl
plateful
  platefuls pl
plate-glass
platform
platinum
platitude
platitudinous
platonic
platonically
platoon
platter
platypus
  platypuses pl
plaudit
plausibility
plausible
plausibly
play
  played

playing
play-off
player
playfellow
playful
playfully
playfulness
playgoer
playgoing
playmate
playwright
plaza
  plazas pl
plea
  pleas pl
plead
pleader
pleasant
pleasantly
pleasantness
pleasantry (joke)
  pleasantries pl
please
  pleased
  pleasing
pleasurable
pleasurably
pleasure
  pleasured
  pleasuring
pleat
plebeian
plebiscite

pledge
  pledged
  pledging
Pleistocene
plenary
  plenaries *pl*
plenipotentiary
  plenipotentiaries *pl*
plenitude
plenteous
plenteously
plentiful
plentifully
plentifulness
plenty
plethora
plethoric
pleura
pleural
pleurisy
pliability
pliable
pliancy
pliant
plied (*from* ply)
pliers
plies
plight
Plimsoll line
plimsoll
plinth
Pliocene
plod

plodded
plodding
plods
plodder
plonk
plop
  plopped
  plopping
  plops
plot
  plots
  plotted
  plotting
plotter
plough
  ploughed
  ploughing
plover
plow *Am*
pluck
pluckily
plucky
  pluckier
  pluckiest
plug
  plugged
  plugging
  plugs
plum
plumage
plumb (to measure
  depth)
plumbago

  plumbagos *pl*
plumber
plumbing
plume
plummet
  plummeted
  plummeting
plummy
plummet
plump
plumper
plumpness
plum pudding
plunder
  plundered
  plundering
plunge
  plunged
  plunging
plunger
pluperfect
plural
pluralism
plurality
plus
  pluses *pl*
plush
plutocracy
  plutocracies *pl*
plutocrat
plutocratic
plutonium
ply

plied

plies

plying

plywood

pneumatic

pneumonia

poach

poached

poaches

poaching

poacher

pock

pocket

pocketed

pocketing

pocket book

pockmarked

pockmark

pod

podge

podgy

podium

podia, podiums *pl*

poem

poesy

poet

poetic

poetical

poetically

poetry

pogrom

poignancy

poignant

poignantly

poinsettia

poinsettias *pl*

point

point-blank

pointed

pointedly

pointless

pointlessly

poise

poised

poison

poisoned

poisoning

poisoner

poisonous

poke

poked

poking

poker

poky

polar

polarisation

polarise

polarised

polarising

polarity

polarization

polarize

polarized

polarizing

pole

polemic

polemical

polemically

police

policed

policing

policeman

policemen *pl*

policewoman

policewomen *pl*

policy

policies *pl*

poliomyelitis

polish

polite

politely

politeness

politer

politic

political

politically

politician

polity

polka

polkas *pl*

poll

pollard

pollen

pollinate

pollinated

pollinating

pollination

pollinator

pollster

pollutant
pollute
  polluted
  polluting
pollution
polo
polonaise
polonium
polony
  polonies *pl*
poltergeist
poltroon
polyandrous
polyandry
polyanthus
polychromatic
polychrome
polyester
polygamist
polygamous
polygamously
polygamy
polyglot
polygon
polymer
polymerisation
polymerise
  polymerised
  polymerising
polymerization
polymerize
  polymerized
  polymerizing

polyp
polyphonic
polyphony
polypus
  polypi *pl*
polystyrene
polysyllabic
polytechnic
polythene
polyunsaturated
pomade
pomatum
  pomatumed
  pomatuming
pomegranate
pommel (of saddle)
pomp
Pompeian
Pompeii
pomposity
pompous
pompously
poncho
  ponchos *pl*
pond (to consider)
ponder
  pondered
  pondering
ponderous
poniard
pontiff
  pontiffs *pl*
pontifical

pontificate
  pontificated
  pontificating
pontification
pontoon
pony
  ponies *pl*
ponytail
poodle
pooh-pooh
  pooh-poohed
  pooh-poohing
pool
  pooled
  pooling
poop
  pooped
  pooping
pooper scooper
poor (lacking wealth)
poorly
poorness
pop
  popped
  popping
  pops
popcorn
pope
popery
pop-eyed
poplar (tree)
poplin
poppers

poppet
poppy
  poppies *pl*
populace
popular
popularisation
popularise
  popularised
  popularising
popularity
popularization
popularize
  popularized
  popularizing
popularly
populate
  populated
  populating
population
populous
porcelain
porch
porcupine
pore (of skin; to look,
    think intently)
  pored
  poring
pork
porker
pornographer
pornographic
pornographically
pornography

porosity
porous
porphyry
porpoise
porridge
porringer
port
portability
portable
portal
portcullis
portend
portent
portentous
porter
porterage
portfolio
  portfolios *pl*
porthole
portico
  porticoes, porticos *pl*
portion
portlier
portliness
portly
portmanteau
  portmanteaus,
    portmanteaux *pl*
portrait
portraiture
portray
  portrayed
  portraying

portrayal
Portugal
Portuguese
pose
  posed
  posing
poser
posh
position
  positioned
  positioning
positive
positively
positivism
positivist
positron
posse
possess
possession
possessive
possessively
possessiveness
possessor
possibility
  possibilities *pl*
possible
possibly
post
postage
postal order
post-date
  post-dated
  post-dating

poste restante
poster
posterior
posterity
postgraduate
post-haste
posthumous
posthumously
post-impressionism
post-impressionist
postman
  postmen *pl*
postmark
postmaster
post-mortem
post-natal
post office
post-paid
postpone
  postponed
  postponing
postponement
postscript
postulant
postulate
  postulated
  postulating
postulation
postural
posture
  postured
  posturing
posturer

postwoman
  postwomen *pl*
posy
  posies *pl*
pot
  pots
  potted
  potting
potable
potash
potassium
potation
potato
  potatoes *pl*
pot-bellied
pot-belly
  pot-bellies *pl*
pot-boiler
potency
potent
potentate
potential
potentiality
potentially
potentiometer
potently
pother
pothole
  potholed
  potholing
potholer
potion
pot-pourri

pottage
potter
  pottered
  pottering
potterer
pottery
  potteries *pl*
pottily
potty (crazy)
  pottier
  pottiest
pouch
pouffe, pouf (cushion)
poulterer
poultice
poultry
pounce
  pounced
  pouncing
pound
poundage
poundal
pour (liquid)
  poured
  pouring
pourboire
pout
  pouted
  pouting
pouter
poverty
powder
  powdered

powdering
powdery
power
  powered
  powering
powerful
powerfully
powerless
powerlessness
powwow
pox
practicability
practicable
practical
practicality
  practicalities *pl*
practically
practice
  practiced *Am*
  practicing *Am*
practise (*eg* piano)
  practised
  practising
practitioner
pragmatic
pragmatical
pragmatically
pragmatism
prairie
praise
  praised
  praising
praiseworthy

praline
pram
prance
  pranced
  prancing
prank
prate
  prated
  prating
prattle
  prattled
  prattling
prattler
prawn
pray (to say prayers)
  prayed
  praying
prayer
preach
preacher
preamble
prearrange
  prearranged
  prearranging
prearrangement
prebend
prebendary
  prebendaries *pl*
precarious
precariously
precariousness
precatory
precaution

precautionary
precede (to go before)
  preceded
  preceding
precedence
precedent
precentor
precept
precession
precinct
precious
precipice
precipitant
precipitate
  precipitated
  precipitating
precipitately
precipitation
precipitous
precipitously
précis
precise
precisely
precision
preclude
  precluded
  precluding
preclusive
precocious
precociousness
precocity
precognition
preconceived

preconception
precursor
precursory
predacious
predator
predatory
predecease
  predeceased
  predeceasing
predecessor
predestination
predestine
  predestined
  predestining
predetermined
predicament
predicate
  predicated
  predicating
predication
predict
predictable
predictably
prediction
predigest
predigestion
predilection
predispose
  predisposed
  predisposing
predisposition
predominance
predominant

predominantly
predominate
  predominated
  predominating
pre-eminence
pre-eminent
pre-eminently
pre-empt
pre-emption
pre-emptive
pre-exist
pre-existence
pre-existent
pre-existing
preen
  preened
  preening
prefab
prefabricate
  prefabricated
  prefabricating
prefabrication
preface
  prefaced
  prefacing
prefect
prefectorial
prefecture
prefer
  preferred
  preferring
  prefers
preferable

preferably
preference
preferential
preferentially
preferment
prefix
  prefixes *pl*
  prefixed
  prefixing
pregnancy
  pregnancies *pl*
pregnant
prehensile
prehension
prehistoric
prehistorically
prehistory
prejudge
  prejudged
  prejudging
prejudice
  prejudiced
  prejudicing
prejudicial
prejudicially
prelacy
  prelacies *pl*
prelate
preliminarily
preliminary
  preliminaries *pl*
prelude
preluding

premarital
premature
prematurely
prematurity
premeditate
  premeditated
  premeditating
premeditation
premier (most
  important; prime
  minister)
première (first
  performance)
  premièred
  premières
  premièring
premiership
premise, premiss
  (logic statement)
  premises,
    premisses pl
premises (eg houses)
premium
  premiums pl
premonition
premonitory
prenatal
prentice
  prenticed
  prenticing
preoccupation
preoccupy
  preoccupied

preoccupies
preoccupying
prepaid (from prepay)
preparation
preparative
preparatorily
preparatory
prepare
  prepared
  preparing
preparedness
prepay
  prepaid
  prepaying
  prepays
prepayable
preponderance
preponderant
preponderantly
preponderate
  preponderated
  preponderating
preposition
prepossess
prepossessing
preposterous
preposterously
prerequisite
prerogative
presage
  presaged
  presaging
presbyter

Presbyterian
prescience
prescient
prescribe (eg
  medicine)
  prescribed
  prescribing
prescription
prescriptive
presence
present
presentable
presentation
presentiment
presently
preservation
preservative
preserve
  preserved
  preserving
preserver
preside
  presided
  presiding
presidency
  presidencies pl
president
presidential
presidio
  presidios pl
presidium
  presidiums pl
press

pressed

pressure

pressurisation

pressurise
  pressurised
  pressurising

pressurization

pressurize
  pressurized
  pressurizing

prestidigitation

prestidigitator

prestige

prestigious

prestissimo
  prestissimos *pl*

presto

pre-stress

pre-stressed

presumably

presume
  presumed
  presuming

presumption

presumptive

presumptuous

presuppose
  presupposed
  presupposing

presupposition

pretence

pretend

pretender

pretense *Am*

pretension

pretentious

pretentiously

preterit *Am*

preterite

preternatural

pretext

prettily

prettiness

pretty
  prettier
  prettiest

pretzel

prevail
  prevailed
  prevailing

prevalence

prevalent

prevaricate
  prevaricated
  prevaricating

prevarication

prevaricator

prevent

preventable

preventative

prevention

preventive

preview

previous

previously

pre-war

prey (plunder)
  preyed
  preying

price
  priced
  pricing

priceless

prick

pricker

prickle
  prickled
  prickling

prickly

pride
  prided
  priding

pried (*from* pry)

pries (*from* pry)

priest

priesthood

priestly

prig

priggish

prim
  primmer
  primmest

prima donna
  prima donnas *pl*

prima facie

primacy

primarily

primary
  primaries *pl*

primate
prime
  primed
  priming
prime minister
primeval
primitive
primitively
primly
primogenitor (earliest
  ancestor)
primogeniture (being
  first born)
primordial
primordially
primrose
primula
  primulas *pl*
prince
princely
princess
principal (chief)
principality
  principalities *pl*
principally
principle (moral
  code)
print
printable
printer
prior
prioress
priority

  priorities *pl*
priory
  priories *pl*
prise
  prised
  prising
prism
prismatic
prison
prisoner
pristine
privacy
private
privateer
privately
privation
privative
privet (hedge)
privilege
privileged
privy
Privy Council
Privy Councillor
prize
  prized
  prizing
prizefight
prizefighter
proactive
probability
probable
probably
probate

probation
probationer
probe
  probed
  probing
probity
problem
problematic
problematical
problematically
proboscis
  proboscises,
    proboscides *pl*
procedural
procedure
proceed
  proceeded
  proceeding
process
procession
processional
processor
pro-choice
proclaim
  proclaimed
  proclaiming
proclamation
proclivity
  proclivities *pl*
procrastinate
  procrastinated
  procrastinating
procrastination

procrastinator
procreate
  procreated
  procreating
procreative
procreator
proctor
proctorial
procurable
procuration
procurator
procure
  procured
  procuring
prod
  prodded
  prodding
  prods
prodigal
prodigality
prodigally
prodigious
prodigiously
prodigiousness
prodigy
  prodigies *pl*
produce
  produced
  producing
producer
product
production
productive

productively
productiveness
productivity
profanation
profane
  profaned
  profaning
profanely
profanity
  profanities *pl*
profess
profession
professional
professionalism
professionally
professor
professorial
proffer
  proffered
  proffering
proficiency
proficient
proficiently
profile
  profiled
  profiling
profit
  profited
  profiting
profitability
profitable
profitably
profiteer

profiteered
profiteering
profitless
profligacy
profligate
profligately
pro forma
profound
profounder
profoundly
profundity
profuse
profusely
profusion
progenitor (ancestor)
progenitrix
progeniture
progeny
prognosis
  prognoses *pl*
prognostic
prognosticate
  prognosticated
  prognosticating
prognostication
program (*Am* and
  computer)
  programmed
  programming
  programs
programme (all senses
  except computer)
  programmed

programming
programmes
programmer
progress
progression
progressive
progressively
prohibit
  prohibited
  prohibiting
prohibition
prohibitionist
prohibitive
prohibitively
project
projectile
projection
projector
prolapsed
proletarian
proletariat
pro-life
proliferate
  proliferated
  proliferating
proliferation
prolific
prolifically
prolification
prolix
prolixity
prologue
prolong

prolongation
promenade
  promenaded
  promenading
promenader
prominence
prominent
prominently
promiscuity
promiscuous
promiscuously
promise
  promised
  promising
promissory
promontory
  promontories *pl*
promote
  promoted
  promoting
promoter
promotion
prompt
prompter
promptitude
promptly
promptness
promulgate
  promulgated
  promulgating
promulgation
promulgator
prone

prong
pronged
pronoun
pronounce
  pronounced
  pronouncing
pronounceable
pronouncement
pronunciation
proof
  proofs *pl*
proof-reader
proof-reading
prop
  propped
  propping
  props
propaganda
propagandist
propagate
  propagated
  propagating
propagation
propagator
propel
  propelled
  propelling
  propels
propellant (rocket fuel)
propellent (driving)
propeller
propensity

propensities *pl*
proper
properly
propertied
property
  properties *pl*
prophecy (prediction)
  prophecies *pl*
prophesy (to predict)
  prophesied
  prophesies
  prophesying
prophet
prophetic
prophetically
prophylactic
prophylaxis
propinquity
  propinquities *pl*
propitiate
  propitiated
  propitiating
propitiator
propitiatory
propitious
propitiously
proponent
proportion
proportional
proportionally
proportionate
proposal
propose

proposed
proposing
proposer
proposition
propound
proprietary (legally
  owned)
proprietor (owner)
proprietress
propriety (decency)
  proprieties *pl*
propulsion
propulsive
pro rata
prorogation
prorogue
  prorogued
  proroguing
prosaic
prosaically
proscenium
proscribe (to outlaw)
  proscribed
  proscribing
proscription
proscriptive
prose
prosecute
  prosecuted
  prosecuting
prosecution
prosecutor
proselyte

proselytise
  proselytised
  proselytising
proselytiser
proselytism
proselytize
  proselytized
  proselytizing
proselytizer
prosily
prosiness
prosody
prospect
prospective
prospector
prospectus
  prospectuses *pl*
prosper
  prospered
  prospering
prosperity
prosperous
prostate (gland)
prostitute
  prostituted
  prostituting
prostitution
prostrate
  prostrated
  prostrating
prostration
prosy
protagonist

protean (variable)
protect
protection
protective
protector
protectorate
protégé
protein (food
  chemical)
pro tempore, pro tem
protest
Protestant
Protestantism
protestation
protester, protestor
protocol
proton
protoplasm
prototype
protozoon
  protozoa *pl*
protract
protractor
protrude
  protruded
  protruding
protrusion
protuberance
protuberant
proud
prouder
proudly
provable

prove
  proved
  proving
proven (in law)
provenance
provender
proverb
proverbial
proverbially
provide
  provided
  providing
providence
provident
providential
providentially
provider
province
provincial
provincialism
provision
provisional
provisionally
proviso
  provisos *pl*
provisory
provocation
provocative
provocatively
provoke
  provoked
  provoking
provost

prow
prowess
prowl
prowler
proximate (nearest)
proximity
proxy
  proxies *pl*
prude
prudence
prudent
prudential
prudentially
prudery
prudish
prune
  pruned
  pruning
prurience
prurient
prussic
pry
  pried
  pries
  prying
psalm
psalmist
psalter (book of
  psalms)
pseudonym
pseudonymity
pseudonymous
psittacosis

syche
psychedelic
psychiatric
psychiatrist
psychiatry
psychic
psychoanalyse
  psychoanalysed
  psychoanalysing
psychoanalysis
psychoanalyst
psychoanalytic
psychoanalytical
psychoanalyze
  psychoanalyzed
  psychoanalyzing
psychological
psychologist
psychology
psychometric
psychopath
psychopathic
psychosis
  psychoses pl
psychosomatic
ptarmigan
pterodactyl
ptomaine
pub
puberty
pubescence
pubescent
pubic

pubis
public
publican
publication
publicise
  publicised
  publicising
publicist
publicity
publicize
  publicized
  publicizing
publish
publisher
puce
puck
pucker
  puckered
  puckering
puckish
pudding
puddle
puerile
puerilely
puerility
puerperal
puff
puffin (sea-bird)
puffiness
puffy
  puffier
  puffiest
pug

pugilism
pugilist
pugnacious
pugnaciously
pugnacity
puisne (judge)
pukka
puling (whining)
pull
pullet
pulley
  pulleys pl
pullover
pullulate
  pullulated
  pullulating
pulmonary
pulp
pulpit
pulsar
pulsate
  pulsated
  pulsating
pulsation
pulse
  pulsed
  pulsing
pulseless
pulverisation
pulverise
  pulverised
  pulverising
pulverization

pulverize
  pulverized
  pulverizing
puma
  pumas *pl*
pumice
pummel
  pummelled
  pummelling
  pummels
  pummeled *Am*
  pummeling *Am*
pump
pumpernickel
pumpkin
pun
  punned
  punning
  puns
punch
punctilious
punctiliously
punctiliousness
punctual
punctuality
punctually
punctuate
  punctuated
  punctuating
punctuation
puncture
  punctured
  puncturing

pundit
pungency
pungent
pungently
punish
punishable
punishment
punitive
punnet (small basket)
punster
punt
punter
puny
  punier
  puniest
pup
pupa
  pupae *pl*
pupate
  pupated
  pupating
pupation
pupil
puppet
puppeteer
puppetry
puppy
  puppies *pl*
purblind
purchasable
purchase
  purchased
  purchasing

purchaser
purdah
pure
purée, puree(food)
  puréed, pureed
  puréeing, pureeing
  purées, purees
purely
purer
purgation
purgative
purgatorial
purgatory
purge
  purged
  purging
purification
purifier
purify
  purified
  purifies
  purifying
purism
purist
Puritan
puritanic
puritanical
puritanism
purity
purl (in knitting)
purloin
purple
purport

purpose
purposeful
purposeless
purposely
purr
purse
  pursed
  pursing
purser
pursuance
pursuant
pursue
  pursued
  pursuing
pursuit
purulence
purulent
purvey
  purveyed
  purveying
  purveys
purveyance
purveyor
purview
pus (from wound)
push
pusher
pushover
pusillanimity
pusillanimous
puss (cat)
pussy
  pussies *pl*

pustule
put (to place)
  puts
  putted
  putting
putative
putrefaction
putrefy
  putrefied
  putrefies
  putrefying
putrescence
putrescent
putrid
putt (in golf)
puttee (leggings)
putter
putty (for glazing)
puzzle
  puzzled
  puzzling
puzzlement
puzzler
pyelitis
pygmy
  pygmies *pl*
pyjamas
pylon
pyramid
pyramidal
pyre
pyrites
pyrotechnics

pyrrhic
python

quack
quackery
quadragenarian
Quadragesima
  Quadragesimas *pl*
quadrangle
quadrangular
quadrant
quadraphonic
quadratic
quadrature
quadrilateral
quadrille
quadruped
quadruple
  quadrupled

quadrupling
quadruplet
quadruplicate
  quadruplicated
  quadruplicating
quadruplication
quaff
quagmire
quail
  quailed
  quailing
quaint
quainter
quaintly
quaintness
quake

quaked
quaking
Quaker
qualification
qualify
  qualified
  qualifies
  qualifying
qualitative
qualitatively
quality
  qualities *pl*
qualm
quandary
  quandaries *pl*
quango
  quangos *pl*
quantifiable
quantification
quantify
  quantified
  quantifies
  quantifying
quantitative
quantitatively
quantity
  quantities *pl*
quantum
  quanta *pl*
quarantine
quarrel
  quarrelled
  quarrelling

quarrels
quarreled *Am*
quarreling *Am*
quarrelsome
quarry
quarries *pl*
quart
quarter
quartered
quartering
quarterly
quartermaster
quartet, quartette
quarto
quartos *pl*
quartz
quartzite
quasar
quash
Quaternary
quatrain
quaver
quavered
quavering
quay (landing place)
quays *pl*
quean (hussy)
queasiness
queasy
queen (sovereign)
queenly
queer
queerly

quell
quench
querulous
querulously
querulousness
query
queries *pl*
queried
queries
querying
quest
question
questioned
questioning
questionable
questionably
questioner
questionnaire
queue
queued
queuing
queuer
qui vive
quibble
quibbled
quibbling
quibbler
quick
quicken
quickened
quickening
quicker
quickly

quickness
quicksand
quicksilver
quid pro quo
quiescence
quiescent
quiet
quieten
quietened
quietening
quieter
quietly
quietude
quietus
quiff
quill
quilt
quince
quinine
quinquennial
quinquennium
quinquenniums,
    quinquennia *pl*
quinsy
quintessence
quintet *m*
quintette *f*
quintuple
quintuplet
quip
quipped
quipping
quips

quire (of paper)
quirk
quisling
quit
  quits
  quitted
  quitting
quite
quittance
quitter
quiver
  quivered
  quivering
Quixote
quixotic
quixotically
quixotism
quiz
  quizzes *pl*
  quizzes
  quizzed
  quizzing
quizzically
quod (prison)
quoit
quorum
  quorums *pl*
quota
  quotas *pl*
quotable
quotation
quote
  quoted

quoting
quotidian
quotient

R

rabbi
  rabbis *pl*
rabbinical
rabbit
rabble
rabid
rabidly
rabies
race (to compete)
  raced
  racing
racecourse
racehorse
raceme
race track
racer
racial
racialism
racialist

racially
racily
racism
racist
rack
racket (disturbance;
  swindle)
racket, racquet
  (*eg* tennis)
racketeer
raconteur
racoon, raccoon
racquet, racket
  (*eg* tennis)
racy
radar
radial
radially
radiance

radiant
radiantly
radiate
  radiated
  radiating
radiation
radiator
radical
radicalism
radically
radio
  radios *pl*
  radioed
  radioing
  radios
radioactive
radioactivity
radiogram
radiographer
radiography
radioisotope
radiologist
radiology
radish
radium
radius
  radii, radiuses *pl*
radon
raffia
raffish
raffle
  raffled
  raffling

raft
rafter
rag
 ragged
 ragging
 rags
ragamuffin
rage
 raged
 raging
ragged
raglan
ragout
rags
ragtime
raid
 raided
 raiding
raider
rail
 railed
 railing
raillery (teasing)
railroad (street)
railway
 railways *pl*
raiment
rain (water)
 rained
 raining
rainbow
rain check
raincoat

rainfall
rainless
rainy
raise (to increase,
   bring up)
 raised
 raising
raisin (dried grape)
raison d'être
rajah, raja
rake
 raked
 raking
rakish
rallentando
 rallentandos *pl*
rally
 rallies *pl*
 rallied
 rallies
 rallying
ram
 rammed
 ramming
 rams
ramble
 rambled
 rambling
rambler
ramekin, ramequin
ramification
ramify
 ramified

ramifies
ramifying
ramp
rampage
 rampaged
 rampaging
rampancy
rampant
rampart
ram-raid
 ram-raided
 ram-raiding
ramrod
ramshackle
ran (*from* run)
ranch
rancher
rancid
rancor *Am*
rancorous
rancour
random
randomly
randy
 randier
 randiest
rang (*from* ring)
range
 ranged
 ranging
rangy
 rangier
 rangiest

rank
ranker
rankle
　rankled
　rankling
ransack
ransom
　ransomed
　ransoming
rant
rap (to knock; music)
　rapped
　rapping
　raps
rapacious
rapacity
rape
　raped
　raping
rapid
rapidity
rapidly
rapier
rapine
rapist
rapport
rapprochement
rapscallion
rapt (engrossed)
rapture
rapturous
rapturously
rare

rarebit (Welsh)
rarefaction
rarefy
　rarefied
　rarefies
　rarefying
rarely
rarer
rarity
　rarities *pl*
rascal
rascality
rase (to destroy)
　rased
　rasing
rash
rasher
rashly
rasp
raspberry
　raspberries *pl*
rat
　rats
　ratted
　ratting
ratan
ratchet
rate
　rated
　rating
rateable, ratable
ratepayer
rather

ratification
ratify
　ratified
　ratifies
　ratifying
ratio
　ratios *pl*
ratiocinate
　ratiocinated
　ratiocinating
ratiocination
ration
　rationed
　rationing
rational (reasonable)
rationale (basic
　reason)
rationalisation
rationalise
　rationalised
　rationalising
rationalism
rationality
rationalization
rationalize
　rationalized
　rationalizing
rationally
rats
rattan
rattle
　rattled
　rattling

rattlesnake
raucous
raucously
raucousness
ravage
  ravaged
  ravaging
ravager
rave
  raved
  raving
ravel
  ravelled
  ravelling
  ravels
  raveled *Am*
  raveling *Am*
raven
ravening
ravenous
ravenously
raver
ravine (gorge)
ravioli
ravish
raw (uncooked)
raw-boned
rawer
rawness
ray (beam)
  rays *pl*
rayon
raze (to destroy)

razed
razing
razor
razzle-dazzle
reach
react
reactance
reaction
reactionary
  reactionaries *pl*
reactivate
  reactivated
  reactivating
reactive
reactor
read (*eg* a book)
  reading
readable
readdress
reader
readily
readiness
readjust
readjustment
readmission
readmit
  readmits
  readmitted
  readmitting
readmittance
ready
  readied
  readies

readying
ready-made
reagent
real (true)
realisable
realisation
realise
  realised
  realising
realism
realist
realistic
realistically
reality
  realities *pl*
realizable
realization
realize
  realized
  realizing
really
realm
ream (of paper)
reap
  reaped
  reaping
reaper
reappear
  reappeared
  reappearing
reappearance
rear
  reared

rearing
rearguard
rearm
rearmed
rearming
rearmament
rearrange
rearranged
rearranging
rearrangement
reason
reasoned
reasoning
reasonable
reasonableness
reasonably
reassemble
reassembled
reassembling
reassess
reassessment
reassurance
reassure
reassured
reassuring
reassuringly
rebate
rebel
rebelled
rebelling
rebels
rebellion
rebellious

rebirth
rebound
rebuff
rebuild
rebuilding
rebuilds
rebuilt
rebuke
rebuked
rebuking
rebut
rebuts
rebutted
rebutting
rebuttal
recalcitrance
recalcitrant
recall
recant
recantation
recap
recapped
recapping
recaps
recapitulate
recapitulated
recapitulating
recapitulation
recapture
recaptured
recapturing
recede
receded

receding
receipt
receivable
receive
received
receiving
receiver
receivership
recent
recently
receptacle
reception
receptionist
receptive
recess
recessed
recession
recessional
recessive
recharge
recharged
recharging
rechargeable
recherché
recidivism
recidivist
recipe
recipient
reciprocal
reciprocally
reciprocate
reciprocated
reciprocating

reciprocation
reciprocity
recital
recitation
recitative
recite
  recited
  reciting
reciter
reckless
recklessly
recklessness
reckon
  reckoned
  reckoning
reckoner
reclaim
  reclaimed
  reclaiming
reclamation
recline
  reclined
  reclining
recluse
reclusion
reclusive
recognisable
recognisance
recognise
  recognised
  recognising
recognition
recognizable

recognizance
recognize
  recognized
  recognizing
recoil
  recoiled
  recoiling
recollect
recollection
recommend
recommendation
recommit
  recommits
  recommitted
  recommitting
recommitment
recommittal
recommitted
recompense
  recompensed
  recompensing
reconcilable
reconcile
  reconciled
  reconciling
reconcilement
reconciliation
recondite
recondition
  reconditioned
  reconditioning
reconnaissance
reconnoiter *Am*

reconnoitered
reconnoitering
reconnoitre
reconnoitred
reconnoitring
reconquer
  reconquered
  reconquering
reconsider
  reconsidered
  reconsidering
reconsideration
reconstruct
reconstruction
record
recorder
record player
re-count (to count
  again)
recount (to tell)
recoup
  recouped
  recouping
recourse
recover
  recovered
  recovering
recovery
  recoveries *pl*
recreant
recreate (create
  again)
recreated

recreating
ecreation
ecreational
ecreative
ecriminate
recriminated
recriminating
ecrimination
ecriminatory
ecrudescence
ecrudescent
ecruit
recruited
recruiting
ectal
ectangle
ectangular
ectifiable
rectification
ectifier
rectify
rectified
rectifies
rectifying
rectilineal
rectilinear
rectitude
rector
rectorial
rectory
rectories *pl*
rectum
rectums *pl*

recumbent
recuperate
recuperated
recuperating
recuperation
recuperative
recur
recurred
recurring
recurs
recurrence
recurrent
recusancy
recusant
recycle
recycled
recycling
red (colour)
redbreast
redden
reddened
reddening
redder
redeem
redeemed
redeeming
redeemable
redeemer
redemption
redeploy
redeployed
redeploying
redeploys

redeployment
redevelop
redeveloped
redeveloping
redevelopment
redid (*from* redo)
rediffusion
redirect
redirection
redistribute
redistributed
redistributing
redistribution
redo
redid
redoes
redoing
redone
redolence
redolent
redouble
redoubled
redoubling
redoubt
redoubtable
redound
redress
reduce
reduced
reducing
reducible
reductio ad absurdum
reduction

redundancy
  redundancies *pl*
redundant
reduplicate
  reduplicated
  reduplicating
reduplication
re-echo
  re-echoed
  re-echoes
  re-echoing
reed (water plant)
reef
reek (smell)
reel (dance; *eg* of
  cotton; to stagger)
re-elect
re-election
re-enter
  re-entered
  re-entering
re-entrant
re-entry
  re-entries *pl*
re-establish
re-establishment
re-examination
re-examine
  re-examined
  re-examining
re-export
re-exportation
refectory

refectories *pl*
refer
  referred
  referring
  refers
referable
referee
  refereed
  refereeing
reference
referendum
  referenda,
    referendums *pl*
refill
refillable
refine
  refined
  refining
refinement
refinery
  refineries *pl*
refit
  refits
  refitted
  refitting
reflate
  reflated
  reflating
reflation
reflationary
reflect
reflection
reflective

reflector
reflex
  reflexes *pl*
reflexive (grammar)
refloat
  refloated
  refloating
reform
reformation
reformatory
  reformatories *pl*
reformed
reformer
refract
refraction
refractive
refractoriness
refractory
refrain
  refrained
  refraining
refresh
refresher
refreshment
refrigerant
refrigerate
  refrigerated
  refrigerating
refrigeration
refrigerator
refuel
  refuelled
  refuelling

refuels
refueled *Am*
refueling *Am*
refuge
refugee
refulgence
refulgent
refund
refurbish
refurbishment
refusal
refuse
refused
refusing
refutable
refutal
refutation
refute
refuted
refuting
regain
regained
regaining
regal (royal)
regale (to entertain)
regaled
regaling
regalia
regally
regard
regardless
regatta
regattas *pl*

regency
regencies *pl*
regenerate
regenerated
regenerating
regeneration
regenerative
regenerator
regent
regicidal
regicide
regime (method of government)
regimen (strict routine)
regiment (of soldiers)
regimental
regimentation
region
regional
regionally
register (record)
registered
registering
registrar (*eg* of college)
registration
registry (where records are kept)
registries *pl*
registry office
regress
regression

regressive
regret
regrets
regretted
regretting
regretful
regretfully
regrettable
regrettably
regular
regularisation
regularise
regularised
regularising
regularity
regularization
regularize
regularized
regularizing
regularly
regulate
regulated
regulating
regulation
regulator
regurgitate
regurgitated
regurgitating
regurgitation
rehabilitate
rehabilitated
rehabilitating
rehabilitation

rehearsal
rehearse
  rehearsed
  rehearsing
reign (to rule)
  reigned
  reigning
reimburse
  reimbursed
  reimbursing
reimbursement
rein (of horse)
reincarnation
reincarnate
  reincarnated
  reincarnating
reindeer
reinforce
  reinforced
  reinforcing
reinforceable
reinforcement
reinstate
  reinstated
  reinstating
reinstatement
reiterate
  reiterated
  reiterating
reiteration
reject
rejection
rejoice

rejoiced
rejoicing
rejoinder
rejuvenate
  rejuvenated
  rejuvenating
rejuvenation
relapse
  relapsed
  relapsing
relate
  related
  relating
relation
relationship
relative
relatively
relativity
relax
  relaxed
  relaxes
  relaxing
relaxation
relaxed
relay
  relayed
  relaying
  relays
release
  released
  releasing
relegate
  relegated

relegating
relegation
relent
relentless
relentlessly
relevance
relevant
reliability
reliable
reliably
reliance
reliant
relic
relief
relieve
  relieved
  relieving
religion
religious
religiously
relinquish
reliquary
  reliquaries *pl*
relish
reluctance
reluctant
reluctantly
rely
  relied
  relies
  relying
remain
  remained

remaining
remainder
  remaindered
  remaindering
remand
remark
remarkable
remarkably
remediable
remedial
remedy
  remedies *pl*
  remedied
  remedies
  remedying
remember
  remembered
  remembering
remembrance
remind
reminder
reminisce
  reminisced
  reminiscing
reminiscence
reminiscent
remiss
remissible
remission
remissness
remit
  remits
  remitted

remitting
remittal
remittance
remnant
remonstrance
remonstrant
remonstrate
  remonstrated
  remonstrating
remonstration
remonstrator
remorse
remorseful
remorseless
remorselessly
remote
remotely
remotest
remount
removable
removal
remove
  removed
  removing
remover
remunerate
  remunerated
  remunerating
remuneration
remunerative
Renaissance
rend
render

rendered
rendering
rendezvous
rendition
renegade (turncoat)
renegation
renege, renegue (to
    deny)
  reneged, renegued
  reneging, reneguing
renew
  renewed
  renewing
renewable
renewal
rennet
renounce
  renounced
  renouncing
renounceable
renouncement
renovate
  renovated
  renovating
renovation
renovator
renown
renowned
rent
rental
rentier
renunciate
  renunciated

renunciating
renunciation
reopen
  reopened
  reopening
reorganisation
reorganise
  reorganised
  reorganising
reorganization
reorganize
  reorganized
  reorganizing
repaid (*from* repay)
repair
  repaired
  repairing
repairer
reparable
reparation
repartee
  repartees *pl*
repast
repatriate
  repatriated
  repatriating
repatriation
repay
  repaid
  repaying
  repays
repayable
repayment

repeal
  repealed
  repealing
repeat
  repeated
  repeating
repeatedly
repeater
repel
  repelled
  repelling
  repels
repellent
repent
repentance
repentant
repercussion
repertoire (list of
  plays)
repertory (theatre)
  repertories *pl*
repetition
repetitious
repetitive
rephrase
  rephrased
  rephrasing
repine
  repined
  repining
replace
  replaced
  replacing

replaceable
replacement
replay
  replays *pl*
  replayed
  replaying
  replays
replenish
replenishment
replete
repletion
replica
  replicas *pl*
reply
  replies *pl*
  replied
  replies
  replying
report
reportable
reportedly
reporter
repose
  reposed
  reposing
repository
  repositories *pl*
repossess
repossession
reprehend
reprehensible
reprehension
represent

representation
representative
repress
repression
repressive
reprieve
  reprieved
  reprieving
reprimand
reprint
reprisal
reproach
reproached
reproachful
reproachfully
reprobate
  reprobated
  reprobating
reprobation
reproduce
  reproduced
  reproducing
reproducible
reproduction
reproductive
reproof (blame)
  reproofs *pl*
reproval
reprove (to scold)
  reproved
  reproving
reprovingly
reptile

reptilian
republic
republican
republicanism
republication
republish
repudiate
  repudiated
  repudiating
repudiation
repugnance
repugnant
repulse
  repulsed
  repulsing
repulsion
repulsive
reputable
reputation
repute
reputedly
request
requiem
requiescat in pace
require
  required
  requiring
requisite
requisition
requital
requite
  requited
  requiting

re-route
  re-routed
  re-routeing
  re-routes
  re-routing
rerun
  reran
  rerunning
  reruns
resat (*from* resit)
rescind
rescission
rescript
rescue
  rescued
  rescuing
rescuer
research
researcher
researching
resemblance
resemble
  resembled
  resembling
resent
resentful
resentment
reservation
reserve
  reserved
  reserving
reservedly
reservist

reservoir

reset
  resets
  resetting

resettle
  resettled
  resettling

resettlement

reside
  resided
  residing

residence

residency
  residencies *pl*

residential

residual

residuary

residue

residuum
  residua *pl*

resign
  resigned
  resigning

resignation

resilience

resilient

resiliently

resin

resinous

resist

resistance

resistant

resister (person)

resistive

resistor (electrical)

resit
  resat
  resits
  resitting

resole
  resoled
  resoling

resolute

resolutely

resolution

resolve
  resolved
  resolving

resonance

resonant

resonate
  resonated
  resonating

resonator

resort

resound

resource

resourceful

respect

respectability

respectable

respectful

respectfully

respective

respectively

respiration

respirator

respiratory

respire
  respired
  respiring

respite

resplendence

resplendent

resplendently

respond

respondent

response

responsibility
  responsibilities *pl*

responsible

responsibly

responsive

rest (sleep)

restaurant

restaurateur

restful

restfully

restfulness

restitution

restive

restively

restiveness

restless

restlessly

restlessness

restoration

restorative

restore

restored
restoring
restorer
restrain
 restrained
 restraining
restraint
restrict
restriction
restrictive
restructure
 restructured
 restructuring
result
resultant
résumé (review)
resume (take up)
 resumed
 resuming
resumption
resurgence
resurgent
resurrect
resurrection
resuscitate
 resuscitated
 resuscitating
resuscitation
retail
 retailed
 retailing
retailer
retain

retained
 retaining
retainer
retaliate
 retaliated
 retaliating
retaliation
retaliatory
retard
retardation
retch (to vomit)
retention
retentive
rethink
 rethinking
 rethinks
 rethought
reticence
reticent
reticule
retina
 retinas *pl*
retinue
retire
 retired
 retiring
retirement
retort
retouch
retrace
 retraced
 retracing
retract

retractable
retractile
retraction
retractor
retread
 retreading
 retreads
 retrod
retreat
 retreated
 retreating
retrench
retrenchment
retribution
retributive
retrievable
retrieval
retrieve
 retrieved
 retrieving
retriever
retroactive
retro-engineer
retrograde
retrogression
retrogressive
retro-rocket
retrospect
retrospection
retrospective
retrospectively
retrovirus
return

returnable
reunion
reunite
  reunited
  reuniting
reusable
reuse
  reused
  reusing
rev
  revs
  revved
  revving
revaluation
revalue
  revalued
  revaluing
revamp
  revamped
  revamping
reveal (to disclose)
  revealed
  revealing
reveille
revel (to make merry)
  revelled
  revelling
  revels
  reveled *Am*
  reveling *Am*
revelation
reveler
reveller

revelry
  revelries *pl*
revenge
  revenged
  revenging
revengeful
revenue
reverberate
  reverberated
  reverberating
reverberation
reverberator
revere (respect)
  revered
  revering
reverence
reverend
reverent
reverential
reverie
revers (turned back
  cloth)
reversal
reverse (back; move
  backwards)
  reversed
  reversing
reversible
reversion
revert
revetment
review (to examine
  critically)

reviewed
reviewing
reviewer
revile
  reviled
  reviling
revise
  revised
  revising
revision
revitalise
  revitalised
  revitalising
revitalize
  revitalized
  revitalizing
revival
revive
  revived
  reviving
revocable
revocation
revoke
  revoked
  revoking
revolt
revolution
revolutionary
  revolutionaries *pl*
revolutionise
  revolutionised
  revolutionising
revolutionize

revolutionized
revolutionizing
revolve
revolved
revolving
revolver
revue (entertainment)
revulsion
reward
rewrite
rewrites
rewriting
rewritten
rewrote
rhapsodise
rhapsodised
rhapsodising
rhapsodize
rhapsodized
rhapsodizing
rhapsody
rhapsodies *pl*
rheostat
rhesus
rhetoric
rhetorical
rhetorically
rheumatic
rheumatism
rheumatoid
rheumy
rhinoceros
rhinoceroses *pl*

rhizome
rhododendron
rhododendrons *pl*
rhomboid
rhombus
rhombuses *pl*
rhubarb
rhyme (verse)
rhymed
rhyming
rhythm
rhythmic
rhythmical
rhythmically
rib
ribbed
ribbing
ribs
ribald
ribaldry
ribbon
rice
rich
riches
richly
richness
rick (of hay)
rick, wrick (to sprain)
ricked, wricked
ricking, wricking
rickets
rickety
rickshaw, ricksha

ricochet
ricocheted,
ricochetted
ricocheting,
ricochetting
rid
ridding
rids
ridable
riddance
ridden
riddle
riddled
riddling
ride
ridden
rides
riding
rode
rider
ridge
ridging
ridicule
ridiculed
ridiculing
ridiculous
ridiculously
rife
riff
riff-raff
rifle
rifled
rifling

rift
rig
  rigged
  rigging
  rigs
right (correct)
right angle
right-angled
righteous
righteousness
rightful
rightfully
rightly
rigid
rigidity
rigidly
rigmarole
rigor *Am*
rigor mortis (stiffness
  after death)
rigorous
rigorously
rigour
rile
  riled
  riling
rim
rime (frost)
rimmed
rind
ring (*eg* a bell)
  rang
  ringing

rings
  rung
ring (to surround)
  ringed
  ringing
  rings
ringer
ringleader
ringlet (of hair)
rink
rinse
  rinsed
  rinsing
riot
  rioted
  rioting
rioter
riotous
riotously
riotousness
R.I.P.
rip
  ripped
  ripping
  rips
ripe
ripely
ripen
  ripened
  ripening
  ripens
ripeness
riper

riposte
ripple
  rippled
  rippling
rise
  rose
  rises
  rising
  risen
riser
risible
risk
riskily
riskiness
risky
  riskier
  riskiest
risotto
  risottos *pl*
risqué
rissole
rite (ceremony)
ritual
ritualism
ritualist
ritualistic
ritually
rival
  rivalled
  rivalling
  rivals
  rivaled *Am*
  rivaling *Am*

rivalry
  rivalries *pl*
river
rivet
  riveted
  riveting
riveter
Riviera
rivulet
roach
  roach, roaches *pl*
road
roadblock
road hog
road map
roadway
  roadways *pl*
roadworthiness
roadworthy
roam
  roamed
  roaming
roan
roar (loud noise)
  roared
  roaring
roast
rob (to steal)
  robbed
  robbing
  robs
robber
robbery

  robberies *pl*
robe (dress)
  robed
  robing
robin
robot
robotics
robust
robustly
robustness
rock
rock and roll
rockery
  rockeries *pl*
rocket
  rocketed
  rocketing
rocketry
rocking horse
rocky
  rockier
  rockiest
rococo
rod
rode (*from* ride)
rodent
rodeo
  rodeos *pl*
roe (deer; of fish)
rogation
rogue
roguery
roguish

roisterer
role (actor's part)
roll
roll-call
roller
roller skate
  roller skated
  roller skating
rollick
roly-poly
  roly-polies *pl*
romance
  romanced
  romancing
romancer
romantic
romantically
romanticise
  romanticised
  romanticising
romanticism
romanticize
  romanticized
  romanticizing
romp
romper
rondo
  rondos *pl*
roo (kangaroo)
rood (crucifix)
roof
  roofs *pl*
rook

rookery
  rookeries *pl*
rookie
room
roomful
roominess
room-mate
room service
roomy
  roomier
  roomiest
roost
rooster (hen)
root (*eg* of a plant)
  rooted
  rooting
rootless
rope
  roped
  roping
rosary
  rosaries *pl*
rose (*from* rise; flower)
rosé (pink)
roseate
rose leaf
  rose leaves *pl*
rosemary
rosette
rosily
rosin
  rosined
  rosining

roster (list)
rostrum
  rostra, rostrums *pl*
rosy
rot
  rots
  rotted
  rotting
rota
  rotas *pl*
Rotarian
rotary
rotatable
rotate
  rotated
  rotating
rotation
rote (procedure)
rotisserie
rotor (of electric
  motor)
rotten
rottenness
rotter
rotund
rotunda
  rotundas *pl*
rotundity
rouble (Russian
  money)
roué
rouge
rough (coarse)

roughage
roughen
  roughened
  roughening
rougher
rough-hewn
roughly
roughness
roughshod
roulette
round
roundabout
roundelay
  roundelays *pl*
rounder
rounders
roundness
rouse
  roused
  rousing
rout (to defeat)
  routed
  routing
route (road taken)
  routed
  routing
route march
routine (procedure)
rove
  roved
  roving
rover
row (boat)

rowdy
  rowdies *pl*
rowdily
rowdiness
rower
rowlock
royal
royalist
royally
royalty
  royalties *pl*
rub
  rubbed
  rubbing
  rubs
rubber
rubbish
rubbishy
rubble
rubicund
ruby
  rubies *pl*
rubric
ruche
  ruched
  ruching
ruck (crease)
rucked
ruckle
  ruckled
  ruckling
rucksack
ruction

rudder
ruddiness
ruddy
  ruddier
  ruddiest
rude (rough)
rudely
rudeness
rudiment
rudimentary
rue (herb; to regret)
  rued
  ruing
rueful
ruefully
ruff (collar)
ruffian
ruffle
  ruffled
  ruffling
rug
rugby
rugged
ruggedness
rugger
ruin destroy)
  ruined
  ruining
ruinous
ruinously
rule
  ruled

  ruling
ruler
rum
rumble
  rumbled
  rumbling
ruminant
ruminate
  ruminated
  ruminating
rummage
  rummaged
  rummaging
rummy
rumor *Am*
rumored *Am*
rumour
rumoured
rump
rumple
  rumpled
  rumpling
rumpus
  rumpuses *pl*
run
  ran
  running
  runs
runabout
runaway
  runaways *pl*
rune (letter)
rung (*from* ring;

ladder)
runic
runner
runner-up
  runners-up *pl*
runny
  runnier
  runniest
runway
  runways *pl*
rupee (Indian money)
rupture
  ruptured
  rupturing
rural
rurally
ruse
rush
rush hour
rusk
russet
rust
rustic
rusticate
  rusticated
  rusticating
rustication
rusticity
rustiness
rustle
  rustled
  rustling
rustler

rustless
rustproof
  rustproofed
  rustproofing
  rustproofs
rusty
  rustier
  rustiest
rut
  ruts
  rutted
  rutting
ruthless
ruthlessly
ruthlessness
rye (grain)

S

Sabbatarian
sabbath
sabbatical
saber *Am*
sable
sabotage
  sabotaged
  sabotaging
saboteur
sabre
sac (pouch)
saccharin
sacerdotal
sachet (small bag)
sack (hessian)
sacked
sacrament
sacramental
sacred

sacredly
sacredness
sacrifice
  sacrificed
  sacrificing
sacrificial
sacrilege
sacrilegious
sacrosanct
sad
  sadder
  saddest
sadden
  saddened
  saddening
saddle
  saddled
  saddling
saddler

saddlery
  saddleries *pl*
sadism
sadist
sadistic
sadly
sadness
safari
  safaris *pl*
safe
safeguard
safely
safer
safety
saffron
sag
  sagged
  sagging
  sags
saga
  sagas *pl*
sagacious
sagaciously
sagacity
sage
sagely
sago
  sagos *pl*
sahib
said (*from* say)
sail (of ship)
sailer (ship)
sailor (man)

saint
sainthood
saintliness
saintly
sake
salaam
　salaamed
　salaaming
salacious
salacity
salad
salamander
salami (sausage)
　salamis pl
salariat
salary (wage)
　salaries pl
sale (at shop)
saleability
saleable
salesman
　salesmen pl
saleswoman
　saleswomen pl
salicin
salicylic
salient
saline
salinity
saliva
salivary
salivate
　salivated

salivating
salivation
sallow
sallowness
sally
　sallies pl
　sallied
　sallies
　sallying
salmon
salmonella
　(bacterium)
salon (drawing room)
saloon (of pub)
salsify
　salsifies pl
salt
salt cellar
saltiness
saltpeter Am
saltpetre
salty
　saltier
　saltiest
salubrious
salubrity
salutary
salutation
salute
　saluted
　saluting
salvage (save)
　salvaged

salvaging
salvation
salve
　salved
　salving
salver
salvo
　salvoes, salvos pl
Samaritan
same
samovar
sample
　sampled
　sampling
sampler
sanatorium
　sanatoriums,
　　sanatoria pl
sanctification
sanctify
　sanctified
　sanctifies
　sanctifying
sanctimonious
sanctimoniously
sanctimoniousness
sanction
　sanctioned
　sanctioning
sanctity
sanctuary
　sanctuaries pl
sanctum

sanctums, sancta *pl*

sand

sandal

sandalwood

sandbag

  sandbagged

  sandbagging

  sandbags

sandpaper

  sandpapered

  sandpapering

sandwich

  sandwiches *pl*

sandy

  sandier

  sandiest

sane (not mad)

sanely

sang (*from* sing)

sang-froid

sanguinary

sanguine

sanitarium

  sanitariums,

    sanitaria *pl*

sanitary

sanitation

sanity

sank (*from* sink)

Santa Claus

sap

  sapped

  sapping

saps

sapience

sapient

sapling

sapper

sapphire

saprophyte

saprophytic

saraband

sarcasm

sarcastic

sarcastically

sarcoma

  sarcomas *pl*

sarcophagus

  sarcophagi *pl*

sardine

sardonic

sardonically

sari

  saris *pl*

sartorial

sash

sat (*from* sit)

Satan (devil)

satanic

satchel

sate

  sated

  sating

sateen (cotton)

satellite

satiable

satiate

  satiated

  satiating

satiation

satiety

satin (silk)

satinette

satire (sarcasm)

satirical

satirically

satirise

  satirised

  satirising

satirist

satirize

  satirized

  satirizing

satisfaction

satisfactorily

satisfactory

satisfiable

satisfy

  satisfied

  satisfies

  satisfying

satsuma

  satsumas *pl*

saturate

  saturated

  saturating

saturation

Saturday

  Saturdays *pl*

saturnine
satyr (a god)
sauce (food)
saucepan
saucer
saucily
sauciness
saucy
  saucier
  sauciest
sauerkraut
sauna (steam bath)
  saunas *pl*
saunter
  sauntered
  sauntering
sausage
sauté (fried)
  sautéed
  sautéing
savage
  savaged
  savaging
savagely
savagery
savant
save
  saved
  saving
saveloy
  saveloys *pl*
saver (keeper)
savior *Am*

saviour (rescuer)
savoir faire
savor (taste) *Am*
  savored
  savoring
  savoriness
savory
  savories *pl*
savour (taste)
  savoured
  savouring
savoury
  savouries *pl*
saw (to cut; tool)
  sawed
  sawing
  sawn
  saws
saxifrage
saxophone
saxophonist
say
  said
  saying
  says
scab
scabbard
scabies
scaffold
scald (burn)
scale
  scaled
  scaling

scallop, scollop
scallywag
scalp
scalpel
scaly
scamp
scamper
  scampered
  scampering
scampi (prawns)
scan
  scanned
  scanning
  scans
scandal
scandalise
  scandalised
  scandalising
scandalize
  scandalized
  scandalizing
scandalmonger
scandalous
scandalously
scanner
scansion
scant
scantily
scantiness
scanty
  scantier
  scantiest
scapegoat

scapegrace
scapula
  scapulas *pl*
scar
  scarred
  scarring
  scars
scarce
scarcely
scarcity
  scarcities *pl*
scare
  scared
  scaring
scarecrow
scarf
  scarfs, scarves *pl*
scarification
scarify
  scarified
  scarifies
  scarifying
scarlatina
scarlet
scarp
scat
  scats
  scatted
  scatting
scathe
  scathed
  scathing
scatheless

scatter
  scattered
  scattering
scatterbrain
scavenge
  scavenged
  scavenging
scavenger
scenario
  scenarios *pl*
scene (view)
scenery
scenic
scent (perfume)
scented
scepsis
scepter *Am*
sceptic (disbeliever)
sceptical
sceptically
scepticism
sceptre
schedule
  scheduled
  scheduling
schematic
schematically
scheme
  schemed
  scheming
schemer
scherzo
  scherzos *pl*

schism
schismatic
schist
schizoid
schizophrenia
schizophrenic
schnapps
scholar
scholarly
scholarship
scholastic
school
  schooled
  schooling
schoolboy
  schoolboys *pl*
schoolgirl
schoolmaster
schoolmistress
schoolteacher
schooner
sciatica
science
scientific
scientifically
scientist
scimitar
scintillate
  scintillated
  scintillating
scintillation
scion
scission (cutting)

scissors
sclerosis
scoff
scoffer
scold (to chide)
scollop, scallop
sconce
scone
scoop
scoot
scooter
scope
scorbutic
scorch
scorcher
score
  scored
  scoring
scoreboard
scorer
scorn
scornful
scornfully
scorpion
Scot
Scotch (whisky)
scotch (to prevent;
  to wedge)
scot-free
Scotland
Scotsman
  Scotsmen *pl*
Scotswoman

Scotswomen *pl*
Scottish
scoundrel
scour (scratch)
  scoured
  scouring
scourer
scourge
  scourged
  scourging
scout
  scouted
  scouting
scowl
scrabble
  scrabbled
  scrabbling
scrag
scraggy
scramble
  scrambled
  scrambling
scrap
  scrapped
  scrapping
  scraps
scrape
  scraped
  scraping
scraper
scrapie (disease in
  sheep)
scrappy

scrappier
scrappiest
scratch
scratched
scrawl
scrawny
  scrawnier
  scrawniest
scream
  screamed
  screaming
screech
screech owl
screed
screen
  screened
  screening
screenplay
  screenplays *pl*
screw
  screwed
  screwing
screwdriver
screwy
scribble
  scribbled
  scribbling
scribbler
scribe
scrimmage
  scrimmaged
  scrimmaging
scrimp

scrip (certificate)
script
scriptural
scripture
scriptwriter
scrofula
scrofulous
scroll
scrotum
  scrotums, scrota *pl*
scrounge
  scrounged
  scrounging
scrounger
scrub
  scrubbed
  scrubbing
  scrubs
scrubby
scruff
scruffily
scruffiness
scruffy
  scruffier
  scruffiest
scrum
scrummage
  scrummaged
  scrummaging
scrumptious
scrunch
scruple
scrupulous

scrupulously
scrupulousness
scrutineer
scrutinise
  scrutinised
  scrutinising
scrutinize
  scrutinized
  scrutinizing
scrutiny
scuba
scud
  scudded
  scudding
  scuds
scuff
  scuffed
scuffle
  scuffled
  scuffling
scull (rowing)
sculler
scullery
  sculleries *pl*
scullion
sculpt
sculptor
sculptress
  sculptresses *pl*
sculpture
scum
scummy
scupper

scuppered
scuppering
scurf
scurrilous
scurrilously
scurry
  scurried
  scurries
  scurrying
scurvily
scurvy
scutcheon,
  escutcheon
scuttle
  scuttled
  scuttling
scythe
  scythed
  scything
sea (ocean)
seaboard
seaborne
seafarer
seafaring
seafood
seagull
seakale
seal
  sealed
  sealing
sea level
sealing wax
sea lion

sealskin
seam (in sewing)
seaman (sailor)
  seamen *pl*
seamanship
seamless
seamstress, sempstress
seamy
seance
seaplane
sear (to scorch)
  seared
  searing
search
searcher
searchlight
seascape
sea serpent
seashore
seasick
seasickness
seaside
season
  seasoned
  seasoning
seasonable
seasonably
seasonal
seasonally
seat
  seated
  seating
seat belt

seaweed
seaworthiness
seaworthy
sebaceous
sec (of wine; dry)
secant, sec. (maths.)
secateurs
secede
  seceded
  seceding
secession
seclude
  secluded
  secluding
seclusion
second
secondarily
secondary
  secondaries *pl*
secondary school
seconder
second guess
second-hand
secondment
second-rate
secrecy
secret
secretaire (desk)
secretarial
secretariat
secretary
  secretaries *pl*
secrete

secreted
  secreting
secretion
secretive
secretively
secretiveness
secretly
sect
sectarian
section
sectional
sector
secular
secure
  secured
  securing
securely
security
  securities *pl*
sedate
  sedated
  sedating
sedately
sedation
sedative
sedentary
sedge
sediment
sedimentary
sedimentation
sedition
seditious
seditiously

seduce
 seduced
 seducing
seducer
seduction
seductive
seductively
sedulity
sedulous
see (to view)
 saw
 seeing
 seen
 sees
seed (of a plant)
 seeded
 seeding
seediness
seedling
seedy
 seedier
 seediest
seek
 seeking
 seeks
 sought
seeker
seem (to appear)
 seemed
 seeming
seemingly
seemliness
seemly

see-saw
 see-sawed
 see-sawing
seen (*from* see)
seep
 seeped
 seeping
seepage
seer (prophet)
seethe
 seethed
 seething
segment
segmentation
segregate
 segregated
 segregating
segregation
segregative
seine (fishing net)
seismic
seismograph
seismologist
seismology
seize
 seized
 seizing
seizure
seldom
select
selection
selective
selectively

selectivity
selector
selenium
self
 selves *pl*
self-addressed
self-assured
self-catering
self-centered *Am*
self-centred
self-conscious
self-consciously
self-consciousness
self-defence
self-defense *Am*
self-employed
self-esteem
self-evident
self-explanatory
self-image
self-important
self-interest
selfish
selfishly
selfishness
selfless
self-made
self-portrait
self-possessed
self-raising (flour)
self-regulating
self-righteous
self-righteousness

selfsame
self-satisfied
self-service
self-starter
self-styled
self-sufficient
self-taught
sell (of goods)
seller (of goods)
Sellotape
sell-out
seltzer
selvedge, selvage
  (edge)
semantic
semaphore
semblance
semen (sperm)
semester
semi-automatic
semibreve
semicircle
semicircular
semicolon
semiconductor
semi-conscious
semi-detached
semi-final
seminal
seminar
seminary
  seminaries *pl*
semi-precious

semiquaver
semi-skilled
semitone
semitropical
semolina
senate
senator
senatorial
send
  sending
  sends
  sent
sender
senile
senility
senior
seniority
senna
  sennas *pl*
sensation
sensational
sensationalism
sensationally
sense
  sensed
  sensing
senseless
senselessly
senselessness
sensibility
sensible
sensibly
sensitise

sensitised
sensitising
sensitive
sensitively
sensitivity
sensitize
  sensitized
  sensitizing
sensor (detecting
  device)
sensory
sensual
sensualist
sensuality
sensually
sensuous
sensuously
sensuousness
sent (*from* send)
sentence
  sentenced
  sentencing
sententious
sententiously
sententiousness
sentience
sentient
sentiment
sentimental
sentimentalise
  sentimentalised
  sentimentalising
sentimentalist

sentimentality
sentimentalize
  sentimentalized
  sentimentalizing
sentimentally
sentinel
sentry
  sentries *pl*
separable
separate
  separated
  separating
separation
separatism
separator
sepia
sepoy
  sepoys *pl*
sepsis
September
septic (infected)
septicaemia
septicemia *Am*
septuagenarian
septum
  septa *pl*
sepulcher *Am*
sepulchral
sepulchre
sequel
sequence
  sequenced
  sequencing

sequential
sequester
  sequestered
  sequestering
sequestrate
  sequestrated
  sequestrating
sequestration
sequestrator
sequin
sequinned
seraglio
  seraglios *pl*
seraph
  seraphs, seraphim *pl*
seraphic
serenade
  serenaded
  serenading
serenader
serendipitous
serendipity
serene
serenely
serenity
serf (land slave)
serfdom
serge (cloth)
sergeant
sergeant major
serial (story in
  instalments)
serialisation

serialise
  serialised
  serialising
serialization
serialize
  serialized
  serializing
serially
series
serif
serious
seriously
seriousness
serjeant (legal officer)
sermon
sermonise
  sermonised
  sermonising
sermonize
  sermonized
  sermonizing
serpent
serpentine
serrated
serration
serried
serum
  sera, serums *pl*
servant
serve
  served
  serving
server

service
  serviced
  servicing
serviceability
serviceable
serviette
servile
servility
servitude
sesame
session (period)
set
  sets
  setting
setback
settee
  settees *pl*
setter
settle
  settled
  settling
settlement
seven
seventeen
seventeenth
seventh
seventieth
seventy
  seventies *pl*
sever (to cut off)
  severed
  severing
several

severally
severance
severe (strict)
severely
severity
sew (to stitch)
  sewed
  sewing
  sewn
  sews
sewage
sewer (drain)
sewing machine
sex
  sexes *pl*
sexagenarian
sexed
sexiness
sexist
sextant
sextet
sexton
sextuple
sexual
sexuality
sexually
sexy
  sexier
  sexiest
shabbier
shabbily
shabbiness
shabby

shabbier
shabbiest
shack
shackle
  shackled
  shackling
shade
  shaded
  shading
shadily
shadow
shadowy
shady
  shadier
  shadiest
shaft
shaggy
  shaggier
  shaggiest
shagreen
Shah
shake (to tremble)
  shaken
  shakes
  shaking
  shook
shaker
shake-up
shakily
shakiness
shaky
shale
shall (will)

shallot
shallow
shallower
shallowness
shalt
sham
  shammed
  shamming
  shams
shamble
  shambled
  shambling
shame
  shamed
  shaming
shamefaced
shameful
shamefully
shameless
shamelessly
shammer
shampoo
  shampooed
  shampooing
  shampoos
shamrock
shandy
shandygaff
shanghai
  shanghaied
  shanghaiing
shan't (shall not)
shank

shantung
shanty
  shanties pl
shanty town
shape
  shaped
  shaping
shapeless
shapeliness
shapely
shard, sherd
share
  shared
  sharing
shareholder
sharer
shark
sharp
sharpen
  sharpened
  sharpening
sharpener
sharper
sharply
sharpshooter
sharp-witted
shatter
  shattered
  shattering
shatter-proof
shave
  shaved
  shaving

shaven
shaver
shawl
she
sheaf
  sheaves pl
shear (to cut)
  sheared
  shearing
  shears
  shorn
shearer
shears
sheath
sheathe
  sheathed
  sheathing
sheath knife
shed
  shedding
  sheds
she'd (she would;
  she had)
sheen
sheep
sheepish
sheepishly
sheepskin
sheer (absolute; steep)
sheet
sheikh, sheik (ruler)
she'll (she will)
shelf

shelves *pl*
shell
shellac
  shellacked
  shellacking
  shellacs
shellfish
shelter
  sheltered
  sheltering
shelterer
shelve
  shelved
  shelving
shenanigan
shepherd
  shepherded
  shepherding
shepherdess
sherbet
sherd, shard
sheriff
  sheriffs *pl*
sherry
  sherries *pl*
she's (she has; she is)
shied (*from* shy)
shield
shies (*from* shy)
shift
shiftily
shiftiness
shifty

shiftier
shiftiest
shilling
shilly-shallier, shilly-
  shallyer
shilly-shally
  shilly-shallied
  shilly-shallies
  shilly-shallying
shimmer
  shimmered
  shimmering
shin
shindy
  shindies *pl*
shine (to give out
  light)
  shines
  shining
  shone
shine (to polish)
  shined
  shines
  shining
shingle
  shingled
  shingling
  shingles
shiny
  shinier
  shiniest
ship
  shipped

shipping
ships
shipmate
shipment
shipper
shipshape
shipwrecked
shipwright
shire (county)
shirk
shirker
shirr
shirring
shirt
shiver
  shivered
  shivering
shivers
shivery
shoal
  shoaled
  shoaling
shock
shock absorber
shocker
shocking
shod
shoddier
shoddily
shoddiness
shoddy
  shoddier
  shoddiest

shoe (footwear)
shoes *pl*
shod
shoed
shoeing
shoes
shoelace
shone (*from* shine)
shoo (scare)
shooed
shooing
shoos
shook (*from* shake)
shoot (*eg* with a gun)
shooting
shoots
shot
shop
shopped
shopping
shops
shopkeeper
shoplifting
shopped
shopper
shore (beach)
shored
shoring
shorn
short
shortage
shortbread
shortcake

short-circuit
short-circuited
short-circuiting
shortcoming
shorten
shortened
shortening
shorter
shorthand
short-lived
shortly
shortness
short-sighted
short-sightedness
short-tempered
shot
shotgun
should
shoulder
shouldered
shouldering
shoulder blade
shouldn't (should
not)
shout
shouted
shouting
shove
shoved
shoving
shovel
shovelled
shovelling

shovels
shoveled *Am*
shoveling *Am*
show
showed
showing
shown
shows
showdown
shower
showery
showily
showman
showmen *pl*
showmanship
showpiece
showy
shrank
shrapnel
shred
shredded
shredding
shreds
shredder
shrew
shrewd
shrewdly
shrewdness
shrewish
shriek
shrieked
shrieking
shrift

shrike
shrill
shriller
shrillness
shrilly
shrimp
shrine
shrink
shrinkage
shrivel
  shrivelled
  shrivelling
  shrivels
  shriveled Am
  shriveling Am
shroud
shrub
shrubbery
  shrubberies pl
shrug
  shrugged
  shrugging
  shrugs
shrunk
shrunken
shuffle
  shuffled
  shuffling
shun
  shunned
  shunning
  shuns
shunt

shut
  shuts
  shutting
shutdown
shutters
shuttle
  shuttled
  shuttling
shuttlecock
shy
  shies pl
shy (timid)
  shied
  shies
  shying
  shyer
  shyest
shyly
shyness
sibilant
sibling
sic (thus)
siccative
sick
sick bay
sicken
  sickened
  sickening
sickle (for reaping)
sickly
sickness
side
  sided

siding
sideboard
sideburns
sidelight
sideline
  sidelined
  sidelining
sidelong
side-splitting
sidestep
  sidestepped
  sidestepping
  sidesteps
sidetrack
sidewalk
sideways
siding
sidle
  sidled
  sidling
siege
sienna
  siennas pl
siesta
  siestas pl
sieve
  sieved
  sieving
sift
sigh
  sighed
  sighing
sight (vision)

sightless
sightlessness
sightliness
sightly
sightseeing
sightseer
sign (mark)
  signed
  signing
signal
  signalled
  signalling
  signals
  signaled *Am*
  signaling *Am*
signaler
signaller
signally
signalman
  signalmen *pl*
signals
signatory
  signatories *pl*
signature
signer
signet (ring)
significance
significant
significantly
signify
  signified
  signifies
  signifying

Signor
Signora
  Signoras *pl*
Signorina
  Signorinas *pl*
signpost
signwriter
signwriting
Sikh
silage
silence
  silenced
  silencing
silencer
silent
silently
silhouette
  silhouetted
  silhouetting
silica (*eg* in sand)
silicate
silicon (chem.
  element)
silicone (compound
  of silicon)
silicosis
silk
silken
silkworm
silky
  silkier
  silkiest
sill

sillabub, syllabub
  (sweet cream)
silliness
silly
  sillier
  silliest
silo
  silos *pl*
silt
silver
  silvered
  silvering
silversmith
silver-tongued
silvery
simian
similar
similarity
  similarities *pl*
similarly
simile
  similes *pl*
similitude
simmer
  simmered
  simmering
simnel
simony
simper
  simpered
  simpering
simple
simple-minded

simpler
simpleton
simplex
simplicity
simplification
simplify
  simplified
  simplifies
  simplifying
simplistic
simply
simulacrum
  simulacra *pl*
simulate
  simulated
  simulating
simulation
simulator
simultaneity
simultaneous
simultaneously
sin
  sinned
  sinning
  sins
since
sincere
sincerely
sincerity
sine, sin (maths.)
sinecure
sine die
sine qua non

sinew
sine wave
sinewy
sinful
sinfully
sinfulness
sing
  sang
  singing
  sings
  sung
singe (to scorch)
  singed
  singeing
  singes
singer
single
  singled
  singling
single-minded
singlet
singleton
singly
singsong
singular
singularity
singularly
sinister
sinisterly
sink
  sank
  sinking
  sinks

  sunk
sinker
sinless
sinner
sinologist
sinology
sinuous (with curves)
sinuously
sinus
  sinuses *pl*
sinusitis
sinusoidal
sinusoidally
sip
  sipped
  sipping
  sips
siphon
  siphoned
  siphoning
sir
sire
  sired
  siring
siren
sirloin
sirocco
  siroccos *pl*
sisal
sister
sisterhood
sister-in-law
  sisters-in-law *pl*

sisterly

sit
  sits
  sat
  sitting
site (location)
sit-in
  sit-ins *pl*
sitter
situate
  situated
  situating
situation
sitz-bath
six
  sixes *pl*
sixteen
sixteenth
sixth
sixthly
sixtieth
sixty
  sixties *pl*
size
  sized
  sizing
sizeable
sizeably
sizzle
  sizzled
  sizzling
skate
  skated

skating
skateboard
skater
skedaddle
  skedaddled
  skedaddling
skein
skeletal
skeleton
skeptic *Am*
skeptical *Am*
skeptically *Am*
skepticism *Am*
sketch
sketcher
sketchily
sketchiness
sketchy
  sketchier
  sketchiest
skew
  skewed
  skewing
skewer
skew-whiff
ski
  skied
  skiing
  skis
skid
  skidded
  skidding
  skids

skied
skier
skiff
skilful
skilfully
skill
skilled
skillet
skillful *Am*
skim
  skimmed
  skimming
  skims
skimp
skimpily
skimpiness
skimpy
  skimpier
  skimpiest
skin
  skinned
  skinning
  skins
skin-deep
skin diver
skin diving
skinflint
skinny
  skinnier
  skinniest
skintight
skip
  skipped

skipping
skips
skipper
skirl
skirmish
skirt
skit
skittish
skittishly
skittishness
skittle
skittle alley
skua
  skuas *pl*
skulduggery
skulk
skull (of head)
skullcap
skunk
sky
  skies *pl*
skydiving
sky-high
skylark
skylight
skyscraper
slab
slack
slacken
  slackened
  slackening
slacker
slackness

slag
  slagged
  slagging
  slags
slain (*from* slay)
slake
  slaked
  slaking
slalom
slam
  slammed
  slamming
  slams
slander
  slandered
  slandering
slanderer
slanderous
slang
slangy
slant
slap
  slapped
  slapping
  slaps
slapdash
slapstick
slash
slat
slate
  slated
  slating
slattern

slatternly
slaughter
  slaughtered
  slaughtering
slaughterhouse
slave
  slaved
  slaving
slaver
  slavered
  slavering
slavery
slavish
slavishly
slavishness
slay (kill)
  slain
  slayed
  slaying
  slays
  slew
sleaze
sleazy
  sleazier
  sleaziest
sled
sledge
sledgehammer
sleek
sleekness
sleep
  sleeps
  slept

sleeping
leeper
leepily
leepiness
leeping partner
leeping draught
leepless
leeplessness
leepover
leepwalk
sleepwalked
sleepwalking
leepwalker
leepy
sleepier
sleepiest
leet
sleeted
sleeting
leeve
leeveless
leigh (sledge)
leight (skill)
lender
lenderness
lept (*from* sleep)
leuth
lew (*from* slay)
lew, slue (to swing around)
slewed
slewing
lice

sliced
slicing
slick
slicker
slide
slid
slides
sliding
slide rule
slight (small)
slighted
slighting
slighter
slightest
slightly
slim
slimmed
slimming
slims
slime (dirt)
slimmer
slimness
slimy
slimier
slimiest
sling
slinging
slings
slung
slink
slinking
slinks
slunk

slip
slipped
slipping
slips
slip-knot
slipper
slipperiness
slippery
slipshod
slipstream
slit
slits
slitting
slither
slithered
slithering
sliver (to break up)
slivered
slivering
slobber
slobbered
slobbering
sloe (fruit)
sloe gin
sloe-eyed
slog
slogged
slogging
slogs
slogan
slogger
sloop (ship)
slop

slopped
slopping
slops
slope
  sloped
  sloping
sloppily
sloppiness
sloppy
  sloppier
  sloppiest
slosh
slot
  slots
  slotted
  slotting
sloth
slothful
slouch
slough (skin)
  sloughed
  sloughing
sloven
slovenliness
slovenly
slow (not fast)
  slowed
  slowing
  slower
  slowest
slowly
sludge
slug

slugged
slugging
slugs
sluggard
sluggish
sluggishly
sluggishness
sluice
  sluiced
  sluicing
slum
  slummed
  slumming
  slums
slumber
  slumbered
  slumbering
slumberous, slumbrous
slump
slung (*from* sling)
slunk (*from* slink)
slur
  slurred
  slurring
  slurs
slurry
slush
slut
sluttish
sly
  slyer
  slyest
  slyly

slyness
smack
small
smallness
smart
smarten
  smartened
  smartening
smartly
smartness
smash
smattering
smear
  smeared
  smearing
smell
smelled
smells
smelly
  smellier
  smelliest
smelt
smidgen, smidgin
smile
  smiled
  smiling
smirch
smirched
smirk
smite
  smites
  smiting
  smitten

smote

mith

mithereens

mithy

smithies *pl*

mock

mocking

mog

mokable

moke

smoked

smoking

mokeless

moker

moking

moky

smokier

smokiest

molder *Am*

smoldered

smoldering

mooth

smoother

moothly

smoothness

morgasbord

smote (*from* smite)

smother

smothered

smothering

smoulder

smouldered

smouldering

smudge

smudged

smudging

smug

smugger

smuggle

smuggled

smuggling

smuggler

smugly

smugness

smut

smuttiness

smutty

smuttier

smuttiest

snack

snaffle

snaffled

snaffling

snag

snagged

snagging

snags

snail

snake

snaked

snaking

snap

snapped

snapping

snaps

snapdragon

snapper

snappily

snappish

snappy

snappier

snappiest

snaps

snapshot

snare

snared

snaring

snarl

snatch

sneak

sneaked

sneaking

sneakers

sneer

sneered

sneering

sneeze

sneezed

sneezing

snicker

snickered

snickering

snide

sniff

sniffle

sniffled

sniffling

snifter

snigger

sniggered
sniggering
snip (to cut)
  snipped
  snipping
  snips
snipe (bird; to shoot)
  sniped
  sniping
snippet
snivel
  snivelled
  snivelling
  snivels
  sniveled Am
  sniveling Am
sniveller
snob
snobbery
  snobberies pl
snobbish
snobbishly
snobbishness
snooker
  snookered
  snookering
snoop
  snooped
  snooping
snooper
snooze
  snoozed
  snoozing

snore
  snored
  snoring
snorer
snorkel
  snorkelled
  snorkelling
  snorkels
  snorkeled Am
  snorkeling Am
snort
snot
snotty
snout
snow
  snowed
  snowing
snowball
snowballing
snowdrop
snowfall
snowflake
snowmobile
snowplough
snowplow Am
snowshoe
  snowshoes pl
snub
  snubbed
  snubbing
  snubs
snub-nosed
snuff

snuffers
snuffle
  snuffled
  snuffling
snug
snuggery
  snuggeries pl
snuggle
  snuggled
  snuggling
snugly
soak
  soaked
  soaking
soap
  soaped
  soaping
soap flakes
soapsuds
soapy
soar (to fly high)
  soared
  soaring
sob
  sobbed
  sobbing
  sobs
sober
  sobered
  sobering
sobriety
sobriquet
soccer

ociability
ociable
ociably
ocial
Social Security
ocialisation
ocialise
  socialised
  socialising
Socialism
Socialist
ocialite
ocialization
ocialize
  socialized
  socializing
ocially
ociety
  societies pl
ocio-economic
sociological
sociologist
sociology
sock
socket
sod (turf)
soda
  sodas pl
soda water
sodden
sodium
sodomy
sofa

sofas pl
soft
softball
soften
  softened
  softening
softer
softly
softness
software
soggy
  soggier
  soggiest
soil
  soiled
  soiling
soirée
sojourn
solace
solacing
solar
solar system
solarium
  solariums, solaria pl
sold (from sell)
solder
  soldered
  soldering
soldering iron
soldier
  soldiered
  soldiering
sole (alone; fish; of

shoe)
solecism
solely
solemn
solemnisation
solemnise
  solemnised
  solemnising
solemnity
  solemnities pl
solemnization
solemnize
  solemnized
  solemnizing
solemnly
solenoid
solicit
  solicited
  soliciting
solicitation
solicitor
solicitous
solicitously
solicitude
solid
solidarity
solidification
solidify
  solidified
  solidifies
  solidifying
solidity
solidly

solid-state
soliloquise
  soliloquies *pl*
soliloquising
soliloquize
  soliloquized
  soliloquizing
soliloquy
  soliloquies *pl*
soling
solitaire (single gem)
solitarily
solitariness
solitary
solitude
solo
  solos, soli *pl*
soloed
soloes
soloing
soloist
solstice
solstitial
solubility
soluble
solution
solvable
solve
  solved
  solving
solvency
solvent
somatic

somber
somberly
somberness
sombre
sombrely
sombreness
sombrero
  sombreros *pl*
some (a few)
somebody
somehow
someone
somersault
somewhat
somewhere
somnambulism
somnambulist
somnolence
somnolent
son (boy child)
sonar
sonata
  sonatas *pl*
sonatina
  sonatinas *pl*
son-in-law
  sons-in-law *pl*
song
songster
sonic
sonnet
sonny
sonority

sonorous
sonorously
soon
  sooner
  soonest
soot
soothe
  soothed
  soothing
soothsayer
sop
  sopped
  sopping
  sops
sophism
sophist
sophisticated
sophistry
sophomore
soporific
soprano
  sopranos *pl*
sorcerer
sorceress
sorcery
sordid
sordidly
sordidness
sore (painful)
sorely
soreness
sorority
sorrel

orrow
orrowful
orrowfully
orrowfulness
orry
  sorrier
  sorriest
ort (kind; to arrange
  in groups)
orter
ortie
  sorties *pl*
ot
ottish
otto voce (in a
  whisper)
oubrette
oufflé
ought (*from* seek)
oul (spirit; music)
oulful
oulfully
oulless
ound
ounder
oundless
oundlessly
oundly
oundness
oundproof
  soundproofed
  soundproofing
  soundproofs

soup
soupçon
sour
source (origin)
  sourced
  sourcing
sourer
sourly
sourness
souse
  soused
  sousing
south
southerly
southern
southerner
southward
souvenir
sou'wester
sovereign
sovereignty
soviet
sow (female pig;
    seeds)
  sowed
  sowing
  sown
  sows
soya
soybean
spa
  spas *pl*
space

spaced
spacing
spacecraft
spaceship
spacesuit
spacious
spaciousness
spade
spaghetti
span
  spanned
  spanning
  spans
spangle
  spangled
  spangling
spaniel
spank
spanner
spar
  sparred
  sparring
  spars
spare
  spared
  sparing
sparingly
spark
sparkle
  sparkled
  sparkling
sparkler
sparrow

sparse

sparsely

spasm

spasmodic

spasmodically

spastic

spat (*from* spit)

spate

spatial

spatter

  spattered

  spattering

spatula

  spatulas *pl*

spavin

spavined

spawn

spay

  spayed

  spaying

  spays

speak

  speaking

  speaks

  spoke

  spoken

speaker

spear

  speared

  spearing

spearhead

spec (gamble)

special

specialisation

specialise

  specialised

  specialising

specialist

speciality

  specialities *pl*

specialization

specialize

  specialized

  specializing

specially

specialty

  specialties *pl*

specie (coins)

species

  species *pl*

specific

specifically

specification

specify

  specified

  specifies

  specifying

specimen

specious (plausible)

speck (fleck)

speckled

spectacle

spectacles

spectacular

spectacularly

spectator

specter *Am*

spectral

spectre

spectroscope

spectroscopic

spectrum

  spectra *pl*

speculate

  speculated

  speculating

speculation

speculative

speculatively

speculator

speech

speechified

speechify

  speechified

  speechifies

  speechifying

speechless

speechlessly

speed

  sped

  speeded

  speeding

  speeds

speedily

speedometer

speedy

  speedier

  speediest

spell

spelled
spelling
spells
spelt
spellbinding
spellbound
speller
spelt
spelter
spend
  spending
  spends
  spent
spender
spendthrift
sperm
spermaceti
sperm whale
spew
  spewed
  spewing
sphagnum
  sphagna *pl*
sphere
spherical
spherically
spheroid
sphincter
sphinx
  sphinxes *pl*
sphygmomanometer
spice
spicily

spiciness
spick and span
spicy
  spicier
  spiciest
spider
spidery
spied (*from* spy)
spigot
spike
  spiked
  spiking
spiky
  spikier
  spikiest
spill
  spilled
  spilling
  spills
  spilt
spillage
spillikin
spin
  spinning
  spins
  spun
spinach
spinal
spinal column
spindle
spindly
spin-dryer, spin-drier
spine

spineless
spinet
spinnaker
spinner
spinneret
spinney
  spinneys *pl*
spinning wheel
spin-off
spinster
spinsterhood
spiraea
  spiraeas *pl*
spiral
  spiralled
  spiralling
  spirals
  spiraled *Am*
  spiraling *Am*
spirally
spire
spirit
  spirited
  spiriting
spiritedly
spiritless
spiritual
spiritualism
spiritualist
spiritualistic
spiritually
spirituous
spirt, spurt

spit
  spits
  spitted
  spitting
spite
spiteful
spitefully
spitefulness
spitfire
spitter
spittle
spittoon
spiv
splash
splashdown
splatter
  splattered
  splattering
splay
  splayed
  splaying
  splays
spleen
splendid
splendidly
splendor *Am*
splendour
splenetic
splice
  spliced
  splicing
splint
splinter

splintered
splintering
split
  splits
  splitting
splurge
  splurged
  splurging
splutter
  spluttered
  spluttering
spoil
  spoiled
  spoiling
  spoils
  spoilt
spoke (*from* speak;
  thin rod)
spoken (*from* speak)
spokeshave
spokesman
  spokesmen *pl*
spokeswoman
  spokeswomen *pl*
spoliation
spoliator
sponge
  sponged
  sponging
sponger
spongy
sponsor
  sponsored

sponsoring
spontaneity
spontaneous
spontaneously
spoof
  spoofed
  spoofing
  spoofer
spool
  spooled
  spooling
spoon
  spooned
  spooning
spoonerism
spoon-feed
  spoon-fed
  spoon-feeding
  spoon-feeds
spoonful
  spoonfuls *pl*
spoor (track)
sporadic
sporadically
spore (for
  reproduction)
sporran
sport
sportive
sportively
sportsman
  sportsmen *pl*
sportsmanship

spot
  spots
  spotted
  spotting
spot check
spotless
spotlessness
spotlight
  spotlighted
  spotlighting
  spotlights
spotlit
spotty
  spottier
  spottiest
spouse
spout
sprain
  sprained
  spraining
sprang (*from* spring)
sprat
sprawl
spray
  sprays *pl*
  sprayed
  spraying
  sprays
sprayer
spread
  spreading
  spreads
spreadeagle

spreadeagled
spreadeagling
spree
sprig
sprightliness
sprightly
  sprightlier
  sprightliest
spring
  sprang
  springing
  springs
  sprung
springboard
spring-clean
  spring-cleaned
  spring-cleaning
springtime
sprinkle
  sprinkled
  sprinkling
sprinkler
sprint
sprinter
sprite
spritzer
sprocket
sprout
  sprouted
  sprouting
spruce
  spruced
  sprucing

sprucely
spruceness
sprue
sprung (*from* spring)
spry
spryer
spryly
spryness
spud
spume
spun (*from* spin)
spunk
spur
  spurred
  spurring
  spurs
spurious
spurn
spurt, spirt
sputnik
sputter
  sputtered
  sputtering
sputum
  sputa *pl*
spy
  spies *pl*
  spied
  spies
  spying
squabble
  squabbled
  squabbling

squad
squadron
squadron leader
squalid
squalidly
squall
squally
squalor
squander
  squandered
  squandering
square
  squared
  squaring
squarely
squash
squat
  squats
  squatted
  squatting
squatter
squaw
squawk
squawker
squeak
  squeaked
  squeaking
squeal
  squealed
  squealing
squeamish
squeamishness
squeegee

squeeze
  squeezed
  squeezing
squelch
squib
squid
squiggle
  squiggled
  squiggling
squill
squint
squire
squirearchy
  squirearchies *pl*
squireen
squirm
squirrel
squirt
stab
  stabbed
  stabbing
  stabs
stabilisation
stabilise
  stabilised
  stabilising
  stabiliser
stability
stabilization
stabilize
  stabilized
  stabilizing
  stabilizer

stable
  stabled
  stabling
staccato
  staccatos *pl*
stack
stadium
  stadiums, stadia *pl*
staff
  staffed
  staffing
  staffs
stag
stage
  staged
  staging
stagecraft
stagey, stagy
stagger
  staggered
  staggering
staggers (sheep
  disease)
stagnant
stagnate
  stagnated
  stagnating
stagnation
staid (steady)
staidly
staidness
stain
  stained

staining

tainless

tair (step)

taircase

take (post; to bet)

  staked

  staking

takeholder

takeholding

talactite

talagmite

tale

  staled

  staling

talemate

taleness

talk (to hunt)

talker

tall

tallion

talwart

tamen

tamina

tammer

  stammered

  stammering

tammerer

tamp

tamp album

tamp collecting

tamp collector

tampede

  stampeded

stampeding

stance

stanchion

stand

standard

standardisation

standardise

  standardised

  standardising

standardization

standardize

  standardized

  standardizing

standby

  standbys *pl*

stank

stanza

  stanzas *pl*

staple

  stapled

  stapling

stapler

star

  starred

  starring

  stars

starboard

starch

stardom

stare (to gaze)

  stared

  staring

stark

starless

starlet

starry

start

starter

startle

  startled

  startling

star turn

starvation

starve

  starved

  starving

starveling

state

  stated

  stating

stateless

stateliness

stately

statement

statesman

  statesmen *pl*

statesmanship

static

station

  stationed

  stationing

stationary (not moving)

stationer

stationery (paper)

stationmaster

statistical
statistically
statistician
statistics
statuary
statue
  statues *pl*
statuesque
statuette
stature
status
  statuses *pl*
status quo
statute (law)
statutory
staunch, stanch
  (loyal; to stop
  bleeding)
staunchly
staunchness
stave
  staved
  staving
stave off
stay
  stayed
  staying
  stays
steadfast
steadfastly
steadfastness
steadier
steadily

steadiness
steady
  steadied
  steadies
  steadying
steak (meat)
steal (to rob)
  stealing
  steals
  stole
  stolen
stealth
stealthily
stealthiness
stealthy
  stealthier
  stealthiest
steam
  steamed
  steaming
steam engine
steamer
steamroller
  steamrollered
  steamrollering
steed
steel (metal; to
  prepare oneself)
  steeled
  steeling
steely
steep
  steeped

steeping
steeper
steeple
steeplechase
steeplejack
steeply
steepness
steer
  steered
  steering
steerable
steerage
steersman
  steersmen *pl*
stele, stela (Greek
  gravestone)
stellar
stem
  stemmed
  stemming
  stems
stench
stencil
  stencilled
  stencilling
  stencils
  stenciled *Am*
  stenciling *Am*
stenographer
stenographic
stenography
stenotype
stentorian

366

step
  stepped
  stepping
  steps
stepbrother
stepfather
stepladder
stepmother
steppe (plain)
stepsister
stereo
stereophonic
stereoscope
stereoscopic
stereotype
  stereotyped
  stereotyping
sterile
sterilisation
sterilise
  sterilised
  sterilising
steriliser
sterility
sterilization
sterilize
  sterilized
  sterilizing
sterilizer
sterling
stern
sterner
sternly

sternness
sternum
  sternums *pl*
steroid
stertorous
stet
stethoscope
stevedore
stew
  stewed
  stewing
steward
stewardess
stick
sticker
stickily
stickiness
stickleback
stickler
sticky
  stickier
  stickiest
sticky (adhesive note)
  stickies *pl*
stiff
stiffen
  stiffened
  stiffening
stiffener
stiffly
stiff-necked
stifle
  stifled

stifling
stigma
  stigmas, stigmata *pl*
stigmatise
  stigmatised
  stigmatising
stigmatize
  stigmatized
  stigmatizing
stile (over a hedge)
stiletto
  stilettos *pl*
still
stillbirth
stillborn
stillness
stilt
stilted
stimulate
  stimulated
  stimulating
stimulation
stimulative
stimulus
  stimuli *pl*
sting
  stings
  stinging
  stung
stinger
stingily
stinginess
stingless

stingy
  stingier
  stingiest
stink
  stank
  stinking
  stinks
  stunk
stinker
stint
stipend
stipendiary
  stipendiaries *pl*
stipple
  stippled
  stippling
stipulate
  stipulated
  stipulating
stipulation
stir
  stirred
  stirring
  stirs
stirrup
stitch
stitched
stoat
stock
Stock Exchange
stockade
stockbroker
stocked

stockholder
stockiness
stockinette, stockinet
stocking
stockist
stockpile
  stockpiled
  stockpiling
stock still
stocktaking
stocky
  stockier
  stockiest
stockyard
stodge
stodgily
stodgy
  stodgier
  stodgiest
stoic
stoical
stoically
stoicism
stoke
  stoked
  stoking
stoker
stole (*from* steal; robe)
stolen (*from* steal)
stolid
stolidity
stolidly
stomach

stomach ache
stone
  stoned
  stoning
stone deaf
stonemason
stonewalling
stonily
stony
  stonier
  stoniest
stood (*from* stand)
stooge
stook
  stooked
  stooking
stool
stoop
  stooped
  stooping
stop
  stopped
  stopping
  stops
stopcock
stopgap
stopover
stoppage
stopper
stop press
stopwatch
storage
store

stored
storing
storekeeper
storey (of a building)
storeys *pl*
stork (bird)
storm
stormbound
stormily
stormy
stormier
stormiest
story (tale; of a
building *Am*)
stories *pl*
storyteller
stoup (flagon)
stout
stoutly
stoutness
stove
stow
stowed
stowing
stowage
stowaway
stowaways *pl*
straddle
straddled
straddling
strafe
strafed
strafing

straggle
straggled
straggling
straggler
straight (direct)
straighten
straightened
straightening
straighter
straightforward
strain
strained
straining
strainer
strait (narrow)
straiten
straitened
straitening
straitjacket
strait-laced
straits (difficulties)
Straits of Dover
strand
stranded
strange
strangely
stranger
strangle
strangled
strangling
stranglehold
strangulate
strangulated

strangulating
strangulation
strap
strapped
strapping
straps
straphanger
stratagem (trickery)
strategic
strategically
strategist
strategy (war tactics)
strategies *pl*
stratification
stratify
stratified
stratifies
stratifying
stratosphere
stratospheric
stratum (layer)
strata *pl*
stratus (cloud)
strati *pl*
straw
strawberry
strawberries *pl*
stray
strayed
straying
strays
streak
streaked

streaking
streaky
stream
  streamed
  streaming
streamline
  streamlined
  streamlining
street
streetcar
streetwise
strength
strengthen
  strengthened
  strengthening
strenuous
strenuously
strenuousness
streptococcal
streptococcus
  streptococci *pl*
streptomycin
stress
stretch
stretcher
strew
  strewed
  strewing
  strewn
  strews
striate
  striated
  striating

striation
stricken
strict
stricter (more
   disciplined)
strictly
strictness
stricture (scolding)
stride
  strides
  striding
  strode
stridency
strident
stridently
strife
strike (to hit)
  strikes
  striking
  struck
strike (affected)
  strikes
  striking
  stricken
strikebound
strike-breaker
strike-breaking
striker
string
  strings
  stringing
  strung
  stringed

stringency
stringent
stringently
stringy
strip
  stripped
  stripping
  strips
stripe
  striped
  striping
stripling
stripper
striptease
strive
  striven
  strives
  striving
  strove
stroboscope
stroboscopic
strode (*from* stride)
stroke
  stroked
  stroking
stroll
stroller
strong
stronger
stronghold
strongly
strontium
strop

stropped
stropping
strops
strove (*from* strive)
struck (*from* strike)
structural
structurally
structure
structured
structuring
strudel
struggle
struggled
struggling
strum
strummed
strumming
strums
strummer
strumpet
strung (*from* string)
strut
struts
strutted
strutting
strychnine
stub
stubbed
stubbing
stubs
stubble
stubborn
stubbornly

stubbornness
stucco
stuccoed
stuccoes
stuccoing
stuck (*from* stick)
stud
studded
studding
studs
student
stud farm
studied
studio
studios *pl*
studious
studiously
study
studies *pl*
studied
studies
studying
stuff
stuffed
stuffier
stuffiness
stuffy
stuffier
stuffiest
stultification
stultify
stultified
stultifies

stultifying
stumble
stumbled
stumbling
stumbling block
stump
stumped
stun
stunned
stunning
stuns
stung (*from* sting)
stunk (*from* stink)
stunt
stunted
stupefaction
stupefy
stupefied
stupefies
stupefying
stupendous
stupendously
stupid
stupider
stupidity
stupor
sturdily
sturdiness
sturdy
sturdier
sturdiest
sturgeon
stutter

stuttered
stuttering
stutterer
sty
  sties *pl*
style (method,
  elegance)
stylise
  stylised
  stylising
stylish
stylishly
stylishness
stylist
stylize
  stylized
  stylizing
stylus (gramophone
  needle)
  styluses, styli *pl*
stymie
  stymied
  stymieing
  stymies
styptic
styrene
suave
suavely
suavity
subaltern
subcommittee
subconscious
subconsciously

subconsciousness
subcontract
subcontractor
subdivide
  subdivided
  subdividing
subdivisible
subdivision
subdual
subdue
  subdued
  subduing
sub-edit
  sub-edited
  sub-editing
sub-editor
subject
subjection
subjective
subjectively
subjectivity
sub judice
subjugate
  subjugated
  subjugating
subjugation
subjunctive
sublet
  sublets
  subletting
sublimate
  sublimated
  sublimating

sublimation
sublime
sublimely
subliminal
sublimity
submarine
submerge
  submerged
  submerging
submergence
submersible
submersion
submission
submissively
submissiveness
submit
  submits
  submitted
  submitting
subnormal
subnormality
subnormally
subordinate
  subordinated
  subordinating
subordination
suborn (to bribe)
subornation
suborner
sub-plot
subpoena
  subpoenaed
  subpoenaing

subpoenas
sub rosa
subscribe
  subscribed
  subscribing
subscriber
subscription
subsequent
subsequently
subservience
subservient
subside
  subsided
  subsiding
subsidence
subsidiary
  subsidiaries pl
subsidies pl
subsidise
  subsidised
  subsidising
subsidize
  subsidized
  subsidizing
subsidy
  subsidies pl
subsist
subsistence
subsoil
subsonic
substance
substandard
substantial

substantially
substantiate
  substantiated
  substantiating
substantiation
substantive
substation
substitute
  substituted
  substituting
substitution
substratum
  substrata pl
substructure
subtenancy
  subtenancies pl
subtenant
subtend
subterfuge
subterranean
subtitle
  subitled
  subtitling
subtle
subtlety (ingenuity)
  subtleties pl
subtly
subtract
subtraction
subtropical
suburb
suburban
suburbanite

suburbia
subvention
subversion
subversive
subvert
subverter
subway
  subways pl
succeed
  succeeded
  succeeding
success
successful
successfully
succession
successive
successively
successor
succinct
succor Am
  succored
  succoring
succour
  succoured
  succouring
succulence
succulent
succumb
  succumbed
  succumbing
such
suck
sucker

suckle
  suckled
  suckling
sucrose
suction
sudden
suddenly
suddenness
suds
sue
  sued
  sues
  suing
suede (kind of
  leather)
suet
suet pudding
suffer
  suffered
  suffering
sufferance
sufferer
suffice
  sufficed
  sufficing
sufficiency
sufficient
sufficiently
suffix
  suffixes *pl*
suffocate
  suffocated
  suffocating

suffocation
suffragan
suffrage
suffragette
suffuse
  suffused
  suffusing
suffusion
sugar
  sugared
  sugaring
sugary
suggest
suggestion
suggestive
suggestively
suicidal
suicide
suit (clothes; to be
    convenient)
  suited
  suiting
suitability
suitable
suitably
suitcase
suite (furniture;
    rooms)
suitor
sulfate *Am*
sulfide *Am*
sulfur *Am*
sulfuretted *Am*

sulfuric acid *Am*
sulk
sulkily
sulkiness
sulky
sullen
sullenly
sullenness
sully
  sullied
  sullies
  sullying
sulphate
sulphide
sulphur
sulphuretted
sulphuric acid
sultan
sultana
  sultanas *pl*
sultanate
sultrier
sultrily
sultriness
sultry
sum (total)
  summed
  summing
  sums
summarily
summariness
summarise
  summarised

summarising

summarize
  summarized
  summarizing

summary (short)
  summaries *pl*

summation

summer

summertime

summery (warm)

summit

summitry

summon
  summoned
  summoning

summons
  summonses *pl*

sump

sumptuary

sumptuous

sumptuously

sumptuousness

sums

sun (star)
  sunned
  sunning
  suns

sunbathe
  sunbathed
  sunbathing

sunbeam

sunburn

sunburned

sunburnt

sundae (ice-cream)
  sundaes *pl*

Sunday

sundial

sundry
  sundries *pl*

sunflower

sung (*from* sing)

sunglasses

sunk (*from* sink)

sunken

sunless

sunlight

sunnier

sunny

sunrise

sunspot

sunstroke

suntan
  suntanned
  suntanning
  suntans

sup
  supped
  supping
  sups

superabundance

superabundant

superannuate
  superannuated
  superannuating

superannuation

superb

superbly

supercargo
  supercargoes *pl*

supercharge
  supercharged
  supercharging

supercilious

superciliously

superciliousness

superconductivity

superconductor

superficial

superficiality

superficially

superfluity

superfluous

superfluously

superglue

superheterodyne

superhuman

superimpose
  superimposed
  superimposing

superimposition

superintend

superintendence

superintendent

superior

superiority

superlative

superlatively

superman

supermen *pl*
supermarket
supernatural
supernaturalism
supernaturally
supernumerary
  supernumeraries *pl*
superpose
  superposed
  superposing
superposition
supersaturate
  supersaturated
  supersaturating
supersaturation
supersede
  superseded
  superseding
supersedence
supersedure
supersonic
superstition
superstitious
superstructure
supervene
  supervened
  supervening
supervention
supervise
  supervised
  supervising
supervision
supervisory

supine
supped
supper
supperless
supplant
supplanter
supple
supplely
supplement
supplementary
supplementation
suppleness
suppliant
supplicate
  supplicated
  supplicating
supplication
supplier
supply
  supplies *pl*
  supplied
  supplies
  supplying
support
supporter
suppose
  supposed
  supposing
supposedly
supposition
suppository
  suppositories *pl*
suppress

suppressible
suppression
suppressor
suppurate
  suppurated
  suppurating
suppuration
supremacy
supreme
supremely
surcharge
  surcharged
  surcharging
sure (certain)
surely
surety
  sureties *pl*
surf (sea)
  surfed
  surfing
surface
  surfaced
  surfacing
surfboard
surfeit
  surfeited
  surfeiting
surfer
surfing
surge (to rush)
  surged
  surging
surgeon

surgery
  surgeries *pl*
surgical
surgically
surlily
surliness
surly
  surlier
  surliest
surmise
  surmised
  surmising
surmount
surname
surpass
surplice (clergyman's)
surplus (excess)
  surpluses *pl*
surprise
  surprised
  surprising
surrealism
surrealist
surrender
  surrendered
  surrendering
surreptitious
surreptitiously
surrogate
surround
surtax
  surtaxes *pl*
surveillance

survey
  surveyed
  surveying
  surveys
surveyor
survival
survive
  survived
  surviving
survivor
susceptibility
susceptible
suspect
suspend
suspender
suspense
suspension
suspicion
suspicious
suspiciously
sustain
  sustained
  sustaining
sustenance
suture
  sutured
  suturing
svelte
swab
  swabbed
  swabbing
  swabs
swaddle

swaddled
swaddling
swag
swagger
  swaggered
  swaggering
swaggerer
swain
swallow
  swallowed
  swallowing
swam (*from* swim)
swamp
swampy
swan
  swanned
  swanning
  swans
swanky
swank
swap, swop
  swapped, swopped
  swapping, swopping
  swaps, swops
sward (of grass)
swarm
swarthily
swarthiness
swarthy
  swarthier
  swarthiest
swash
swashbuckler

swastika
  swastikas *pl*
swat (a fly)
  swats
  swatted
  swatting
swath, swathe (strip)
swathe (to bandage)
  swathed
  swathing
swatter
sway
  swayed
  swaying
  sways
swear
  swearing
  swears
swore
  sworn
sweat
  sweated
  sweating
sweater
sweaty
  sweatier
  sweatiest
swede (kind of turnip)
Swede (person from
  Sweden)
Swedish
sweep
  sweeping

sweeps
swept
sweeper
sweepstake
sweet (sugary)
sweet pea
sweetbread
sweeten
  sweetened
  sweetening
sweeter
sweetheart
sweetly
sweetmeat
swell
  swelled
  swelling
  swells
  swollen
swelter
  sweltered
  sweltering
swept (*from* sweep)
swerve
  swerved
  swerving
swift
swifter
swiftly
swiftness
swig
  swigged
  swigging

swigs
swill
swim
  swam
  swimming
  swims
  swims
  swum
swimmer
swimmingly
swindle
  swindled
  swindling
swindler
swine
swing
  swinging
  swings
  swung
swingeing (huge)
swinish
swipe
  swiped
  swiping
swirl
  swirled
  swirling
switch
switchback
switchboard
swivel
  swivelled
  swivelling

swivels
swiveled *Am*
swiveling *Am*
swizzle
swollen (*from* swell)
swoon
swooned
swooning
swoop
swooped
swooping
swop, swap
swopped, swapped
swopping, swapping
swops, swaps
sword
swore (*from* swear)
sworn (*from* swear)
swot (to study hard)
swots
swotted
swotting
swotter
swum (*from* swim)
swung (*from* swing)
sybarite
sybaritic
sycamore
sycophant
syllabic
syllable (part of a
word)
syllabub, sillabub

syllabus
syllabuses, syllabi *pl*
syllogism
sylph
symbiosis
symbol (sign)
symbolic
symbolical
symbolically
symbolise
symbolised
symbolising
symbolism
symbolize
symbolized
symbolizing
symmetrical
symmetrically
symmetry
symmetries *pl*
sympathetic
sympathetically
sympathise
sympathised
sympathising
sympathiser
sympathize
sympathized
sympathizing
sympathizer
sympathy
sympathies *pl*
symphonic

symphony
symphonies *pl*
symposium
symposia *pl*
symptom
symptomatic
synagogue
synchromesh
synchronisation
synchronise
synchronised
synchronising
synchronism
synchronization
synchronize
synchronized
synchronizing
synchronous
synchronously
syncopate
syncopated
syncopating
syncopation
syncope
syndicalism
syndicate
syndication
syndrome
synod
synonym
synonymous
synopsis
synopses *pl*

syntactic
syntax
synthesis
  syntheses *pl*
synthesise
  synthesised
  synthesising
synthesize
  synthesized
  synthesizing
synthetic
synthetically
syphilis
syphilitic
syringe
  syringed
  syringing
syrup
syrupy
system
systematic
systematically
systematise
  systematised
  systematising
systematize
  systematized
  systematizing
systole

tab
  tabbed
  tabbing
  tabs
tabby
  tabbies *pl*
tabernacle
table
  tabled
  tabling
table d'hôte
tableau
  tableaux *pl*
tablespoon
tablespoonful
  tablespoonfuls *pl*
tablet
tabloid
taboo

taboos *pl*
  tabooed
  tabooing
  taboos
tabulate
  tabulated
  tabulating
tabulation
tabulator
tachycardia
tacit
tacitly
taciturn
taciturnity
tack
tackiness
tackle
  tackled
  tackling

tackler
tacky (sticky)
taco
  tacos *pl*
tact
tactful
tactfully
tactic
tactical
tactician
tactile
tactless
tactlessly
tadpole
taffeta
tag
  tagged
  tagging
  tags
tagliatelle
tail (of animal)
  tailed
  tailing
tailless
tailor
  tailored
  tailoring
tailor-made
taint
  tainted
take
  taken
  takes

taking
took
take-off
taker
talc
talcum
tale (story)
talent
talented
talisman
 talismans *pl*
talk
talkative
talkativeness
talker
tall
tallness
tallow
tally
 tallies *pl*
 tallied
 tallies
 tallying
tally-ho
talon
tambourine
tame
 tamed
 taming
tameable
tameness
tamer
tam-o'-shanter

tamp
tamper
 tampered
 tampering
tampon
tan
 tanned
 tanning
 tans
tandem
tang
tangent, tan
tangential
tangentially
tangerine
tangibility
tangible
tangibly
tangle
 tangled
 tangling
tango
 tangos *pl*
 tangoed
 tangoing
 tangos
tank
tankage
tankard
tanker
tankful
 tankfuls *pl*
tanner

tannery
 tanneries *pl*
tannic
tannin
tantalise
 tantalised
 tantalising
 tantalisingly
tantalize
 tantalized
 tantalizing
 tantalizingly
tantalum
tantalus
 tantaluses *pl*
tantamount
tantrum
 tantrums *pl*
tap
 tapped
 tapping
 taps
tape
 taped
 taping
tape-recorder
taper
 tapered
 tapering
tapestry
 tapestries *pl*
tapeworm
tapioca

tappet

tap root

taproom

tapster

tar

  tarred

  tarring

  tars

tarantella (dance)

  tarantellas *pl*

tarantula (spider)

  tarantulas *pl*

tardily

tardiness

tardy

tare (weight)

target

tariff

  tariffs *pl*

tarmac

tarn

tarnish

tarnished

tarot

tarpaulin

tarragon

tarry

  tarried

  tarries

  tarrying

tart

tartan

tartar

tartaric

tartness

tartrate

task

task force

taskmaster

tassel

tasseled *Am*

tasselled

taste

  tasted

  tasting

tasteful

tastefully

tastefulness

tasteless

taster

tasty

  tastier

  tastiest

tatter

tatterdemalion

tattered

tattle

  tattled

  tattling

tattoo

  tattoos *pl*

  tattooed

  tattooing

  tattoos

tattooist

tatty

tattier

tattiest

taught (*from* teach)

taunt

taupe

taut (tight)

tauten

  tautened

  tautening

tautly

tautness

tautological

tautology

  tautologies *pl*

tavern

tawdrily

tawdry

tawny

tax

  taxes *pl*

  taxed

  taxes

  taxing

taxable

taxation

tax collector

tax-deductible

taxi

  taxis *pl*

  taxied

  taxiing

  taxis

taxicab

taxidermist
taxidermy
taximeter
taxonomy
  taxonomies *pl*
taxpayer
tea (drink)
tea bag
teach
  taught
  teaches
  teaching
teacher
teacup
teak
tea leaf
  tea leaves *pl*
tea party
  tea parties *pl*
teapot
team (*eg* of players)
team-mate
teamster
teamwork
tear (to rip; crying)
  tearing
  tears
  tore
  torn
tearful
tearfully
tearfulness
tearless

tease
  teased
  teasing
teaser
teaspoon
teaspoonful
  teaspoonfuls *pl*
teat
technical
technicality
  technicalities *pl*
technically
technician
Technicolor
technique
technocracy
  technocracies *pl*
technological
technologically
technology
  technologies *pl*
teddy bear
Te Deum
tedious
tediously
tediousness
tedium
tee (in golf)
  teed
  teeing
teem (to be
  abundant)
  teemed

  teeming
teenage
teenager
teens (age)
teeth (*from* tooth)
teethe
  teethed
  teething
teetotal
teetotaler *Am*
teetotalism
teetotaller
telecommunications
telegram
telegraph
telegraphic
telemeter
telepathic
telepathy
telephone
  telephoned
  telephoning
telephonic
telephonist
telephony
telephoto
teleprinter
teleprompter
telescope
  telescoped
  telescoping
telescopic
telescopy

teletext
teletype
televise
  televised
  televising
television
teleworker
teleworking
telex
  telexes *pl*
  telexed
  telexes
  telexing
tell
  telling
  tells
  told
tell-tale
temerity
temper
  tempered
  tempering
tempera
temperament
temperamental
temperamentally
temperance
temperate
temperature
tempest
tempestuous
template
temple

tempo
  tempi, tempos *pl*
temporal
temporally
temporarily
temporary
temporise
  temporised
  temporising
temporiser
temporize
  temporized
  temporizing
temporizer
tempt
temptation
tempter
temptress
tempus fugit
ten
tenability
tenable
tenacious
tenaciously
tenacity
tenancy
  tenancies *pl*
tenant
tenantry
tendency
  tendencies *pl*
tendentious
tender

tendered
tendering
tenderer
tender-hearted
tenderise
  tenderised
  tenderising
tenderize
  tenderized
  tenderizing
tenderly
tendon
tendril
tenement
tenet
tenfold
tennis
tennis court
tennis racket
tenon
tenon saw
tenor
tense
  tensed
  tensing
tensely
tenseness
tensile
tension
tent
tentacle
tentative
tentatively

tenterhooks
tenth
tenthly
tenuity
tenuous
tenuously
tenure
tepid
tepidly
tercentenary
tercentennial
term
termagant
terminable
terminal
terminally
terminate
  terminated
  terminating
termination
terminological
terminology
  terminologies *pl*
terminus
  termini, terminuses
    pl
termite
tern (bird)
terra firma
terrace
  terraced
  terracing
terracotta

terrain
terrapin
terrestrial
terrible
terribly
terrier
terrific
terrifically
terrify
  terrified
  terrifies
  terrifying
territorial
territorially
territory
  territories *pl*
terror
terrorisation
terrorise
  terrorised
  terrorising
terrorism
terrorist
terrorization
terrorize
  terrorized
  terrorizing
terse
tersely
terseness
tertian
Tertiary
test

testament
testamentary
testate
testator
testatrix
  testatrices *pl*
testicle
testicular
testify
  testified
  testifies
  testifying
testily
testimonial
testimony
  testimonies *pl*
testiness
test tube
testy
tetanus
tetany
tetchily
tetchiness
tetchy
tête-à-tête
tether
  tethered
  tethering
tetragon
tetragonal
tetrahedral
tetrahedron
tetralogy

tetralogies *pl*
tetrarch
tetrarchy
  tetrarchies *pl*
tetrode
Teuton
Teutonic
text
textile
textual
textually
texture
than
thank
thankful
thankfully
thankfulness
thankless
thank offering
thanksgiving
that
thatch
thatcher
thaw
  thawed
  thawing
theater *Am*
theatre
theatrical
theatrically
thee
theft
their (of them)

theirs
theism
theist
them
thematic
theme
themed
themselves
then
thence
thenceforth
thenceforward
theocracy
  theocracies *pl*
theodolite
theologian
theological
theologist
theology
theosophical
theorem
theoretic
theoretical
theoretically
theoretician
theorise
  theorised
  theorising
theorize
  theorized
  theorizing
theory
  theories *pl*

theosophist
theosophy
therapeutic
therapist
therapy
  therapies *pl*
there (at that place)
thereabouts
thereafter
thereby
therefore
thereupon
therm
thermal
thermally
thermionic
thermite
thermocouple
thermodynamic
thermometer
Thermos
thermostat
thesaurus
  thesauri *pl*
these
thesis
  theses *pl*
they
they'd (they would;
  they had)
they'll (they will)
they're (they are)
they've (they have)

thick
thicken
  thickened
  thickening
thickener
thicker
thicket
thickheaded
thickly
thickness
thickset
thick-skinned
thief
  thieves *pl*
thieve
  thieved
  thieving
thigh
thimble
thin
  thinned
  thinning
  thins
thine
thing
think
  thinking
  thinks
thought
thinker
thinner
thin-skinned
third

thirdly
thirst
thirstily
thirsty
  thirstier
  thirstiest
thirteen
thirteenth
thirtieth
thirty
  thirties *pl*
thirty-something
this
thistle
thither
thong
thoracic
thorax
  thoraxes *pl*
thorn
thornless
thorny
  thornier
  thorniest
thorough (absolute)
thoroughbred
thoroughfare
thoroughgoing
thoroughly
thoroughness
those
thou (you)
though (in spite of)

thought (*from* think)
thoughtful
thoughtfully
thoughtfulness
thoughtless
thoughtlessness
thought-reader
thought-reading
thousand
thousandth
thrash
thread
  threaded
  threading
threadbare
threat
threaten
  threatened
  threatening
three
three-cornered
three-dimensional
threefold
three-quarters
three-ply
threescore
thresh
thresher
threshold
threw (*from* throw)
thrice
thrift
thriftily

thriftless
thrifty
  thriftier
  thriftiest
thrill
thrilled
thriller
thrilling
thrive
  thrived
  thriving
throat
throb
  throbbed
  throbbing
  throbs
throe (suffering)
  throes *pl*
thrombosis
  thromboses *pl*
throne (chair)
throng
throttle
  throttled
  throttling
throttler
through (from end
  to end)
throughout
throve
throw (to fling)
  threw
  throwing

  thrown
  throws
thrush
thrust
thud
  thudded
  thudding
  thuds
thug
thuggery
thumb
  thumbed
  thumbing
thump
  thumped
  thumping
thunder
  thundered
  thundering
thunderbolt
thunderer
thunderstorm
thunderstruck
thundery
Thursday
  Thursdays *pl*
thus
thwart
thwarted
thy
thyme (herb)
thyroid
thyself

tiara
  tiaras *pl*
tibia
  tibias *pl*
tic (twitch)
tick (insect; sound of
  clock; credit)
ticked
ticker
ticker tape
ticket
  ticketed
  ticketing
ticket collector
tickle
  tickled
  tickling
ticklish
tidal
titbit
tiddler
tiddlywinks
tide (ocean)
tideless
tidily
tidiness
tidings
tidy
  tidied
  tidies
  tidying
  tidier
  tidiest

tie (to bind)
  tied
  ties
  tying
tie-dye
  tie-dyed
  tie-dying
tier (row of seats)
tierce (set of three)
tiered
tiff
tiffin
tiger
tight
tighten
  tightened
  tightening
tighter
tight-laced
tight-lipped
tightly
tightrope
tights
tigress
tyke (dog)
tile
  tiled
  tiling
till
tillable
tillage
tiller
tilt

tilth
timber
timbered
timbre (quality of
  sound)
time (clock)
  timed
  timing
time-honored *Am*
time-honoured
timekeeper
timeless
timely
timepiece
timer
time warp
timid
timidity
timidly
timorous
timorously
timorousness
timpani
timpanist
tin
  tinned
  tinning
  tins
tincture
tinder
tinfoil
tinge
  tinged

  tingeing
tingle
  tingled
  tingling
tinker
  tinkered
  tinkering
tinkle
  tinkled
  tinkling
tinnitus
tinny
  tinnier
  tinniest
tinplate
tinsel
tinseled *Am*
tinselled
tint
tin tack
tinted
tintinnabulation
tiny
  tinier
  tiniest
tip
  tipped
  tipping
  tips
tip-off
tipped-off
tipper
tippet

tipple
  tippled
  tippling
tippler
tipsily
tipsiness
tipstaff
  tipstaffs, tipstaves *pl*
tipster
tipsy
tiptoe
  tiptoed
  tiptoeing
  tiptoes
tiptop
tirade
tire (to get tired;
   tyre *Am*)
  tired
  tiring
tiredness
tireless
tirelessly
tiresome
tiresomely
tissue
tit
tit-for-tat
titan
titanic
titbit
tithe
  tithed

tithing
Titian (painter)
titillate
  titillated
  titillating
titillation
titivate (to smarten)
  titivated
  titivating
titivation
title
  titled
titmouse
  titmice *pl*
titrate
  titrated
  titrating
titration
titter
  tittered
  tittering
tittle-tattle
  tittle-tattled
  tittle-tattling
titular
to (towards)
to and fro
toad
toadstool
toady
toadying
toast
toaster

tobacco
tobacconist
toboggan
  tobogganed
  tobogganing
tobogganer
tobogganist
toccata
  toccatas *pl*
tocsin (alarm bell)
today
toddle
  toddled
  toddling
toddler
toddy (drink)
  toddies *pl*
to-do
toe (foot)
  toed
  toeing
  toes
toehold
toff
toffee
tog
together
togged
togged up
toggery
toggle
togs (clothes)
toil

toiled
toiling
toiler
toilet
toiletry
  toiletries *pl*
token
told (*from* tell)
tolerable
tolerably
tolerance
tolerant
tolerantly
tolerate
  tolerated
  tolerating
toleration
toll
toll call (telephone)
tomahawk
tomato
  tomatoes *pl*
tomato sauce
tomb
tombola
  tombolas *pl*
tomboy
  tomboys *pl*
tombstone
tom-cat
tome (volume)
tomfoolery
tomorrow

tomtit
ton (imperial weight)
tonal
tonality
tone (sound)
toneless
tongs (pincers)
tongue (in mouth)
  tongued
  tongues
  tonguing
tongue-tied
tonic
tonight
tonnage
tonne (metric ton)
tonsil
tonsillectomy
tonsillitis
tonsorial
tonsure
too (also)
took (*from* take)
tool
  tooled
  tooling
tooth
toothache
toothless
toothsome
tootle
  tootled
  tootling

top
  topped
  topping
  tops
toper (drinker)
top-heavy
topiary
topic
topical
topically
topknot
topless
topmost
top-notch
topographer
topographic
topography
topper
topple
  toppled
  toppling
topsy-turvy
toque (small hat)
torch
tore (*from* tear)
toreador
torment
tormentor
torn (*from* tear)
tornado
  tornadoes *pl*
torpedo
  torpedoes *pl*

torpedoed

torpedoes

torpedoing

torpid

torpidity

torpidly

torpidness

torpor

torque (twisting)

torrent

torrential

torrid

torsion

torso

  torsos *pl*

tort (law)

tortilla

  tortillas *pl*

tortoise

tortoiseshell

tortuosity

tortuous

tortuously

tortuousness

torture

  tortured

  torturing

torturer

tosh

toss

tossed

toss-up

tot

tots

  totted

  totting

total

  totalled

  totalling

  totals

  totaled *Am*

  totaling *Am*

totalisator

totalitarian

totality

totalizator

totally

tote

totem

totter

  tottered

  tottering

touch

touché

touched

touchy

  touchier

  touchiest

tough

toughen

  toughened

  toughening

tougher

toughly

toughness

toupee

tour (trip)

  toured

  touring

tour de force

tourism

tourist

tournament

tournedos

tourniquet

tousle

  tousled

  tousling

tout

  touted

  touting

touter

tow (pull)

  towed

  towing

towage

toward

towards

towel

  towelled

  towelling

  towels

  toweled *Am*

  toweling *Am*

tower

  towered

  towering

Town Hall

town

townie
township
townspeople
tow-path
toxaemia
toxemia *Am*
toxic
toxicologist
toxicology
toxin (poison)
toy
  toys *pl*
  toyed
  toying
  toys
toyshop
trace
  traced
  tracing
traceable
tracer
tracery
trachea (windpipe)
  tracheas *pl*
trachoma
track
tract
tractable
traction
traction engine
tractor
trade
  traded

  trading
trademark
trader
tradesman
  tradesmen *pl*
tradition
traditional
traditionally
traduce
  traduced
  traducing
traducer
traffic
trafficker
trafficking
tragedian *m*
tragedienne *f*
tragedy
  tragedies *pl*
tragic
tragically
tragicomedy
tragicomic
trail
  trailed
  trailing
trailblazer
trailer
train
  trained
  training
trainee
trainer

traipse
  traipsed
  traipsing
trait
traitor
traitorous
trajectory
  trajectories *pl*
tram
tramcar
trammel
  trammelled
  trammelling
  trammels
  trammeled *Am*
  trammeling *Am*
tramp
trample
  trampled
  trampling
trampoline
trance
tranquil
tranquilization *Am*
tranquilize *Am*
  tranquilized
  tranquilizing
tranquilizer *Am*
tranquillisation
tranquillise
  tranquillised
  tranquillising
tranquilliser

tranquillity
tranquillization
tranquillize
  tranquillized
  tranquillizing
tranquillizer
tranquilly
transact
transaction
transatlantic
transceiver
transcend
transcendent
transcendental
transcontinental
transept
transsexual
transfer
  transferred
  transferring
  transfers
transferable
transference
transfiguration
transfigure
  transfigured
  transfiguring
transfix

transfixed
transfixes
transfixing
transform
transformation
transformer
transfuse
  transfused
  transfusing
transfusion
transgress
transgression
transgressor
tranship
  transhipped
  transhipping
  tranships
transhipment
transience
transient
transistor
transistorisation
transistorise
  transistorised
  transistorising
transistorization
transistorize
  transistorized
  transistorizing
transit
transition
transitional
transitive

transitorily
translatable
translate
  translated
  translating
translation
translator
transliterate
  transliterated
  transliterating
transliteration
translucence
translucent
transmigrate
  transmigrated
  transmigrating
transmigration
transmission
transmit
  transmits
  transmitted
  transmitting
transmitter
transmutation
transmute
  transmuted
  transmuting
transoceanic
transom
transpacific
transparence
transparency
transparent

transparently
transpiration
transpire
  transpired
  transpiring
transplant
transplantation
transport
transportable
transportation
transporter
transpose
  transposed
  transposing
transposition
transubstantiate
transubstantiation
transverse
transversely
transvestism
transvestite
trap
  trapped
  trapping
  traps
trapeze
trapezium
trapper
trash
trauma
  traumas *pl*
traumatic
travail (painful effort)

travel
  travelled
  travelling
  travels
  traveled *Am*
  traveling *Am*
traveller
travelogue
traverse
  traversed
  traversing
travesty
  travesties *pl*
trawl
  trawled
  trawling
  trawls
trawler
tray
  trays *pl*
treacherous
treacherously
treachery
  treacheries *pl*
treacle
treacly
tread
  treading
  treads
  trod
  trodden
treadle
treason

treasonable
treasonably
treasure
  treasured
  treasuring
treasurer
treasury
  treasuries *pl*
treat
  treated
  treating
treatable
treatise
treatment
treaty
  treaties *pl*
treble
trebly
tree
trefoil
trek
  trekked
  trekking
  treks
trekker
Trekkie
trellis
tremble
  trembled
  trembling
tremendous
tremendously
tremolo

tremolos *pl*
tremor
tremulous
tremulously
tremulousness
trench
trenchancy
trenchant
trenchantly
trencher
trend
trendy
 trendier
 trendiest
trepan
 trepanned
 trepanning
 trepans
trepidation
trespass
trespassed
trespasser
trestle
trial
trials
triangle
triangular
triangulate
 triangulated
 triangulating
triangulation
tribal
tribalism

tribe
tribulation
tribunal
tribune
tributary
 tributaries *pl*
tribute
trice
trick
trickery
trickily
trickle
 trickled
 trickling
trickster
tricky
 trickier
 trickiest
tricycle
trident
tried (*from* try)
triennial
trier
tries (*from* try)
trifle
 trifled
 trifling
trifler
trigger
 triggered
 triggering
trigonometric
trigonometrical

trigonometry
trill
trilogy
 trilogies *pl*
trim
 trimmed
 trimming
 trims
trimmer
trinity
 trinities *pl*
trinket
trio
 trios *pl*
triode
trip
 tripped
 tripping
 trips
tripartite
tripe
triphthong
triple
 tripled
 tripling
triplet
triplicate
triplication
triply
tripod
tripodal
tripos
tripper

triptych (picture)
triptyque (travel
  document)
trite
tritely
triumph
triumphal
triumphant
triumphantly
triumvirate
trivia
trivial
trivialise
  trivialised
  trivialising
triviality
  trivialities *pl*
trivialize
  trivialized
  trivializing
trivially
trod (*from* tread)
trodden (*from* tread)
troll
trolley
  trolleys *pl*
trollop
trombone
troop (soldiers)
  trooped
  trooping
trooper
trophy

trophies *pl*
tropic
tropical
tropism
troposphere
tropospheric
trot
  trots
  trotted
  trotting
trotter
troubadour
trouble
  troubled
  troubling
troublesome
trough
trounce
  trounced
  trouncing
troupe (of actors)
trouper
trousers
trousseau
  trousseaus,
    trousseaux *pl*
trout
trowel
truancy
truant
truce
truck
truckle

truckling
truculence
truculent
truculently
trudge
  trudged
  trudging
true
true-blue
truer
truffle
truism
truly
trump
trumped-up
trumpery
trumpet
  trumpeted
  trumpeting
trumpeter
truncate
  truncated
  truncating
truncation
truncheon
trundle
  trundled
  trundling
trunk
trunnion
truss
  trussed
trust

trustee
trusteeship
trustful
trustfully
trustworthiness
trustworthy
truth
truthful
truthfully
truthfulness
try
  tries *pl*
  tried
  tries
  trying
try-out
tryst
tsetse fly
  tsetse flies *pl*
T-shirt
tub
tuba (music)
  tubas *pl*
tubbiness
tubby
  tubbier
  tubbiest
tube
tuber (swelling)
tubercle
tubercular
tuberculosis
tuberculous

tubing
tubular
tuck
Tuesday
  Tuesdays *pl*
tuft
tufted
tug
  tugged
  tugging
  tugs
tuition
tulip
tumble
  tumbled
  tumbling
tumbler
tumescence
tumescent
tumor *Am*
tumour
tumult
tumultuous
tun (barrel)
tuna
  tuna, tunas *pl*
tundra
tune
  tuned
  tuning
tune up
tuneful
tunefully

tunefulness
tuner
tungsten
tunic
tunnel
  tunnelled
  tunnelling
  tunnels
  tunneled *Am*
  tunneling *Am*
  tunneler *Am*
  tunneling *Am*
  tunnelled
  tunneller
tunny
  tunny, tunnies *pl*
turban
turbaned
turbid
turbidity
turbine
turbo-alternator
turbo-generator
turbojet
turboprop
turbot
turbulence
turbulent
tureen
turf
  turfs, turves *pl*
turfed
turgid

turkey
  turkeys *pl*
turmeric
turmoil
turn (to rotate)
turncoat
turner
turnip
turnstile
turntable
turpentine
turpitude
turps
turquoise
turret
turreted
turtle
tusk
tussah *Am*
tussle
  tussled
  tussling
tussore
tutelage
tutelary
tutor
  tutored
  tutoring
tutorial
tutti-frutti
tutu
  tutus *pl*
tuxedo

  tuxedoes, tuxedos *pl*
twaddle
twain
tweak
  tweaked
  tweaking
tweed
tweezers
twelfth
twelve
twentieth
twenty
  twenties *pl*
twice
twiddle
  twiddled
  twiddling
twig
twilight
twilit
twill (fabric)
'twill (it will)
twin
  twinned
  twinning
  twins
twine (thread)
twinge
twinkle
  twinkled
  twinkling
twirl
twist

twister
twit
twitch
twitter
  twittered
  twittering
two (number)
twofold
tycoon
tying (*from* tie)
tyke (dog)
tympanum (eardrum)
  tympanums,
    tympana *pl*
type
  typed
  typing
typecast
  typecasting
typescript
typewriter
typewriting
typewritten
typhoid
typhoon
typhus
typical
typically
typify
  typified
  typifies
  typifying
typist

typographic
typography
tyrannical
tyrannically
tyrannise
    tyrannised
    tyrannising
tyranniser
tyrannize
    tyrannized
    tyrannizing
tyrannous
tyranny
    tyrannies *pl*
tyrant
tyre (on car)
tyro
    tyros *pl*
tzar, tsar, czar
tzigane

ubiquitous
ubiquity
udder
ugliness
ugly
  uglier
  ugliest
ukase
ukulele
ulcer
ulcerated
ulceration
ulcerous
Ulster
ulterior
ultimate
ultimately
ultimatum
  ultimatums,

ultimata *pl*
ultra-conservative
ultramarine
ultramicroscopic
ultra-modern
ultrasonic
ultraviolet
umber
umbilical
umbilicus
  umbilici,
    umbilicuses *pl*
umbrage
umbrella
  umbrellas *pl*
umpire
  umpired
  umpiring
umpteen

umpteenth
unable
unabridged
unacceptable
unaccompanied
unaccountable
unaccountably
unaccustomed
unacquainted
unaffected
unafraid
unalterable
unanimity
unanimous
unanimously
unanswerable
unanswered
unapproachable
unarmed
unashamed
unasked
unassisted
unassuming
unattached
unattainable
unattended
unauthorised
unauthorized
unavailable
unavailing
unavoidable
unaware
unawares

unbalanced
unbearable
unbearably
unbeatable
unbeaten
unbecoming
unbeknown
unbelievable
unbelievably
unbeliever
unbend
unbent
unbiased
unbidden
unblemished
unblushing
unborn
unbounded
unbowed
unbroken
unburdened
unburied
unbuttoned
uncannily
uncanniness
uncanny
unceremonious
uncertain
uncertainty
 uncertainties *pl*
unchangeable
unchanged
uncharitable

uncharted
unchristian
uncivilised
uncivilized
unclaimed
uncle
unclean
uncomfortable
uncomfortably
uncommitted
uncommon
uncommonly
uncommunicative
uncompleted
uncompromising
unconcern
unconditional
unconditionally
unconfirmed
uncongenial
unconnected
unconquerable
unconscious
unconsciously
unconsciousness
unconstitutional
unconstitutionally
uncontrollable
uncontrollably
uncontrolled
unconventional
unconventionally
uncooperative

uncoordinated
uncorroborated
uncouple
 uncoupled
 uncoupling
uncouth
uncouthly
uncouthness
uncover
 uncovered
 uncovering
uncritical
uncritically
unction
unctuous
unctuously
unctuousness
uncultivated
undated
undaunted
undecided
undefended
undeniable
undeniably
under
underarm
undercarriage
underclothes
underclothing
undercover
undercurrent
undercut
 undercuts

undercutting
underdeveloped
underdog
underdone
underexposed
undergo
  undergoes
  undergoing
  undergone
  underwent
undergraduate
underground
undergrowth
underhand
underlay
underlie
  underlain
  underlay
  underlies
  underlying
underline
  underlined
  underlining
underling
undermanned
undermanning
undermine
  undermined
  undermining
underneath
undernourished
undernourishment
underpass

underprivileged
underrate
  underrated
  underrating
undersigned
understand
  understanding
  understands
  understood
understandable
understatement
understrapper
understudied
understudy
  understudies *pl*
  understudied
  understudies
  understudying
undertake
  undertaken
  undertakes
  undertaking
  undertook
undertaker
underwater
underwear
underweight
underwent
underworld
underwrite
  underwrites
  underwriting
  underwritten

underwrote
underwriter
undeserved
undesirable
undesirably
undetermined
undeterred
undigested
undignified
undisciplined
undo
  undid
  undoes
  undoing
  undone
undoubted
undoubtedly
undress
undressed
undue
undulate
  undulated
  undulating
undulation
undulatory
unduly
undying
unearned
unearth
unearthly
uneasily
uneasy
uneatable

uneconomic
uneconomical
uneconomically
uneducated
unemployable
unemployed
unemployment
unenterprising
unequal
unequaled *Am*
unequalled
unequally
unerring
uneven
unevenly
unevenness
uneventful
unexceptionable
unexceptional
unexpected
unfailing
unfair
unfairly
unfairness
unfaithful
unfaithfully
unfaithfulness
unfashionable
unfasten
  unfastened
  unfastening
unfavorable *Am*
unfavorably *Am*

unfavourable
unfavourably
unfeeling
unfeelingly
unfeigned
unfit
  unfits
  unfitted
  unfitting
unfitness
unfold
unforeseen
unforgettable
unforgettably
unfortunate
unfortunately
unfounded
unfriendliness
unfriendly
unfurl
unfurled
unfurnished
ungainly
ungodly
ungovernable
ungrammatical
ungrammatically
ungrateful
ungratefully
unguarded
unguent
unhappily
unhappiness

unhappy
  unhappier
  unhappiest
unharmed
unhealthy
  unhealthier
  unhealthiest
unheard-of
unhinge
unhinged
unhoped-for
unicellular
unicorn
unidentifiable
unidentified
unification
unified
uniform
uniformity
uniformly
unify
  unified
  unifies
  unifying
unilateral
unilaterally
unimpeachable
unimpeachably
uninhabited
uninhibited
uninspiring
unintelligibility
unintelligible

unintelligibly
union
unionisation
unionise
  unionised
  unionising
unionism
unionist
unionization
unionize
  unionized
  unionizing
unique
uniquely
uniqueness
unison
unit
unitary
unite
  united
  uniting
unity
universal
universality
universally
universe
university
  universities *pl*
unjust
unjustifiable
unjustifiably
unjustified
unkempt

unkind
unkindly
unkindness
unknowing
unknown
unlawful
unlawfully
unleaded
unleavened
unless
unlettered
unlicensed
unlike
unlikelihood
unlikely
unlimited
unload
  unloaded
  unloading
unlock
unlocked
unluckily
unlucky
  unluckier
  unluckiest
unmanageable
unmarried
unmask
unmentionable
unmistakable
unmistakably
unmitigated
unmoved

unnamed
unnatural
unnaturally
unnecessarily
unnecessary
unnerved
unnerving
unnumbered
unobservant
unobtrusive
unobtrusively
unobtrusiveness
unoccupied
unofficial
unofficially
unopened
unpack
unpacked
unpaid
unparalleled
unparliamentary
unpleasant
unpleasantly
unpleasantness
unprecedented
unprejudiced
unprepared
unprincipled
unprintable
unprofessional
unprofessionally
unqualified
unquestionable

nquestionably
nravel
  unravelled
  unravelling
  unravels
  unraveled *Am*
  unraveling *Am*
nreadable
nreadiness
nready
nreal
nrealistic
nrealistically
nreasonable
nreasonably
nrecognisable
nrecognised
nrecognizable
nrecognized
nreliable
nreliably
nreserved
nreservedly
nresponsive
nrest
nrestrained
nrighteous
nripe
nrivaled *Am*
nrivalled
nruffled
nruly
  unrulier

unruliest
unsafe
unsaid
unsatisfactorily
unsatisfactoriness
unsatisfactory
unsatisfied
unsavoriness *Am*
unsavory *Am*
unsavouriness
unsavoury
unscathed
unscientific
unscientifically
unscrupulous
unscrupulously
unscrupulousness
unseasonable
unseasonably
unseeing
unseemliness
unseemly
  unseemlier
  unseemliest
unseen
unserviceable
unsettle
  unsettled
  unsettling
unsightliness
unsightly
  unsightlier
  unsightliness

unskilful
unskilfully
unskilled
unskillful *Am*
unskillfully *Am*
unsociable
unsociably
unsophisticated
unspeakable
unspeakably
unspoiled
unstable
unstably
unsteadily
unsteadiness
unsteady
unsubstantiated
unsuccessful
unsuccessfully
unsuitable
unsuitably
unsupported
unsuspected
untactful
untactfully
untenable
unthinkable
untidiness
untidy
  untidier
  untidiest
untie
  untied

unties
untying
until
untimely
unto
untold
untouchable
untoward
untraceable
untrue
untruth
untruthful
untruthfully
unusual
unusually
unveil
  unveiled
  unveiling
unwanted
unwarily
unwarranted
unwary
  unwarier
  unwariest
unwell
unwholesome
unwieldiness
unwieldy
  unwieldier
  unwieldiest
unwind
unwinding
unwise

unwisely
unwitting
unwittingly
unwonted (unusual)
unworkable
unworldliness
unworldly
unworthily
unworthiness
unworthy
  unworthier
  unworthiest
unwound
unwrap
  unwrapped
  unwrapping
  unwraps
unwritten
up-to-date
upbraid
  upbraided
  upbraiding
upbringing
update
  updated
  updating
upheaval
uphold
  upheld
  upholding
  upholds
uphill
upholster

upholstered
upholstering
upholsterer
upholstery
upkeep
upon
upper
uppercut
uppermost
uppish
uppishness
upright
uprightness
uprising
uproar
uproarious
upset
  upsets
  upsetting
upshot
upside
upside down
upstairs
upstart
uptight
upward
upwards
uraemia
uranium
urban (town)
urbane (polite)
urbanely
urbanity

urchin
urea
uremia *Am*
urethra
 urethrae *pl*
urge
 urged
 urging
urgency
urgent
urgently
urinal
urinary
urinate
 urinated
 urinating
urine
urn (pot)
urologist
urology
usable
usage
use
 used
 using
useful
usefully
usefulness
useless
uselessly
uselessness
user
usher

ushered
ushering
usherette
ushers
usual
usually
usurer
usurious
usurp
usurpation
usurper
usury
utensil
uterine
uterus
 uteri *pl*
utilisable
utilisation
utilise
 utilised
 utilising
utilitarian
utility
 utilities *pl*
utilizable
utilization
utilize
 utilized
 utilizing
utmost
Utopia
Utopian
utter

uttered
uttering
utterance
utterly
uttermost
uvula
 uvulae *pl*
uvular
uxorious

vacancy
  vacancies *pl*
vacant
vacate
  vacated
  vacating
vacation (holiday)
vaccinate (to
  inoculate)
  vaccinated
  vaccinating
vaccination
vaccine
vacillate
  vacillated
  vacillating
vacillation
vacuity
vacuole

vacuous
vacuum
  vacuums, vacua *pl*
vade-mecum
  vade-mecums *pl*
vagabond
vagabondage
vagary
  vagaries *pl*
vagina
  vaginas *pl*
vagrancy
vagrant
vague
vaguely
vagueness
vaguer
vain (conceited;
  useless)

vainer
vainglorious
vainglory
vainly
valance (frill)
vale (valley)
valediction
valedictory
valence (chem.)
valency
  valencies *pl*
valentine
valerian
valet
  valeted
  valeting
valetudinarian
Valhalla
valiant
valiantly
valid
validate
  validated
  validating
validation
validity
valise
valley
  valleys *pl*
valor *Am*
valorous
valour
valuable

aluation
alue
  valued
  valuing
alueless
aluer
alve
alvular
amp
ampire
an
andal
andalise
  vandalised
  vandalising
vandalism
vandalize
  vandalized
  vandalizing
vane (weathercock)
vanguard
vanilla
vanish
vanity
  vanities *pl*
vanquish
vantage
vapid
vapor *Am*
vaporisation
vaporise
  vaporised
  vaporising

vaporiser
vaporization
  vaporize
  vaporized
  vaporizing
vaporizer
vaporous
vapour
variability
variable
variance
variant
variation
varicolored *Am*
varicoloured
varicose
varicose veins
varied
variegated
variegation
variety
  varieties *pl*
various
varlet
varnish
varsity
  varsities *pl*
vary
  varied
  varies
  varying
vascular
vase

vaseline
vast
vaster
vastly
vastness
V.A.T., VAT
vat (tank)
Vatican
vaudeville
vault
vaunt
veal
vector
vectorial
veer
  veered
  veering
vegetable
vegetarian
vegetarianism
vegetate
  vegetated
  vegetating
vegetation
vegetative
vehemence
vehement
vehicle
vehicular
veil (cover)
  veiled
  veiling
vein (blood vessel;

manner; thin
strip)
veiny
  veinier
  veiniest
Velcro
vellum
velocity
  velocities *pl*
velour
velvet
velveteen
velvety
venal
venality
venally
vend
vended
vender
vendetta
  vendettas *pl*
vendor (seller)
veneer
  veneered
  veneering
venerable
venerate
  venerated
  venerating
veneration
venereal (disease)
vengeance
vengeful

venial (pardonable)
venison
venom
venomous
venous
vent
ventilate
  ventilated
  ventilating
ventilation
ventilator
ventral
ventrally
ventricle
ventricular
ventriloquism
ventriloquist
venture
  ventured
  venturing
venturer
venturesome
venue
veracious (honest)
veracity
veranda
  verandas *pl*
verb
verbal
verbalise
  verbalised
  verbalising
verbalize

verbalized
verbalizing
verbally
verbatim
verbena
  verbenas *pl*
verbiage
verbose
verbosity
verdancy
verdant
verdict
verdigris
verdure
verdurous
verge
  verged
  verging
verger
verifiable
verification
verify
  verified
  verifies
  verifying
verily
verisimilitude
veritable
veritably
verity
  verities *pl*
vermicelli
vermilion

ermin
erminous
ermouth
ernacular
ernal
ernier
eronal
erruca
verrucae *pl*
ersatile
ersatility
erse
ersed
ersification
ersifier
ersify
versified
versifies
versifying
ersion
ersus (against)
ertebra
vertebrae *pl*
ertebral
ertebrate
ertex
vertices, vertexes *pl*
ertical
ertically
ertiginous
ertigo
erve
ery

vesper
vessel
vest
vestibule
vestige
vestigial
vestment
vestry
vestries *pl*
vesture
vet
vets
vetted
vetting
vetch
veteran
veterinary surgeon
veterinary
veto
vetoes *pl*
vetoed
vetoes
vetoing
vex
vexed
vexing
vexation
vexatious
via
viability
viable
viaduct
vial (tube)

viand
vibrant
vibrate
vibrated
vibrating
vibration
vibrato
vibrator
vibratory
vicar
vicarage
vicarious
vice
vice versa
vice-chancellor
vice-president
vice-presidential
viceregal
viceroy
viceroys *pl*
viceroyalty
vichyssoise
vicinity
vicinities *pl*
vicious (evil)
viciously
viciousness
vicissitude
victim
victimisation
victimise
victimised
victimising

victimization
victimize
  victimized
  victimizing
victor
victorious
victory
  victories *pl*
victuals
victualer *Am*
victualler
video
  videos *pl*
videocassette
videodisc
video frequency
video player
video recorder
video signal
videotape
videotext
vie (to compete with)
  vied
  vies
  vying
view
viewer
viewpoint
vigil
vigilance
vigilant
vigilante
vigilantly

vignette
vigor *Am*
vigorous
vigorously
vigorousness
vigour
vile (bad)
vilely
vileness
viler
vilification
vilifier
vilify
  vilified
  vilifies
  vilifying
villa
  villas *pl*
village
villager
villain
villainous
villainously
villainy
villein (serf)
vim
vinaigrette
vindicate
  vindicated
  vindicating
vindication
vindicator
vindictive

vindictively
vindictiveness
vine
vinegar
vinegary
vinery
  vineries *pl*
vineyard
viniculture
vinous
vintage
vintner
vinyl
viol
viola
  violas *pl*
viola da gamba
  viola da gambas *pl*
violate
  violated
  violating
violation
violator
violence
violent
violently
violet
violin
violoncello
  violoncellos *pl*
V.I.P., VIP
viper
virago

viragoes, viragos *pl*
viral
virgin
virginal (harpsichord)
virginity
  virginities *pl*
virile
virility
virtu (love of art)
virtual
virtually
virtue (goodness)
virtuosity
virtuoso
  virtuosi, virtuosos *pl*
virtuous
virtuously
virulence
virulent
virulently
virus
  viruses *pl*
vis-à-vis
visa
  visas *pl*
visage
viscera
visceral
viscid
viscidity
viscosity
viscount
viscountess

viscous (thick)
visage
vise *Am*
  vised
  vising
visibility
visible
visibly
vision
visionary
  visionaries *pl*
visit
  visited
  visiting
visitation
visitor
visor
vista
  vistas *pl*
visual
visualisation
visualise
  visualised
  visualising
visualization
visualize
  visualized
  visualizing
visually
vital
vitalisation
vitalise
  vitalised

vitalising
vitality
vitalization
vitalize
  vitalized
  vitalizing
vitally
vitals
vitamin
vitiate
  vitiated
  vitiating
vitiation
viticulture
vitreous
vitrification
vitrify
  vitrified
  vitrifies
  vitrifying
vitriol
vitriolic
vituperate
  vituperated
  vituperating
vituperation
vituperative
vivace
viva voce
vivacious
vivacity
vivid
vividly

vividness
vivify
  vivified
  vivifies
  vivifying
viviparous
vivisect
vivisection
vivisector
vixen
vizier
vocabulary
  vocabularies *pl*
vocal
vocal cord
vocalisation
vocalise
  vocalised
  vocalising
vocalist
vocalization
vocalize
  vocalized
  vocalizing
vocally
vocation
vocational
vocative
vociferate
  vociferated
  vociferating
vociferation
vociferous

vociferously
vociferousness
vodka
  vodkas *pl*
vogue
voice
  voiced
  voicing
voiceless
voiceprint
void
voidable
voile
volatile
volatilise
  volatilised
  volatilising
volatility
volatilize
  volatilized
  volatilizing
vol-au-vent
volcanic
volcano
  volcanoes *pl*
volition
volley
  volleys *pl*
volleyball
volt
voltage
voltaic
volte-face

voltmeter
volubility
voluble
volubly
volume
volumetric
voluminous
voluntarily
voluntary
volunteer
  volunteered
  volunteering
  volunteers
voluptuary
  voluptuaries *pl*
voluptuous
voluptuously
voluptuousness
vomit
  vomited
  vomiting
voodoo
voracious (greedy)
voraciously
voracity
vortex (whirlwind)
  vortexes, vortices *pl*
votary
  votaries *pl*
vote
  voted
  voting
voter

votive

vouch

voucher

vouchsafe

  vouchsafed

  vouchsafing

vow

  vowed

  vowing

vowel

voyage

  voyaged

  voyaging

voyager

voyeur

vulcanisation

vulcanise

  vulcanised

  vulcanising

vulcanization

vulcanize

  vulcanized

  vulcanizing

vulgar

vulgarisation

vulgarise

  vulgarised

  vulgarising

vulgarising

vulgarism

vulgarity

vulgarization

vulgarize

  vulgarized

  vulgarizing

vulnerability

vulnerable

vulpine

vulture

vulva

  vulvas *pl*

vying (*from* vie)

wacky
  wackier
  wackiest
wad
wadding
waddle
  waddled
  waddling
wade
  waded
  wading
wader
wafer
waffle
  waffled
  waffling
waft
wag
  wagged

wagging
wags
wage
  waged
  waging
wager
  wagered
  wagering
wages
waggish
waggle
  waggled
  waggling
waggoner
wagon
wagoner
wagonette,
  waggonette
wagon-lit

wagtail
waif
  waifs *pl*
wail (to cry)
  wailed
  wailing
wainscot
wainscoting
waist (body)
waistcoat
wait (at table; bide
  time)
  waited
  waiting
waiter
waitress
waits (street singers)
waive (to forgo)
  waived
  waiving
waiver (in law)
wake
  waking
  woke
  woken
  wakes
  waked *Am*
wakeful
wakefulness
walk
walker
walking stick
walkover

wall
wallaby
  wallabies *pl*
wallah
wallet
wallflower
wallop
  walloped
  walloping
wallow
  wallowed
  wallowing
wallpaper
wally
  wallies *pl*
walnut
walrus
  walruses *pl*
waltz
  waltzes *pl*
wan (pale)
wand
wander (to walk)
  wandered
  wandering
wanderer
wanderlust
wane
  waned
  waning
wangle
  wangled
  wangling

wangler
wanness
want
wanting
wanton (free and
  easy)
wantonly
wantonness
war
  warred
  warring
  wars
warble
  warbled
  warbling
warbler
ward
warden
warder
wardress
wardrobe
ware
  wares *pl*
warehouse
warfare
warier
warily
wariness
warm (heat)
warmer
warm-hearted
warmly
warmonger

warmongering
warmth
warm-up
warn (signal)
warning
warp
warped
warrant
warranty
  warranties *pl*
warring
warren
warrior
wart (lump)
wary
  warier
  wariest
wash
washable
washer
wasn't (was not)
wasp
waspish
wassail
wastage
waste (to squander)
  wasted
  wasting
wasteful
wastefully
wastefulness
waster
wastrel

watch
watcher
watchful
watchfully
watchfulness
watchmaker
watchword
water
  watered
  watering
water-borne
water closet
watercolour
watercress
waterfall
waterlogged
watermark
waterproof
watershed
water-ski
  water-skied
  water-skiing
  water-skis
watertight
waterworks
watt (unit of power)
wattage
wattle
wattmeter
wave (ocean)
  waved
  waving
waveform

wavelength
waver (to sway)
  wavered
  wavering
  waverer
  wavy
wax
  waxed
  waxes
  waxing
waxwork
way (method; route)
  ways *pl*
wayfare
wayfarer
wayfaring
waylaid
waylay
  waylaid
  waylaying
  waylays
wayside
wayward
waywardness
we (us)
weak (feeble)
weaken
  weakened
  weakening
weaker
weak-kneed
weakling
weakly (feebly)

weak-minded
weakness
weal (scar; welfare)
weald (former forest)
wealth
wealthy
  wealthier
  wealthiest
wean
  weaned
  weaning
weapon
weaponry
wear (clothes)
  wearing
  wears
  wore
  worn
wear and tear
wearable
wearier
wearily
weariness
wearisome
weary
  wearier
  weariest
weasel
weather (climate)
  weathered
  weathering
weather-beaten
weathercock

weave (cloth)
  weaves
  weaving
  wove
  woven
weaver
we'd (we had; we
  would)
we'll (we will)
we're (we are)
we've (we have)
web
  webbed
  webbing
web-footed
wed (to marry)
  wedded
  wedding
  weds
wedge
  wedged
  wedging
wedlock
Wednesday
  Wednesdays *pl*
wee (tiny)
week (seven day)
weekday
  weekdays *pl*
weekend
weekly (each week)
  weeklies *pl*
weep

weeping
weeps
wept
weevil
weft
weigh
  weighed
  weighing
weighbridge
weight
  (measurement)
weightily
weightless
weightlessness
weighty
  weightier
  weightiest
weir (across a river)
weird
weirdly
weirdness
welcome
  welcomed
  welcoming
weld
welder
welfare
welkin
well
we'll (we will)
well-being
well-born
well-bred

wellingtons
well-known
well-made
well-meant
well-nigh
well-read
well-to-do
Welsh
welsher
welt
welter
welterweight
wen (swelling)
wench
went (*from* go)
wept (*from* weep)
were (*from* be)
we're (we are)
weren't (were not)
werewolf
  werewolves *pl*
west
westerly
western
westernisation
westernise
  westernised
  westernising
westernization
westernize
  westernized
  westernizing
westward

wet (damp)
  wets
  wetted
  wetting
wet blanket
wether (sheep)
wetness
wetsuit
whack
whacked
whacko
whale (sea mammal)
whalebone
whaler
whaling
wharf
  wharfs, wharves *pl*
wharfage
wharfinger
what (question)
whatever
whatnot
whatsoever
wheat
wheaten
wheatmeal
wheedle
  wheedled
  wheedling
wheel
  wheeled
  wheeling
wheelbarrow

wheelchair
wheelwright
wheeze
  wheezed
  wheezing
wheezily
whelk
whelp
when (question)
whence
whenever
whensoever
where (place)
whereabouts
whereas
whereat
wherefore
whereupon
wherever
wherewithal
wherry
  wherries *pl*
whet (to sharpen)
  whets
  whetted
  whetting
whether (if)
whetstone
whey (from milk)
which (what)
whichever
whiff
Whig

while (time)
  whiled
  whiling
whilst
whim
whimper
  whimpered
  whimpering
whimsical
whimsy
  whimsies *pl*
whine (to cry)
  whined
  whining
whinny
  whinnied
  whinnies
  whinnying
whip
  whipped
  whipping
  whips
whipcord
whip hand
whippet (dog)
whir
whirl (spin)
whirligig
whirlpool
whirlwind
whirr
whisk
whisker

whiskered
whiskey (other
  makes)
  whiskeys *pl*
whisky (Scotch)
  whiskies *pl*
whisper
  whispered
  whispering
whisperer
whist
whistle
  whistled
  whistling
whistler
Whit
whit (small amount)
white
whitebait
white-haired
whiten
  whitened
  whitening
whiter
whitewash
whither (where to)
whiting (fish)
whitlow
Whitsun
whittle
  whittled
  whittling
whizz

whizzed
whizzes
whizzing
who
whoever
whole (entire)
whole-hearted
wholemeal
wholesale
wholesaler
wholesome
wholesomely
wholesomeness
wholly (entirely)
whom
who's (who is or has)
whoop (to shout)
  whooped
  whooping
whoopee
whooping cough
whopper
whore
whoremonger
whoring
whorl (circle)
whortleberry
  whortleberries *pl*
whose
why
wick
wicked (bad)
wickedly

wickedness
wicker
wickerwork
wicket (cricket)
wicketkeeper
wide
wide awake
widely
widen
  widened
  widening
wider
widespread
width
widow
widowed
widower
wield
wife
  wives *pl*
wig (false hair)
wiggle
  wiggled
  wiggling
wigwam
wild
wildebeest
wilder
wilderness
wildfire
wild-goose chase
wildlife

wildly
wildness
wile (trick)
wilful
wilfully
wilfulness
wiliness
will
willful *Am*
willfully *Am*
willfulness *Am*
willing
willingly
willingness
will-o'-the-wisp
willow
willowy
willpower
willy-nilly
wilt (thou)
wilt (to droop)
wily
wimple
win
  winning
  wins
  won
wince
  winced
  wincing
winch
wind
  winding

winds
  wound
winder
windfall
windlass
windless
windmill
window
window-pane
window-shopping
window sill
windscreen
windward
windy
  windier
  windiest
wine (drink)
wine-cellar
wing
wingspan
wingspread
wink
winkle
  winkled
  winkling
winner
winnow
  winnowed
  winnowing
winsome
winsomely
winsomeness
winter

wintered
  wintering
wintry
wipe
  wiped
  wiping
wire
wireless
wiriness
wiry
wisdom
wise
wiseacre
wisecrack
wisely
wiser
wish
wishful
wishfully
wishy-washy
wisp
wisteria
  wisterias *pl*
wistful
wistfully
wistfulness
wit (humour)
witch (magician)
  witches *pl*
witchcraft
witchery
  witcheries *pl*
with

withal
withdraw
  withdrawing
  withdrawn
  withdraws
  withdrew
withdrawal
wither (to shrivel)
  withered
  withering
withers (of a horse)
withhold
  withheld
  withholding
  withholds
within
without
withstand
  withstanding
  withstands
  withstood
witless
witness
witness box
  witness boxes *pl*
witticism
wittily
wittiness
witty
  wittier
  wittiest
wizard
wizardry

wizened
woad
wobble
  wobbled
  wobbling
woe
woebegone
woeful
woefully
woke (*from* wake)
woken (*from* wake)
wold (open hilly
  country)
wolf
  wolves *pl*
woman
  women *pl*
womanly
womankind
womb
womenfolk
won (*from* win)
wonder (to think)
  wondered
  wondering
wonderful
wonderfully
wondrous
wont (accustomed)
won't (will not)
wonted
woo
  wooed

wooing
  woos
wood (timber)
wooden
woodenly
woodenness
woodland
wooer
woofer
wool
woolen *Am*
woollen
woolliness
woolly
word
wordily
wordy
wore (*from* wear)
work
workable
workaholic
worker
workman
  workmen *pl*
workmanship
workshop
world
worldliness
worldly
worldly-wise
world-wide
worm (creature)
worm-eaten

worn (*from* wear)
worn-out
worrier
worry
  worries *pl*
  worried
  worries
  worrying
worse
worsen
  worsened
  worsening
worship
  worshipped
  worshipping
  worships
  worshiped *Am*
  worshiping *Am*
worshiper
worshipful
worshipper
worst
worsted
worth
worthier
worthily
worthless
worthwhile
worthy
  worthier
  worthiest
would
wouldn't (would not)

wound
wounded
wound-up
wove (*from* weave)
woven (*from* weave)
woven
wrack (seaweed)
wraith (ghost)
wrangle
  wrangled
  wrangling
wrangler
wrap (to cover)
  wrapped
  wrapping
  wraps
wraparound
wrapper
wrath (anger)
wrathful
wreak (to inflict)
wreath (of flowers)
  wreaths *pl*
wreathe (twist)
  wreathed
  wreathing
wreck
wreckage
wrecked
wrecker
wren
wrench
wrest (to snatch)

wrestle
  wrestled
  wrestling
wrestler
wretch
wretched
wretchedly
wretchedness
wriggle
  wriggled
  wriggling
wriggler
wring (to twist)
  wringing
  wrings
  wrung
wrinkle
  wrinkled
  wrinkling
wrinkly
wrist
wristband
wristlet
wrist-watch
writ (legal document)
write (letter)
  writes
  writing
  written
  wrote
write-up
writer
writhe

writhed
writhing
wrong
 wronged
 wronging
wrongdoer
wrongdoing
wrongful
wrongfully
wrote (*from* write)
wrought (shaped)
wrung (*from* wring)
wry (twisted)
wryly
wryness
Wurlitzer

xenophobe
xenophobia
xenophobic
Xerox
  Xeroxes *pl*
Xmas
X-ray
  X-rays *pl*
  X-rayed
  X-raying
  X-rays
xylophone

yacht
yachtsman
  yachtsmen *pl*
Yankee
yap
  yapped
  yapping
  yaps
yard
yardage
yardstick
yarn
yashmak
yawl
yawn
  yawned
  yawning
yea
year

yearling
year-long
yearly
year-round
yearn
yeast
yell
yellow
yelp
yen (longing)
yeoman
  yeomen *pl*
yeomanry
  yeomanries *pl*
yes
yesterday
  yesterdays *pl*
yesteryear
yet

yeti
yew (tree)
Yiddish
yield
yippee
yodel
  yodelled
  yodelling
  yodels
  yodeled *Am*
  yodeling *Am*
yodeler *Am*
yodeller
yoga
yogi
yoghurt, yogurt
yoke (fitted on neck)
yokel (peasant)
yolk (of egg)
yonder
yore (long ago)
you (person)
you'd (you had)
you'll (you will)
young
  younger
  youngest
youngster
you're (you are)
your
yours
yourself
  yourselves *pl*

zoos *pl*
zoological
zoologist
zoology
zoom
  zoomed
  zooming
zoom lens
zygote

zany
  zanies *pl*
zeal
zealot
zealous
zebra
  zebras *pl*
zebra crossing
zen
zenith
zephyr
  zephyrs *pl*
zero
  zeros *pl*
zest
zestful
zigzag
  zigzagged
  zigzagging

zigzags
zimmer frame
zinc
zinnia
  zinnias *pl*
Zion
Zionism
Zionist
zip
  zipped
  zipping
  zips
zipper
zither
zodiac
zombie
zonal
zone
zoo